When
GOD
Builds a
CHURCH

FOREWORDS BY MAX LUCADO
AND THOM S. RAINER

When GOD Builds a CHURCH

10 Principles for Growing a Dynamic Church

The Remarkable Story of Southeast Christian Church

BOB RUSSELL

WITH RUSTY RUSSELL

HOWARD
PUBLISHING CO.

Our purpose at Howard Publishing is to:
- *Increase faith* in the hearts of growing Christians
- *Inspire holiness* in the lives of believers
- *Instill hope* in the hearts of struggling people everywhere
  Because He's coming again!

When God Builds a Church © 2000 by Bob Russell
All rights reserved. Printed in the United States of America

Published by Howard Publishing Co., Inc.,
3117 North 7th Street, West Monroe, Louisiana 71291-2227

00 01 02 03 04 05 06 07 08 09   10 9 8 7 6 5 4 3 2 1

Library of Congress Cataloging-in-Publication Data
    Russell, Bob, 1943-
        When God builds a church : 10 principles for growing a dynamic church / Bob Russell with Rusty Russell.
            p. cm.
        Includes bibliographical references.
        ISBN: 1-58229-125-X
        1. Church growth. I. Russell, Rusty, 1967- II. Title.

    BV652.25 .R87 2000
    254'.5—dc21

                                                            00-035093

Edited by Ron Durham
Interior design by Stephanie Denney

Unless otherwise identified, Scripture quotations are from the Holy Bible, New International Version © 1973, 1978, 1984 by International Bible Society. Used by permission of Zondervan Bible Publishers. Other Scripture quotations are from the Holy Bible, Authorized King James Version (KJV). Public domain.

CONTENTS

FOREWORD

MAX LUCADO

AUTHOR AND MINISTER

I have an old Mustang I love to drive. One might wonder why. The heater doesn't work. The air conditioning isn't from the factory. No FM radio, just AM. No power brakes or cruise control.

It's certainly not as comfortable as a newer model. When it comes to gadgets and gizmos, my old Mustang has little to offer.

But when it comes to understandability, it has plenty.

"Understandability"?

Not a word usually associated with cars. But if you're a mechanic no-brain like I am, you appreciate a car you can understand.

In this age of hi-tech compressors and computerized parts, you appreciate the familiarity of spark plugs, points, and V-8 engines.

When it comes to books on our Lord's church, you appreciate the same. Bob and Rusty Russell have given us an understandable book on church dynamics.

No gizmos, no gimmicks, just rock-solid, time-tested, Bible-based principles. Principles quaried out of the gold mine known as Southeast Christian Church.

The Lord is using this wonderful congregation to remind us that he does great things with willing hearts.

Bob Russell and the church elders are humble, godly, devoted men. No one is more surprised and grateful than they are at the phenomenal growth of this church.

Ask them the secret of success, and they say, "What secret?" Raise the hood on this reliable vehicle of grace, and you'll see a familiar engine you can understand and imitate.

Bob Russell's three decades of dedicated service to one church inspires us all. Southeast Christian's high-road commitment to the gospel reminds us all: Church dynamics isn't rocket science. It's understandable and applicable. You've just got to look at the right car.

FOREWORD

THOM S. RAINER

DEAN, BILLY GRAHAM SCHOOL OF EVANGELISM,
MISSIONS, AND CHURCH GROWTH

The manuscript of *When God Builds a Church* is set aside for the moment. The lengthy flight from Cincinnati to Los Angeles has provided me the opportunity to read a major portion of the book a second time. But this time I had to pause. I needed time with God.

You see, the story of Southeast Christian Church in Louisville, Kentucky, reminded me once again of the greatness of the God we serve. The book let me remember again the love of our Savior Jesus Christ. Though on a crowded plane with more than one hundred people, I turned to the window and prayed.

Southeast Christian Church is the story of what God can do when his people are obedient and when his leaders are pure. It is not the story of how megachurches operate or what the latest church growth fad may be or of a church built on personalities.

The first time I met Bob Russell, I had the same reaction that hundreds of others experience. This man is certainly not what I expected. I was impressed with his humility more than any other factor. No superego here, just a humble man seeking to serve God and others.

But then again, such is the story of Southeast Christian Church. Yes, the church is among the largest congregations in North America. The story, however, is not about its size but about the great work God desires to do among his people.

I have had the opportunity to study and write about thousands of churches in North America. Many times I will note a church's dynamic leadership, its wonderful organization, or its impressive array of ministries. But when I finished reading *When God Builds a Church*, I did not think as much about the greatness of a church as I did the greatness of the God who built it.

Read this book for instruction. Read this book for edification. Read this book to understand the timeless principles God uses to build a church. But above all, read this book to be reminded of the magnificent God who builds churches and changes lives.

ACKNOWLEDGMENTS

The role of senior minister is a lot like the quarterback of a football team. When the team does well, the quarterback gets more glory than he deserves; when the team does poorly, the quarterback gets more blame than he deserves.

Since I'm the senior minister, I get to be the one who writes the book. But I don't want to take the glory for what God has done through many faithful staff members and volunteers over the past thirty-seven years. I've tried to tell about many of them, but there's no way I could list them all. I'm privileged to lead the greatest church staff imaginable and to work with the greatest body of elders ever assembled. They're much like the linemen on a good football team—faithfully working hard to make the quarterback look good. Thanks to all of you on staff and in leadership at Southeast!

I'm also thankful for the extra time that many of Southeast's leaders gave us in helping with this book. John Foster, Dave Stone, Greg Allen, Debbie Carper, the leadership team, and many other staff members and volunteers interviewed with us and critiqued rough drafts.

My son Rusty has worked hard on this book for the last six months and wants to thank his wife for putting up with the extra load. I need to thank my wife, too, for putting up with the extra load for the past thirty-three years! Kellie and Judy, thank you, and we love you. Phil, Lisa, Charlie, and the two babies on the way—we love you too. Thanks for keeping us balanced—in love with what we're doing but remembering that there are more important things.

This is our first work with Howard Publishing, and we have been thoroughly impressed. Thank you, Denny and Philis Boultinghouse, all of you at Howard Publishing, and our editor, Ron Durham, for doing all things with excellence.

And thank you, Lord. To God be the glory; great things he has done.

Introduction

A DRAMATIC BEGINNING

I'll never forget the first time I met H. W. "Butch" Dabney that afternoon in Cincinnati, Ohio, during a break at a conference on evangelism in 1965. "Hi, I'm Butch Dabney," he said. "I'm the chairman of the pulpit committee of a new church in Louisville, Kentucky, and I'd like to talk to you about our church. Do you have a minute?"

Butch, who was then in his early forties, was personable, confident, relaxed, and quick-witted. And he had a contagious enthusiasm for the Lord and the new church he had helped start—Southeast Christian Church in Louisville. Little did I know that I had just met a man who would become for me a spiritual mentor and lifelong friend.

"Southeast is going to be such a special church," Butch assured me. "We started just three years ago with fifty members from the South Louisville Christian Church. Among those members were several experienced and devoted leaders who really want the church to honor Christ and grow. Although we're currently meeting in the basement of a house, we've grown to 125 people and are in the process of building a new church building that will seat four hundred." Butch spoke with conviction and enthusiasm as he continued, "We believe that what we do for the Lord should be our very best. We also believe we have the potential to be a powerful church, and we've been praying for the right minister. That's where you come in."

The situation at Southeast sounded ideal, but I knew what I had to say. "Your church sounds wonderful, and I'm sure it's going to do great things, but I know it can't be the Lord's will for me right now. In June, I became the first full-time minister of a congregation here in Ohio, and I committed to stay at least a year. It can't be God's will for me to break that promise." Butch and I parted company, and I didn't think I'd ever see him again.

Several months later I received a long-distance phone call. "Hi, I'm Butch Dabney. Remember me? I talked with you at the conference on evangelism several months ago. Well, we still haven't found a minister. Two women from our church came to hear you preach last Sunday and gave a glowing report. Sometime in the next few weeks, we'd like for you to come down and look over our situation. If it seems like a good fit, we'd be willing to wait until June when your year's commitment is up. Will you come?"

Although I had a lot of apprehension about preaching in the suburbs of a large city, this was obviously an open door through which God was prodding me to walk. "Yes!" I said without hesitation. "I'll be happy to take a look."

When I became a part of the ministry at Southeast in June of 1966, I was not quite twenty-three years old! But Butch Dabney assured me that the church was hungry to love a minister and poised to grow. He was right. The people were supportive and loving, and that's why I've been able to stay for thirty-four years. They endured some very immature sermons in those early years and helped me smooth out a lot of rough edges, and we grew together.

GOD DOES IMMEASURABLY MORE

Southeast Christian Church was founded in 1962 when the leaders of its parent church (South Louisville Christian Church) felt the need to start a congregation on the growing eastern side of Louisville. After much prayer and planning, fifty people agreed to leave that established and growing congregation to start Southeast Christian Church.

The Sunday before the new congregation was to have its first service, Olin Hay, the minister at South Louisville, asked all those who were joining the new church to stand. When he looked out over the congregation, he was a little overwhelmed. He hadn't realized that so many were leaving. Among those who felt led to help start this new church were some of his most influential leaders. The fifty people included a worship leader, four elders, several deacons, and Butch Dabney—Olin's own brother-in-law! But Olin bowed in prayer and asked God to bless this new congregation. And God began to bless it in an outstanding way.

Since 1966, Southeast Christian Church has grown from 125 to over 13,500 in worship. We have gone through five building programs and two complete relocation projects, the last of which cost over ninety million dollars (including land, construction costs, and architects' fees). We have gone from an annual budget of eighteen thousand dollars to an annual budget of eighteen million dollars.

There have been many great joys and a few deep sorrows. Butch Dabney is now a retired elder, but he is still a mentor and friend to me. Our families are still close. He's like a father, and his sons are like brothers to me. And I have discovered that God's Word is true—"God does immeasurably more than all we ask or imagine."

On Christmas Eve, 1998, Southeast moved into a new facility. We desperately needed the room to grow. Before the move we had been cramming ten thousand people into a twenty-two-hundred-seat auditorium in five weekend services. In several of those services, people had to sit in the aisles, and as many as five hundred people were worshiping in the fellowship hall, watching the service on closed-circuit television. We had parking and traffic problems. We were shuttling people from off-site parking locations and housing adult Bible fellowship classes in neighborhood schools. We were even dealing with space problems during the week, without adequate room to house all the Bible studies, training programs, support group meetings, and activities we wanted to offer.

Our new facility includes a worship center that holds over nine thousand people, plenty of classroom space, an activities center, and two large fellowship halls. Attendance jumped by three thousand people in the first few weeks. We wondered if we would sustain that leap. Now, one year later, not only are we sustaining that growth, but we are also seeing many of those three thousand new people come forward to become a part of the church. When they come to shake my hand at the invitation time, I'll say, "How long have you been attending?" I am shocked at how many never attended our church before we moved into our new facility, which makes me all the more thankful that we chose to follow God's leading and build that new building.

While I was a student at Cincinnati Bible Seminary, I once visited a church that had five hundred people. I walked away saying, "That's just too big." I grew up attending a rural congregation in northwest Pennsylvania that until recent years never had more than one hundred members. I decided during my senior year of high school to enter the ministry, assuming I would return to that area of the country and help to pastor another small rural congregation. When people ask me today if I ever dreamed I'd be preaching to fourteen thousand people, I just laugh and say, "Not in my wildest imaginations." I often look around at what God is doing, consider my roots and my limitations, and say to myself, *What in the world am I doing here? How did I get here? God must have a sense of humor!*

BACK TO THE BASICS—THE PURPOSE OF THIS BOOK

One of my favorite movies is *Hoosiers*, where Gene Hackman plays the part of Norman Dale, a former college coach with a tainted past who is hired to coach a rural high-school basketball team from Hickory, Indiana. Coach Dale leads the team all the way to the state finals. On the day of the semifinals, the team arrives at Butler Field House, the huge inner-city arena where they're to play in just a couple of hours. When the players enter the arena, their jaws fall slack and their eyes open wide. Gawking at the seats, the stand-alone goals, the suspended scoreboard, and the lights, they are awestruck and intimidated.

Coach Dale instructs one of his players to take a tape measure and determine the distance between the free-throw line and the goal. "What's the distance?" he asks.

"Fifteen feet," the player says.

Dale then tells the smallest player on the team to climb on the shoulders of a taller player so they can measure the goal. "How high is it?" he asks.

"Ten feet," the player says.

Coach Dale says, "I believe you'll find these are the exact same measurements as our gym back in Hickory."

The team members share in some nervous laughter, and everybody begins to relax. As they exit the gym, Coach Dale turns to his assistant and whispers, "Sure is big, isn't it!"

I don't know what monumental challenges lie ahead in this new millennium. But I know we're still playing the same game. It's the same Bible we are teaching, the same truth we are proclaiming, the same Lord we are exalting. For the church to be the church—in any millennium—we must follow certain principles. If we ignore even one of these essential principles, we'll become something other than a church, with no defining characteristic to separate us from a country club or civic organization.

I'm convinced that if your church is characterized by the ten principles outlined in this book, regardless of the methods you choose to implement them, God will bless your efforts.

Many church leaders go to conferences looking for a quick fix or easy solutions to their problems. They hope to discover some fresh program, some unique gimmick that will jump-start their church—contemporary music with a band, shorter or longer sermons, expository preaching or thematic preaching, small groups, or technological enhancements in the service. Discussing those ideas may be helpful, but what works in one culture or one area of the United States may not work in another. What one church adapts as positive change may be a source of division in another.

The methods we have implemented at Southeast Christian Church may or may not work at your church. You can't fight Goliath wearing Saul's armor. You can't minister with someone else's style. You have to be yourself and adapt to the culture around you. But the principles that undergird those methods—the ten principles discussed in this book—should be enlisted by every congregation that intends to glorify Jesus Christ. Although I will share with you some specific ways our church has tried to apply these principles, you must remember that the secret ingredients are the principles themselves, not the applications.

Rick Warren, in his excellent book *The Purpose Driven Church*, warned church leaders not to try to copycat someone else's church. He said, "You cannot grow a church trying to be someone else." But then he identified what you *can* learn from observing other congregations.

> You can learn principles. As the old cliché says, "Methods are many, principles are few; methods change often, principles never do." If a principle is biblical, I believe it is transcultural. It will work anywhere. It's wise to learn and apply principles from watching how God is working around the world. While you cannot grow a church trying to be someone else, you can

grow a church by using principles someone else discovered and then filtering them through your personality and context.[1]

Amen, Rick! That's what I want to communicate in this book. I want to focus on those principles Rick Warren was talking about.

Many churches have changed their methods to try to reach a new generation and have failed to see any results. But I challenge you to find one church characterized by these ten principles that isn't a healthy, God-honoring, growing congregation. Someday the megachurch may become a thing of the past. Our culture may change, and we may discover a better way to make disciples for Jesus Christ. Right now God is using some very large congregations to reach thousands for Christ and to revive the hearts of thousands more. But regardless of the future of the megachurch, the ten principles that I share in this book will remain true.

Twice a year we host a leadership conference. About fifteen hundred people from churches all over the world attend. Our conference is unique in that it is designed primarily for lay leaders. When pastors go to conferences, they get energized with new ideas and a renewed vision for ministry, then return to a church board that is resistant to change. But our conference helps a church's lay leaders get on the same page as their ministers—and that's usually the first step toward positive change.

We do have a track for preachers at our conference, but about 75 percent of those who attend are elders, deacons, Sunday-school teachers, volunteer music directors, and committee chairpersons. Hundreds of those church leaders have reported back to us about the dramatic growth their churches have experienced after implementing the ten principles I discuss in this book.

My Reluctance to Write This Book

When it was first suggested to me that I write a book about the principles that have helped Southeast Christian Church become the church it is today, I was reluctant to do so for several reasons.

God's Definition of Success Is Different

God doesn't define success in the same terms that we do. Although we rejoice over our numerical growth, we know that God doesn't measure success in terms of attendance, offerings, or size of buildings. He measures effectiveness in terms of faithfulness to His Word, conformity to Jesus Christ, and ministry to those in need.

What If Someone Thinks We're Boasting?

When we talk about the blessings our church has enjoyed, some readers will interpret it as boasting. The apostle Paul wrote, "May I never boast except in the cross of our Lord Jesus Christ, through which the world has been crucified to me, and I to the world" (Gal. 6:14). But Paul did reluctantly boast about what he had witnessed God doing in his presence (2 Cor. 11:10).

God has done a remarkable thing in our church, and he deserves praise. When a church that has stayed true to God's Word grows from fifty people to almost fourteen thousand, builds a 770,000-square-foot facility, gives forty-two million dollars over its regular giving to finance the new building, and has over twenty-four hundred new members in one year, it's obvious that God is doing something significant.

If someone interprets describing all this as boasting, then we have failed to communicate that we're only speaking of how the Lord has blessed us. The Bible commands, "Praise be to the God and Father of our Lord Jesus Christ, who has blessed us in the heavenly realms with every spiritual blessing in Christ" (Eph. 1:3).

I recently met a couple who had listened to me for years on the radio in a city several hundred miles away. They decided to come visit our church, and they were awestruck. The husband said to me, "Bob, we can't get over this place. Only God can do this. I mean, Bob, you're good, but you're not that good!" He's right. It's the Lord who is building the church, not me. I am grateful for the opportunity to make a contribution, but the glory goes to Jesus Christ.

Misconceptions about Megachurches

I have read several articles claiming that most megachurches have grown primarily through "stealing sheep" from other congregations. If you've read those same articles, you might be reading this book with a certain amount of skepticism. I can't speak for other megachurches—I can only report what has happened at Southeast—but through interviews and surveys with our new members, we estimate that 50 percent of them were not involved in any church before coming to Southeast. The other half had their names on a church roll somewhere, but most of them had not actively participated for years. Others left their church because of increased liberalism and were looking for a place where the Scriptures are believed and taught. I heard a preacher in a growing church say, "We don't steal sheep, but we do plant grass!" If people hungry for spiritual food find it in our fellowship, then we certainly welcome them.

Very few of our new members have left an active involvement with a Bible-believing church to come to Southeast. In fact, a megachurch often acts as a funnel to feed other smaller congregations in its area. People often visit Southeast knowing they can remain anonymous and are introduced to Christ. But later they may decide that the church is too far from their home or too big, and they find another church closer to their home or more suited to their needs.

After both of our relocations, we helped support the two smaller churches that bought our previous sites. Several hundred people stayed behind and became involved in those two churches. We sent them a letter thanking them for their contribution to our church and wishing them the very best in their new church families. Our primary concern is that people grow in Christ.

It's Hard to Explain God's Blessings

When God works, it's very difficult to explain why or how it happens. I get amused when "experts" attempt to analyze church growth.

Sometimes they even analyze Southeast as an example. They try to reduce all that has happened to us to a formula. But I've been in the middle of miraculous growth for thirty years, and I can't really explain it myself. Jesus compared the movement of the Holy Spirit to the wind: "The wind blows wherever it pleases," he said. "You hear its sound, but you cannot tell where it comes from or where it is going" (John 3:8).

When I came to Southeast in 1966, I didn't say to the board, "We're going to implement these ten principles and watch our church grow as a result." I didn't have these ten things in mind. But over the years as we began to grow, people started asking why. Why is Southeast growing at such a remarkable pace when other churches aren't? What's the difference?

While I can't explain why God chose to bless us in such a miraculous way, this book is an attempt to explain the basic spiritual principles that have enabled God to pour out His blessings upon us. When Jesus went to Nazareth, he could do no mighty work there because of their unbelief. That tells me that our unbelief and failures can inhibit the work that God wants to do in our midst. I am confident that God wants to do even greater works in other places if he is invited and allowed to do so.

God Wants to Bless Your Church beyond Your Imagination

Many churches in America are dead. They aren't evangelizing, they've quit sending missionaries to the field, and they're having financial problems. The reason for their failure is that at least one of the principles in this book hasn't been followed. Their leaders aren't humble people with vision and a desire to change, the congregation doesn't get along, they don't worship God, they don't give generously, they don't care about evangelism, they don't do things with excellence, or God's truth isn't being spoken from the pulpit.

But I thank God that there are also many churches in America that are very much alive. They're worshiping God, loving one another, and winning people to Christ. Regardless of their size, the ten principles in this book characterize their church. And God has blessed them beyond their wildest dreams—not just with numbers, but with growth in the hearts and souls of the people. Southeast is just one among thousands of such churches.

When these principles are implemented, regardless of the size of your church, I'm convinced that God will bless you more than you could ask or imagine. It's my prayer that he will use this book to prepare you and your congregation for an even greater outpouring of the Holy Spirit in your church.

Several years ago, a young intern went back to seminary after spending several months serving with us. He said his friends immediately hounded him with questions about his experience. "What did you learn from being at Southeast Christian Church? Did you learn about preaching? Administration? What was your most significant lesson?"

He answered, "I think what I really learned is what a church can be."

I'm hoping that's what you will gain from reading this book. I hope you won't see this as a story about a big church, but a vision of what your church can be. Your church may not grow to be fourteen thousand people. Maybe it will grow even larger! But regardless of the size, God can bless your church more than you ever asked or imagined. I hope our story will inspire you to lift your sights and increase your faith.

I can't tell you how honored I am that you have picked up this book. Whether you are a seminary student, church planter, minister, missionary, elder, deacon, or volunteer worker, I hope this book will be an encouragement to you. I pray you will learn something that will help your church better fulfill its mission. May your congregation be instrumental in bringing scores of souls to Jesus Christ and helping them get better acquainted.

❖ Believe the Truth (The World Doesn't)

❖ Teach the Truth (Many Churches Don't)

❖ Apply the Truth (Most Teachers Don't)

1

TRUTH:
Proclaim God's Word as Truth and Apply It to People's Lives

Several months before we moved into our new church building in 1998, our ministry staff met at the new site for a special staff meeting. Most of the building still wasn't carpeted, and some of the rooms still had no drywall. We handed out hard hats, magic markers, and a few Bibles. We instructed staff members to go to the classrooms and offices in the building where they would be working and write Scripture verses on the concrete floors. I said, "Someday soon the scriptures will be covered with carpet. But I hope you will always remember what you have written today. And what we do today will be a visible reminder that we are always to stand on God's Word."

The staff really got into it. Some of them used cans of spray paint they had brought so the words would show up better. (They acted as if they had some experience, which bothered me a little!) Those in the children's ministry wrote things like, "Let the little

13

children come to me...for the kingdom of heaven belongs to such as these."

In the education wing, the adult education ministers wrote things like, "Study to show yourself approved unto God," and "Your Word have I hid in my heart that I might not sin against you."

In the music practice rooms, the music ministers wrote, "Sing and make music unto the Lord," and "Let everything that has breath praise the Lord."

In the offices of the preaching team, we wrote passages like, "Preach the Word in season and out of season," and "Watch your life and doctrine closely...if you do, you will save both yourself and your hearers."

One of our single ladies who worked in the children's ministry wrote her favorite verse on the floor of her office: "It is not good for a man to be alone"!

The "scriptures-on-the-floor" idea caught on, and soon hundreds of church members followed suit. In a matter of weeks, there were scriptures all over the concrete floors—down hallways, on stairways, on the steps leading up to the pulpit. I saw moms and dads bring their children to the building just to write their favorite scriptures on the concrete floors. We actually considered asking people to stop because they started writing in places we hadn't planned to cover with carpet! But we decided it wasn't a good idea to make people quit writing scriptures!

I heard of class officers gathering in their future classrooms, praying together, and writing scriptures on the floor. Small groups chose special places in the building to write their favorite scriptures. When you walked through the building, all the floors looked like they were covered with graffiti. But instead of curse words, they were covered with God's Word. The building became a dramatic reminder to all of us that our church has been called to stand upon the Word of God.

One of our small groups had volunteered to help clean the building one afternoon. As they were preparing to leave, Marty Rice, prayer leader of the group, said, "Why don't we write down a scripture reference in one of the rooms before we leave?"

They found a small room that didn't have any scriptures yet. Rick Nally, one of the group members, said, "How about the passage where Jesus said, 'Where two or three of you are gathered in my name, there am I in the midst of you'?"

Marty asked, "What's the reference?"

"I think it's Matthew 18:28," Rick said. Marty stooped and wrote, "Matthew 18:28" and the group's name on the floor in permanent marker.

Later that evening at a restaurant, Rick brought in his Bible from the car to double-check the reference. He said, "Oh no. It's Matthew 18:20, not 18:28."

Someone asked the obvious question: "What's verse 28 say?"

Rick read, "When that servant went out, he found one of his fellow servants who owed him a hundred denarii. He grabbed him and began to choke him. 'Pay back what you owe me!' he demanded."

I suppose if you are ever in our building and, while standing in a certain classroom, suddenly have the urge to choke someone, you'll know why!

I believe the greatest reason God has chosen to bless Southeast Christian Church and thousands of other evangelical churches around the world is that we have been serious about upholding the absolute truth of God's Word. In a very real sense, we've continued to stand on the Word of God.

Believe the Truth (The World Doesn't)

I'm writing this chapter just weeks after two teenagers in Littleton, Colorado, killed twelve of their classmates and one teacher at Columbine High School before turning the guns on themselves. Following the shooting, Vice President Al Gore was asked by Larry

King why America was so attracted to violence. Gore responded, "It's because of our evolutionary heritage. It's the nature of tooth and claw." A liberal preacher on the same show was asked what he believed needed to be done. He said, "We just need to build up the kids' self-esteem. It doesn't really matter what religion you are; just tell kids they're good and wonderful and beautiful."

The truth is that man has a sin problem that can only be transformed by Jesus Christ. As Franklin Graham said, "When we empty the public schools of the moral teachings and the standards of our holy God, they are indeed very dangerous places."[1] It's true that kids need to be loved. But they are not just "good and wonderful"; they are also sinners—as all of us are (Rom. 3:23). Youth need to be told the truth—that there is an all-powerful God in the universe to whom we will some day give an account; that there is a standard of right and wrong; that we have all violated that standard; and that unless we repent and trust in Christ, we face the wrath of God.

I've heard author Frank Peretti compare our culture's hunger for biblical absolutes to the need for authority on a neighborhood playground in the summertime. Posted on the fence of the playground are some rules: "No hitting. No profanity. Only age ten and under on the monkey bars. Only age eight and older on the basketball court. Ten-minute limit on the tetherball court." The rules work well because mingling through the crowd of children is Mrs. Kravitz. She has a keen eye, and if you misbehave, she will give you a pink slip. Two pink slips and you're out of the playground for the summer.

But take Mrs. Kravitz out of the picture. How long do you think it will take before the rules begin to be violated? "Hey, he hit me!" "She spit on me!" "Hey, get those big kids off the monkey bars! Little kids are getting hurt!" "Hey, he cut the tetherball off!"

Who will soon rule the playground? The biggest, the strongest, the most antagonistic. That's what is happening in our society, because there is no regard for the rules. The Ten Commandments are no longer obeyed, and the Bible is no longer respected as a source of authority in our culture, largely because it is not preached from our pulpits as the Word of God. Preachers don't have the ability to "hand out pink slips," but we do have a duty to uphold the truth of God's Word and sound a clear warning as to what judgment God will bring if his rules are disobeyed. Since preachers haven't faithfully done that, our culture has taken the rules off the fence. The Ten Commandments have been completely removed from public life and even outlawed in public places. And there is no longer any fear of God's authority.

Paul described those who have no fear of God: "Their feet are swift to shed blood; ruin and misery mark their ways, and the way of peace they do not know. There is no fear of God before their eyes" (Rom. 3:15–18). One of America's founders said that people will either be governed by the Bible or the bayonet. A nation of people who refuse to govern themselves will need to have a strong police force to prevent anarchy. That's why our president recently proposed adding one hundred thousand police officers to the streets of America's cities.

Bob Vernon, former assistant police chief of the Los Angeles Police Department, once suggested a theory of "parallel lines" in comparing the church with the culture. He indicated that the church is to be above the world and that we usually do stay above the world to a certain extent. But as the world's values nosedive, we are tempted to accommodate our values so that we're just a *little* above the world, instead of maintaining the high standard of truth that God prescribed in his Word.

The challenge is to retain high biblical standards regardless of how far the world "slouches toward Gomorrah," as Judge Robert Bork put it. John said, "See that what you have heard from the beginning remains in you. If it does, you also will remain in the Son and in the Father. And this is what he promised us—even eternal life" (1 John 2:24–25).

Certain transcendent truths are absolute—the inspiration of Scripture, the historical creation of man, the deity of Jesus Christ, the plan of salvation, the Ten Commandments. These have been given by God as unchanging truths, and they should not be compromised. The church must stand firm in the faith and "preach the Word…in season and out of season" (2 Tim. 4:2). When you do, you will be labeled fundamental, narrow-minded, and bigoted. But Jesus said, "Small is the gate and narrow the road that leads to life, and only a few find it" (Matt. 7:14).

Resist the Temptation to Compromise the Truth

It's not just liberal preachers like the one I heard on *Larry King Live* who are tempted to compromise the truth. We all get into tight situations and are tempted to take the easy way out by saying what we know people want to hear. A wealthy businessman in our community who had pledged a million dollars to our building fund came to me before it was collected and asked me to perform his wedding…his third wedding. Because of the circumstances surrounding his previous divorce, his situation didn't fit into our marriage policy. It was really tempting to try to find a way to accommodate his request. But I decided to follow the policy. (Partly, I confess, because I was afraid the elders would fire me if I didn't follow their guidelines!)

There are times in every church when the leaders are tempted to water down the truth. There will be influential people you want to accommodate. There will be brilliant, likable theological liberals you want to impress. There will be arrogant, angry conservatives you wish you could debate, because even though you may agree with their stance, you hate their demeanor. There will be seekers and believers you won't want to alienate by taking an unpopular stand on a controversial issue.

Despite the real temptation to say just what itching ears want to hear or to say nothing at all, it is imperative that the church be a place where the truth is unashamedly proclaimed. As Paul said, "If the trumpet does not sound a clear call, who will get ready for battle?" (1 Cor. 14:8).

At our annual staff retreat, I always have a kind of "State of the Church" address. In it I encourage the staff, talk about what has gone well in the past year, and try to cast a vision for the coming year. Each year I remind the staff how important it is that they maintain their personal integrity in all they do, lest they themselves become a hindrance to the great work God is doing in our church.

This past year I also asked them to renew their commitment to biblical truth. "When you came on staff," I said, "you signed a document indicating your belief that the Bible is the Word of God. But sometimes people change. Maybe you've taken some graduate classes at a liberal seminary that have led you to question the infallibility of the Bible, or perhaps something else has happened in your life to cause you to waver from your confidence in God's Word. If so, I hope you'll have enough integrity to step down from your position."

Gerd Lüdemann, a prominent German theologian, recently declared, "I no longer describe myself as a Christian." Lüdemann taught for several years at Vanderbilt University and is currently the professor of New Testament and director of the Institute of Early Christian Studies at Göttingen University in Germany. After spending years undermining the Christian faith as a liberal Christian professor, Lüdemann finally decided to do the honest thing. "A Christian is someone who prays to Christ and believes in what is promised by Christian doctrine," Lüdemann admitted. "So I asked myself: 'Do I pray to Jesus? Do I pray to the God of the Bible?' And I don't do that. Quite the reverse."[2]

Liberalism has destroyed too many churches. Many liberals will not be as honest as Gerd Lüdemann was. Instead they continue to pretend they are believers in Christ when they are not. Charles Colson said the number one question in our society today is this: *Is there any absolute truth?* It's imperative that every leader in your church be committed to the Bible as God's Word, the source of absolute truth.

An exciting movement called the Alpha Project is sweeping some formerly liberal, mainline churches. It's a call to fundamental Christianity that is revitalizing some old, formerly dying churches. It began in England and has now taken root in two thousand churches in America. Church leaders are recognizing that liberalism has been a dismal failure, so they are returning to the "alpha" (beginning) beliefs. "Churches that have embraced the program claim it can change lives, jump-start the faith of lukewarm Christians, and bring agnostics and atheists into the fold." Many leaders at formerly liberal churches have begun offering the Alpha courses in efforts to "stem the tide of declining membership and attendance."

Be Ready to Face Opposition

The Alpha Project has drawn criticism from liberal Christians who have taken issue with the course's hard line on divorce, abortion, and homosexuality; its stance that the Bible is literally true; its claim that Christianity is the exclusive path of salvation; and its "lopsided" emphasis on the Holy Spirit.[3] This criticism shouldn't surprise anyone. Jesus promised that those who followed him and stood for truth would be opposed (see John 15:20).

The erosion of truth we saw in the 1990s will only worsen in the next millennium. According to the postmodern mind, there are no absolutes. *You can believe what you want to believe,* the popular thinking goes, *but don't impose your values on me.* The most important virtue to the postmodernist is *tolerance.* To be dogmatic about anything—no matter how true it might be—is considered the height of arrogance and intolerance. That means you can expect increased hostility and opposition if you dare to speak the truth.

A preacher doesn't often get the opportunity to speak openly about

Christ in a public high-school classroom these days, but my son Rusty was asked recently to speak to a local high-school humanities class during a series on world religions. The school is a "magnet" school that attempts to attract the intellectual and artistic elite among our county's teenagers. It's full of National Merit Scholars and some of the sharpest young minds in the area.

After Rusty's lecture, in which he explained the basic beliefs of Christianity and shared the gospel with thirty teenagers, he asked if there were any questions. The students bombarded him with some harsh questions about his claim that Jesus was the "only way" to heaven. He answered, "Jesus said, 'I am the way, the truth and the life; no one comes to the Father except by me.' Either he was telling the truth or he wasn't. Yes, it's exclusive, but that's what he claimed. I'd invite you to search the Scriptures and the historical evidence to see if Jesus' claims were valid. If he was speaking the truth, we'd better follow him." But no matter how logical and polite Rusty tried to be, most of the students still insisted that it was wrong of him to contend that any way was the "true" way.

"I used to be a Christian, but I'm not anymore," one student said. "I just can't accept a religion that tries to claim it's the only true one." Others said similar things about growing up in Christian homes only to reject Christianity because of its exclusiveness. Whether it was true or not didn't matter. To claim that you or anyone else—even Christ himself—has the only handle on the truth is to be intolerant and therefore wrong, according to their system of values.

Several months ago Dave Stone (our preaching associate) and I preached a sermon series titled "Stepping Up and Speaking Out about Moral Issues." The series dealt with topics like racism, abortion, homosexuality, and divorce. Around the office we subtitled it "How to Empty the Church in Five Weeks." But we were wrong. People came and brought their friends. Several responded to the invitation. People would say, "We're so thankful to be a part of a church that takes a stand for God's truth." We tried to speak the truth in love, but we were determined to speak the truth. And God blessed us.

But not everyone was happy with us. On Christmas Eve, 1998, when we held our first services in our new facility, over five thousand people came to the first of five services held that day. I was team preaching with Dave Stone. Christmas Eve is normally a challenging time to deliver a message, so to add some creativity, we had decided to stand side by side and preach alternate points of the sermon. In the middle of one of my points about the humility of Jesus, a man stood up in the balcony and began shouting. "That's absurd!" he yelled. "Jesus was humble and compassionate, and that's exactly what you're not!"

I had never met the man, so I wondered how he knew me so well! He continued to shout. I was finished with my point, so I just looked at Dave while the man shouted, and I said, "Your turn."

Dave had a brilliant, and I think Spirit-led, response. "You can listen to this man," he said calmly to the congregation, "but what you need to do is measure everything that is said—whether by us or someone else—by the truth of God's Word." The congregation stood and applauded, drowning out the heckler.

Our security team did an excellent job, and the heckler was escorted out within thirty seconds. Once outside, the man said, "I know my rights. I want to see a policeman." He was told, "All seven of us are policemen. Which one would you like to talk to?" The man was arrested for disturbing the peace and had to spend a few hours in jail.

The service continued, and everything went smoothly, but afterward, the primary topic of conversation for most people was the incident with the heckler. He had successfully tarnished our first service in the new facility. The AP newswire carried a story, picked up by several major newspapers across the country, with a headline that read, "Heckler mars first service."

Several weeks later that heckler was interviewed by a local gay-and-lesbian magazine. He said he had interrupted our services because he had to speak out against the intolerance of our church. Although he admitted he had never been to our church before, he was angered by our stance that homosexual behavior is a sin against God.

When you stand for truth, you will be opposed. But Jesus said, "Blessed are you when people insult you, persecute you and falsely say all kinds of evil against you because of me. Rejoice and be glad, because great is your reward in heaven, for in the same way they persecuted the prophets who were before you" (Matt. 5:11–12). God has promised that he will bless the church that proclaims his truth. In this case, we were able to see that promise fulfilled almost overnight. In the year following that incident with the heckler, our attendance jumped by three thousand people at our weekend services, we've had over two thousand additions to the church, and the Holy Spirit has permeated our congregation.

God promised Isaiah that as the rain falls and produces a crop, "so is my word that goes out from my mouth: It will not return to me empty, but will accomplish what I desire and achieve the purpose for which I sent it" (Isa. 55:11). We should say with Paul, "I am not ashamed of the gospel, because it is the power of God for the salvation of everyone who believes: first for the Jew, then for the Gentile" (Rom. 1:16).

TEACH THE TRUTH (MANY CHURCHES DON'T)

Have you ever been invited to someone's home for an evening party thinking that dinner was going to be served and you were mistaken? You arrive hungry only to realize it's an open house with only a few finger foods or desserts on the table. You try to fill up on the finger foods, but they don't satisfy. You walk away hungry and say to yourself, *I need to stop by a fast-food restaurant and get a hamburger or something!*

The Importance of Preaching

Many people leave church feeling empty every week. They come hungry for the Word of God, but when they aren't fed, they go empty, hungry, and frustrated. Eventually, unless all they want out of church is the security of tradition or an entertainment fix, they will drift away in an effort to find a place that's offering some substance.

I've noticed a disturbing trend among our churches and Christian colleges. We have discovered worship, and that is good, but some leaders are so enthusiastic about praise and worship that they want to omit the preaching altogether! A Bible-college professor recently told me that almost all of their student-led chapels, about four out of five, had no preaching at all. An "all-singing" service is certainly appropriate occasionally, but to rarely be exposed to preaching—especially on a campus that is supposed to be training the preachers of the next generation— seems way out of balance.

Jesus was a preacher. In fact, in Luke 4:43, Jesus said, "I must preach the good news...because *that is why I was sent*" (author's emphasis)." John the Baptist was a preacher. Paul was a preacher. While Paul was in prison, he bemoaned the fact that some were preaching out of impure motives. Then he concluded, "But what does it matter? The important thing is that in every way, whether from false motives or true, Christ is preached. And because of this I rejoice" (Phil. 1:18).

Instill the Desire to Preach in Young People

When I was in elementary school, the preacher at my church was an eighty-year-old man named D. P. Shaffer. He had been at the church for decades. He was a great man and respected in the community. I remember that he was a very dignified man with a shock of white hair. His hands trembled and his voice quaked from palsy.

One children's day at our church, when I was in the first grade, I quoted a large portion of John 14 in front of the congregation. He met me in the hall, patted me on the head, and said, "You are going to make a good preacher someday." That idea lay dormant in my mind until the end of my senior year in high school when I was suddenly struck with the idea that I should be a preacher.

Although I love preaching, I can relate to what Paul said: "When I preach the gospel, I cannot boast, for I am compelled to preach. Woe to me if I do not preach the gospel! If I preach voluntarily, I have a reward; if not voluntarily, I am simply discharging the trust committed to me" (1 Cor. 9:16–17).

Preaching is an essential ministry of the church and should be held in high regard. We need to develop in our young people not only a hunger for worship but a desire to be fed God's Word through good preaching. And we need to creatively instill in their minds the idea that God could use them someday to spread the gospel.

Use a Lot of Scripture

I remember a second thing D. P. Shaffer said, but only because my mother would quote him. Once an arrogant young preacher delivered a sermon in our church that contained almost no Scripture. My mother, who rarely spoke a negative word to anyone, said to him afterward, "I remember what D. P. Shaffer used to say about preaching: 'Whenever you preach, always use a lot of Scripture, because that's one thing you know is true.'"

Paul commanded Timothy,

> In the presence of God and of Christ Jesus, who will judge the living and the dead, and in view of his appearing and his kingdom, I give you this charge: Preach the Word; be prepared in season and out of season; correct, rebuke and encourage— with great patience and careful instruction. For the time will come when men will not put up with sound doctrine. Instead, to suit their own desires, they will gather around them a great number of teachers to say what their itching ears want to hear. They will turn their ears away from the truth and turn aside to myths. But you, keep your head in all situations,

endure hardship, do the work of an evangelist, discharge all the duties of your ministry. (2 Tim. 4:1–5)

Ground People in the Truth of God's Word

God has ordained the church to be a place of truth. Jesus commanded us to go into all the world and preach the gospel (Mark 16:15). And that gospel doesn't change, regardless of how far the values of our culture erode. Do your best to see that the members of your church, from age zero to one hundred, are grounded in God's Word. Make sure they understand the Bible and have adopted a biblical view of the world.

- In your nursery, don't just baby-sit the kids for an hour. Find a curriculum like Palma Smiley where infants are taught Bible songs and each week learn to respectfully pat the Bible "because the Bible is true."

- In your preschool, don't just play games. Children are sponges, soaking up everything around them. Teach them to memorize Scripture, take the time to plan lessons, and design creative activities that help them learn the Bible stories you want them to remember.

- In your elementary programs, use all the resources available— drama, videos, crafts—to teach your kids God's Word.

- In your youth ministry, don't just entertain your teenagers or rely on gimmicks to get them involved. Teach them God's Word.

- In your counseling, don't just listen. Tell them what God's Word says.

- Provide adult Bible classes that deepen people's understanding of God's truth. Create in them a hunger for the Word of God.

Train your teachers to know God's Word and equip them to communicate it creatively and effectively.

Every ministry should find a way to deepen people's understanding of God's truths so that Christians will be equipped to face this changing world with a solid biblical foundation that does not change—"Then we will no longer be infants, tossed back and forth by the waves, and blown here and there by every wind of teaching and by the cunning and craftiness of men in their deceitful scheming. Instead, speaking the truth in love, we will in all things grow up into him who is the Head, that is, Christ" (Eph. 4:14–15).

Balance Strong Stands with God's Grace

Paul exhorted the church to always speak "the truth in love" (Eph. 4:15). One of the reasons we've been able to continue growing while taking a strong biblical stand on moral issues is that we've done our best to shower people with the grace of God. Someone who has been convicted of God's truth is ready to receive God's grace. Conversely, someone who has heard only about God's grace cannot appreciate it. Grace can only be understood in the context of God's truth.

About six months before our new building was finished, I walked out on the roof and went up to the base of the forty-foot-high cross that sits atop our worship center. I love that cross because it is actually a part of the structure. The base of the cross descends thirty-two feet below the roof into the superstructure and acts like a keystone. It supports the twelve trusses that come to the center and symbolizes that the cross of Christ must be the cornerstone of our church. The cross is directly over the pulpit, symbolizing that we preach under the authority of the cross.

But as I stood at the base of that cross and looked out over the roof, I saw something that put goose bumps on my arms. Unknown to me, the company that had provided the insulation for the roof was the

Grace Ice and Watershield Company. The insulation comes in six-foot sheets, and the word "GRACE" is printed in bold letters on every sheet. As I looked out from the cross, I saw the words GRACE, GRACE, GRACE, GRACE, GRACE...hundreds of times. I thought, *Maybe the Lord is trying to tell me something!* (Even I could catch the symbolism in that!) The church is to be covered with God's grace.

Jesus is described as being "full of grace and truth" (John 1:14). That's the kind of God we need to be portraying from our pulpits—a God of grace and truth.

Years ago I was trying to communicate the fact that we're all sinners saved by God's grace. I said:

> I am an expert with the TV's remote control. I hate watching ads. I can watch three programs simultaneously and get the gist of all three. But I confess that sometimes late at night when I'm channel surfing, I'm tempted to stop when the girls are attractive or scantily clad. (That's why I don't have premium movie channels in my home. I know I'm too weak to resist the temptation if it's right there all the time.) When I yield to that temptation to lust, I feel cheapened, guilty, and unworthy. I need God's forgiveness. Steve Brown says, "Pray for the strong, because they are weak." I've never had an affair. I've never been to an adult bookstore. I'm not addicted to pornography. But I am tempted. I can understand those who crash in those areas. But there's good news: Jesus Christ can forgive the past and empower us to win the victory in the future.

A few weeks after I used that illustration, a physician who is a member of our church walked up to me. He said, "I bought that tape and shared it with a friend of mine, because we both struggle with that same temptation. It was so helpful to know that you struggle too. We realized that it's a daily battle that we can win. And God can forgive us and use us even though the flesh has dragged us down on occasion and we're imperfect."

The apostle Paul said that Jesus came into the world to save sinners and that he, Paul, was the worst sinner of all (see 1 Tim. 1:15). When we preach as sinners saved by grace, instead of superior saints with a condescending spirit, people are encouraged to trust in Christ's love.

Be careful that you don't go too far in your efforts to convince people that you, too, are in need of God's grace. We don't need to exaggerate our sins—they're bad enough as they are. You may have some past sins that you shouldn't share. If God has buried our sins in the deepest sea, we don't need to be dredging them up. Share your spiritual victories too. Keep a balance so that people see the real you but still respect you as their leader. People have a right to expect a higher level of spirituality among their leaders, but your preaching and teaching should always be full of grace.

When I was eight years old, I was riding home from church on Christmas Eve with the rest of my family. I was in the backseat by the door of our old 1948 Nash Rambler. I kept staring at the door handle, wondering what would happen if I just pulled up a little on the handle. (I was interested in aerodynamics, of course.) The back doors of the '48 Rambler opened right into the wind, the opposite of car doors today. They came to be known later as "suicide doors." My curiosity finally got the best of me. I lifted up just a little and—whoosh!—the air ripped that car door open into the oncoming traffic. I grabbed the security rope on the back of the seat and dived onto the floor. My dad brought the car to a screeching halt, and my mother turned around and cried, "Oh, where's Bobby? Where's Bobby?!"

My sisters said, "Oh, Mother, he's all right. He's down here on the floor."

My dad got out of the car, took a few deep breaths, and just leaned up against the car for a minute or two. He drove the rest of the way home without saying a word. I knew I was in deep trouble. All the way home my older sisters kept saying, "What kind of an idiot would open up a car door while the car is going fifty miles an hour?"

When we got home, I jumped out of the car, ran into the house, and stood behind the Christmas tree for protection. My dad came in, walked straight over to me, picked me up, and gave me the biggest hug I can ever remember him giving me. He kept saying over and over again, "I'm sure glad you didn't fall out of that car, son."

I was glad too! And I was also glad for my dad's grace-filled reaction. It's not hard for me to imagine a God of grace because my earthly father was so full of grace. When I picture dying and standing before God, I don't imagine him as an angry judge with a clipboard listing all the idiotic and sinful things I have done in my lifetime. I picture God like the father of the prodigal son, opening his arms, saying, "Welcome home. All is forgiven. Let's celebrate."

APPLY THE TRUTH (MOST TEACHERS DON'T)

The Word of God has tremendous power when the preacher or teacher applies it in a way that builds a bridge to the daily lives of the listeners. "For the word of God is living and active. Sharper than any double-edged sword, it penetrates even to dividing soul and spirit, joints and marrow; it judges the thoughts and attitudes of the heart" (Heb. 4:12).

Jesus, the greatest preacher of all time, was a master at applying biblical principles to the lives of his listeners. When Jesus read the Scripture in the synagogue, he made a direct application to the attitudes of his listeners toward the Gentiles. It was a Gentile widow who helped Elijah, Jesus noted. And it was a Gentile leper that Elisha healed. The Jews in his audience were convicted, not just because Jesus read the Scripture and explained what it meant, but because he connected it to their racist attitudes. In fact, they were so convicted that they tried to kill him! But they certainly didn't ignore him.

Ask, "How Does This Apply?"

Don Hinkle, a popular youth speaker, used to train his audience to yell out upon his cue, "So what? Who cares? Where does that touch me?" He would then proceed to tell them how the message should apply to their personal lives. Whether you're preaching to thousands of adults or teaching a small group of preschoolers, make sure your lesson applies to the daily lives of those who are listening. When you're preparing the lesson, picture them asking, "So what? Who cares? Where does that touch me?" How does the lesson you've prepared apply to their daily lives?

There are three parts to good preaching and teaching: Exposition of text (explaining the passage), illustration of truth, and application to life. A lot of preaching I've heard is heavy on exposition, and occasionally has some illustrations, but has no application to life. Your lessons will not be as effective in changing the hearts, minds, and lives of your hearers if you don't answer the question, *Where does that touch me?*

My friend Bob Shannon, former minister of First Christian Church in Largo, Florida, has often said, "I don't go into the pulpit to explain a passage of Scripture. I go into the pulpit to meet a need. It just so happens that for every need, there is a passage of Scripture that can meet it."

John Stott wrote a book about preaching with a great title: *Between Two Worlds.*[4] The preacher's task is to build a bridge between the spiritual world of the Bible and the world in which we live. When you are studying a passage of Scripture, ask yourself, *How does this apply to me? And how does it apply to those I will be teaching?* Pray that God will reveal to you specific ways the passage should make a difference in people's lives.

Apply the Scripture to Monday

We preachers are inclined to give mainly "Sunday" applications, applying Scripture to the activities of the church. Suppose you were preaching or teaching from the passage where Jesus commanded his followers to deny themselves (Matt. 16:24). If we try to apply that passage, we'll usually implore people to attend church, tithe, volunteer to teach a Sunday-school class, or sign up to visit prospects. But the application we make should focus on the day-to-day lifestyles of our listeners. How can listeners deny themselves Monday through Saturday?

For example, you might say, "Instead of watching television tomorrow night, take time to help your wife fold the clothes. Instead of eating out three times a week, consider fasting one of those times and giving the money to a needy college student. Instead of goofing off at work when you have nothing else to do, decide you're going to assist a colleague who seems overloaded." When people see the gospel is relevant to Monday, not just Sunday, then the Word of God begins to come alive to them.

Include Brief Examples of Practical Application

Suppose you're preaching or teaching about covetousness as I was several months ago. If you say, "We all know what it is to be jealous of this or that which belongs to another," some people will build the bridge to their own situation. But if you were to come up with three or four one-word examples of what we covet, the application would be even more relevant. Suppose you say, "You know, sometimes we're jealous of another person's house, appearance, children, mate, or even talents." Those suggestions become like pylons, enabling the bridge to be built more quickly and effectively.

Two or three specific, one-sentence examples will make the application even better. You might say,

> Some of you are perfectly content living in your house until you go to a "Homearama" show where some architectural marvel is on display, then you come home discontented with your own house. Some of you are perfectly happy with your mate, but then you go to a party and see someone else's spouse who is more attractive or more romantic, and you come home critical and envious. Some of you have wonderful children, but when you see other children who get better grades or are more athletic, you churn with envy and discontentment. You might

love your church, but then you visit a church that seems more alive, and you start picking at the little problems at your church.

Such one-line examples of application can really cultivate the soil of the heart to receive God's truth.

Get the Illustrations from the Application

I find that my best illustrations often emerge from my effort to find examples of application. While I was preparing the sermon on coveting, I started to write, "You may be content with your seat at a ball game, and then you see someone with a better seat...." Then I remembered a time it happened to me. It was a very important University of Louisville basketball game. Signs at the gate said, "Ball Game Sold Out." Scalpers outside the arena were getting twice the ticket price. I took my seat in row 23 and sat for a few minutes thinking about how blessed I was to be in this exciting atmosphere.

Then just before the game started, I looked across the arena and saw Chuck Lee, one of our associate ministers, sitting at mid court, on the third row! I thought to myself, *How did he get those seats? He's not as big a fan of the Louisville Cardinals as I am. Wow, those are great seats! I wish I weren't up so high. I'd like to be closer to center court. This guy in front of me is so tall and has a huge head. He's hard to see around.* Before the game started I almost made myself miserable. I almost fired Chuck Lee!

When I used that story as an illustration, people smiled because they knew exactly what I was feeling. It made it easy to build a bridge to their own personal lives because they've felt the same way.

Last fall I preached a sermon on King David and Nathan the prophet. If you've been preaching or teaching for very long, you've probably told that story. Several months after David committed adultery with Bathsheba, Nathan was sent to confront him. He told David a touching story about a rich man who stole his neighbor's pet lamb and cooked it for dinner. When David's anger boiled toward the rich man, Nathan pointed his finger at David and said, "You are the man." David, convicted by Nathan's story, confessed and repented of his sin.

That's an interesting story to tell in a lesson or sermon, but a *great* lesson will also explain how that story should make a difference in your life. We've often preached about repentance and confession, using David as an example, but what about the example of Nathan? What do we learn from him?

As I was preparing the introduction, I wrote, "This is an important topic we're discussing today because someday you may have to confront someone you love who is caught in a sin." That's something we don't talk much about—confronting in love the person who is caught in a sin. But the Bible is clear that we have a responsibility to hold one another accountable, to correct and rebuke one another, to confront in love, and to restore people from sin. If you see a brother caught in a sin and you say, "It's none of my business," you don't really care about your brother, and you're ignoring Christ's command. (See Luke 17:3; 2 Tim. 4:2; Gal. 6:1.)

So one of the applications to the sermon on Nathan and David is that there will be times when you have to confront someone you love. But a good sermon will take that application a step further and give examples. I tried to think of times when people might have to confront someone they see committing a sin, and I began to write down ideas in my manuscript. "If you know that your friend is having an affair, or you discover that someone is embezzling money from his business, or you're a student and you see someone cheating on a test, what do you do?" Then I remembered visiting the Air Force Academy in Colorado Springs. Etched on the wall is their slogan, "We will not lie, cheat, or steal, or *tolerate those who do*" (emphasis mine). That's a great illustration of how even people outside the church realize the need to confront those who have done wrong.

Then I remembered that a young man in our church, Josh Kolarcik, is attending the Air Force Academy. His father once told me a story about his son taking tests there. He once told his dad that whenever they're taking a test, they all keep their heads down and nobody ever looks up. Ken said, "Why is that, son? Are they afraid they'll be tempted to cheat?"

"No, Dad," Josh answered, "We're afraid we will see someone else cheating and have to turn him in."

That's a great story, and it made a good illustration in the sermon because it helped me bring to light situations that might arise in everyday life when we are called upon to confront someone who has sinned. We don't go looking for people's faults. In fact, we prefer not to find any. But sometimes we can't ignore them, and we must lovingly confront. The illustration that seemed to drive home biblical truth came about as I was considering the application of the truth to people's lives and thinking of specific examples.

Give Practical Steps to Victory

It's not enough to correctly diagnose the problem. Faithful proclamation also needs to suggest practical steps that can enable people to be "more than conquerors" in Christ. Jesus would say:

Don't lust. If your right eye offends you, cut it out.

Don't worry. Instead, remember God's providence, keep your priorities straight, develop an eternal perspective, and live one day at a time.

Don't pray to be seen. Rather, go into your closet and close the door and pray to your Father in secret.

Let's return to the coveting sermon. You can say, "We shouldn't covet." But it's better to give some tangible things people can do to develop a lifestyle of contentment: "Count your blessings. Encourage those who have more. Minister to someone who has less. Remember what you really deserve as a sinner saved by grace. Develop a servant's heart." Most of us don't give this kind of practical help, but it is these points that help people understand the relevance of the Word of God.

Be careful not to go to the opposite extreme. I've heard some preachers who, if they were preaching about covetousness, would take almost their entire sermon to talk about practical ways to overcome the problem. People need to understand what coveting is, be taught God's Word about why coveting is wrong, and then be told how to overcome it. If you go straight to the application, your sermon will seem like one big dessert with no meat. But after you have laid the groundwork, sharing points of application along the way, make sure to take the time to give practical steps to victory at the end.

This style of preaching takes extra time and effort. Coming up with creative application is hard work. But this is the point where preaching becomes a helpful ministry that transforms lives, and not just an interesting discourse.

A man called me one Sunday afternoon a few years ago and said, "We've been coming to your church about six months. But we have a son who is a teenager and has been rebellious. We practically forced him to come to church today. Now he's really mad at us because he insists that we talked to you and made you preach about the very things he's having problems with. Would you explain to him that we've never met you?" I hadn't yet met the man who called, never even talked to him at all, let alone had a conversation with him about his son. But there's something about the power of the Holy Spirit working through the Word of God that convicted that teenager.

I can't tell you how many times I've heard people say, "I was having a problem in my life, and you preached about that very subject that day. I couldn't believe it!" I'll think back about the sermon that day. It really had almost nothing to say about their particular problem, but just one passage of Scripture—one thought from God's Word—was used by the Holy Spirit to convict or encourage.

Preaching is a powerful calling. We desperately need churches with preachers and teachers who will believe God's Word, teach God's Word, and apply God's Word to the everyday lives of those who are listening. And God has been faithful in using this conviction to grow this congregation of his people.

- ❖ We Gather for Worship to Glorify God

- ❖ Genuine Worship Inspires the Worshiper

- ❖ Four Legitimate Expectations from Worship

- ❖ How to Create an Atmosphere of Worship

- ❖ Choose a Music Style Suited to Your Worshipers

2

WORSHIP:
Worship God Every Week
in Spirit and in Truth

O ur worship leader, Greg Allen, has a lot of musical ability, and his voice is enjoyable to sing along with. But there was a period of several months when we let Greg lead our worship even though he couldn't sing at all!

In 1994 we learned that Greg had developed a polyp on one of his vocal cords. For the next three years, he endured three surgeries to try to correct the problem. Each surgery was surrounded by long periods of voice rest. For two months he was not allowed to speak at all. He later talked about how difficult it was to endure Christmas holidays without being able to speak. When his girls were so excited about Christmas day, he could only smile. He said, "The Bible says, 'Out of the abundance of the heart the mouth speaks.' When you feel something, you want to say it, and it was really difficult not to be able to express my love and joy during those times."

For sixteen months out of those three years, Greg

led our worship services even though the vocal team behind him did all the singing. (I'm convinced that some of our congregation never figured out Greg was lip-syncing!) Why on earth would we allow a guy to lead worship who can't even sing? We have so many people at Southeast with musical talent, even people who have musical degrees and experience in leading choirs. But there is something much more important than musical ability in leading people to worship God. We didn't hire Greg to lead worship because he could sing. We hired him because his integrity, sincerity, and personality qualified him in a special way to lead people to worship God.

The primary reason for attending a church service should be to worship God. The psalmist wrote, "Come, let us bow down in worship, let us kneel before the LORD our Maker; for he is our God and we are the people of his pasture, the flock under his care" (Ps. 95:6–7). Worship is more than just singing a few songs, performing a few rituals, and enduring a sermon. We come to experience the presence of God, to acknowledge his authority in our lives, and to worship him as our Creator.

Tim Kelly said, "Worship is taking our affection off our idols and putting it on God." When we worship God we acknowledge that there is a Creator who has authority over us and to whom we are accountable. We humble ourselves in his presence and praise him for his goodness. We renew our pledge to obey his commands and seek his honor.

William Temple said, "Worship is the submission of all our nature to God." What we do in one hour of corporate worship each week is to be a reflection of what we as individuals are doing the other 167 hours a week. In fact, God despises corporate worship if the worshipers have hearts that are not right with him:

> I hate, I despise your religious feasts; I cannot stand your assemblies. Even though you bring me burnt offerings and grain offerings, I will not accept them. Though you bring choice fellowship offerings, I will have no regard for them.

Away with the noise of your songs! I will not listen to the music of your harps. But let justice roll on like a river, righteousness like a never-failing stream! (Amos 5:21–24).

So worship is much more than singing songs to God. Paul told us to offer our "bodies as living sacrifices, holy and pleasing to God," saying, "this is your spiritual act of *worship*" (Rom. 12:1, author's emphasis). Worship is not something we do one hour a week, but a lifestyle that we offer to God. Paul then commanded, "Do not conform any longer to the pattern of this world, but be transformed by the renewing of your mind" (Rom.12:2). Worship should transform the worshiper.

Jesus said we are to be the light of the world. During the week, we're thousands of little lights trying to light the world. When we gather for corporate worship, we should create one giant light that honors God, and we should get recharged for the week ahead so we can return to being little lights for him.

Trying to write a chapter on corporate worship is intimidating, because I know how divisive and emotionally charged this issue can be. You may have even turned straight to this chapter just to see if my ideas about corporate worship align with yours. You might be wondering, *Does he think we ought to abandon all the hymns? Does he try to say we all have to have drama? Does he demand that all churches must put the lyrics on a screen? What does he say about musical styles?*

I hope I don't disappoint you, but I'm not going to answer many of those questions in this chapter. Style of music, how many instruments you use, whether or not you have a drama and words on a screen—all of those are secondary issues when it comes to testing whether or not your church has a healthy view of worship. Primarily, we should be asking three questions about corporate worship:

1. Does our worship honor God?
2. Does it inspire, uplift, and transform the worshiper?
3. Is it powerful enough to draw visitors closer to an encounter with Jesus Christ?

WE GATHER FOR WORSHIP TO GLORIFY GOD

The primary purpose of worship is not to entertain those sitting in the pews but to glorify God. We sometimes evaluate a worship service like it's a performance to be rated. *Did you like the song she sang? That was a great (or terrible) drama. I thought the sermon today was about a seven on a scale of one to ten.* We see those on stage as performers in front of an audience. But that's not the purpose of worship.

The University of Kentucky basketball team won the National Championship a couple of years ago. A few days later there was a celebration in Rupp Arena to honor the team. The audience cheered wildly for each player when he was introduced. The fans carried banners. They painted their faces and proudly wore blue-and-white outfits. They tried to get autographs. Not one fan walked away saying, "That event was a dud. It did nothing for me." The event was a success, not because the performance was great (they didn't play any basketball at all) or the players' speeches were inspiring (most of them weren't very good speakers), but because everyone understood why they were there. The purpose was not to please the fans but to honor the team. People walked away saying, "That was great! I hope the team understands how much we appreciate them!"

The Scriptures command us: "Ascribe to the LORD the glory due his name; worship the LORD in the splendor of his holiness" (Ps. 29:2). "Fear God and give him glory, because the hour of his judgment has come. Worship him who made the heavens, the earth, the sea and the springs of water" (Rev. 14:7).

Most people view worship as though God were the prompter, the leader is the performer, and the congregation is the audience. In reality, the leader is the prompter, the congregation are the performers, and God is the audience. We worship to bring glory to God and express our gratitude for his goodness. Our goal is to please him. When we understand that purpose, we're a lot more likely to walk away saying, "That was great! I hope God knows how much we appreciate him!"

In biblical worship, two ingredients always seem to be present: *a sense of awe* and *a sense of joy*.

A Sense of Awe

I met President Ronald Reagan once. My first reaction was not to say, "Hi, Ronnie! How's the Pres?" I knew he was just a human being, but there is something about the office of president that commands respect. I said, "It's nice to meet you, Mr. President." I mention this because I hear people say, "I can't wait till I can see God face to face. I'm just going to leap into his arms and give him a great big hug." But in Scripture, whenever someone came face to face with God (or even with an angel, one of God's messengers), the first reaction was not love but fear. There was a deep sense of awe and respect and even a genuine dread at the thought of being in the presence of someone so holy and powerful. When we come into the presence of the King of kings and the Lord of the presidents, our appropriate response is one of wonderment and reverence.

Isaiah wrote,

> In the year that King Uzziah died, I saw the Lord seated on a throne, high and exalted, and the train of his robe filled the temple. Above him were seraphs, each with six wings: With two wings they covered their faces, with two they covered their feet, and with two they were flying. And they were calling to one another: "Holy, holy, holy is the LORD Almighty; the whole earth is full of his glory." At the sound of their voices the doorposts and thresholds shook and the temple was filled with smoke.
>
> "Woe to me!" I cried. "I am ruined! For I am a man of unclean lips, and I live among a people of unclean lips, and my eyes have seen the King, the LORD Almighty." (Isa. 6:1–5)

The presence of God is awesome. He is so much more powerful and holy than we are. Haven't you ever stood outside on a clear night, looked up to the heavens and thought, *God is so big!?* Haven't you marveled at the omniscience and omnipotence of God, as the psalmist did?

> When I consider your heavens, the work of your fingers, the moon and the stars, which you have set in place, what is man that you are mindful of him, the son of man that you care for him? You made him a little lower than the heavenly beings and crowned him with glory and honor. You made him ruler over the works of your hands; you put everything under his feet: all flocks and herds, and the beasts of the field, the birds of the air, and the fish of the sea, all that swim the paths of the seas. O LORD, our Lord, how majestic is your name in all the earth! (Ps. 8:3–9)

A Sense of Joy

Awe in the presence of God doesn't rule out a sense of gladness. Biblical worship is characterized by an overwhelming sense of joy in the hearts of God's people. Not only was the early church filled with a sense of awe (Acts 2:43), they also "broke bread in their homes and ate together with glad and sincere hearts, praising God and enjoying the favor of all the people" (Acts 2:46–47). Their hearts were glad because the God of the universe had visited them in the form of Jesus Christ. They weren't worshiping a terrifying, unpredictable force that would destroy them at a whim, but a faithful, personal God of grace who loved them and had saved them through Jesus Christ. God cared enough about them that he died for them! They had an eternal purpose for living. They could shout with the psalmist,

> Shout for joy to the LORD, all the earth. Worship the LORD with gladness; come before him with joyful songs. Know that the LORD is God. It is he who made us, and we are his; we are his people, the sheep of his pasture. Enter his gates with thanksgiving and his courts with praise; give thanks to him and praise his

name. For the LORD is good and his love endures forever; his faithfulness continues through all generations. (Ps. 100)

The Source of Controversy

The failure to understand these two sides of worship and their corresponding musical styles is at the heart of much controversy in churches today. If you come from a formal, liturgical background, you are used to an emphasis on the "reverence and awe" side of worship. When you enter a church, you expect quietness and an atmosphere of "holiness." The leader quotes Psalm 46:10: "Be still, and know that I am God," and Hebrews 12:28–29: "Let us...worship God acceptably with reverence and awe, for our 'God is a consuming fire.'" So if you visit a congregation where people are talking and laughing loudly when you enter, where they clap after a special song and some even raise their hands during the singing, you think it's inappropriate and irreverent.

But if you grew up in a more charismatic church, you're accustomed to the emphasis on the joy of worship. The leader quotes Psalm 47:1: "Clap your hands, all you nations; shout to God with cries of joy," and Psalm 5:11: "But let all who take refuge in you be glad; let them ever sing for joy. Spread your protection over them, that those who love your name may rejoice in you." A charismatic who visits a church that's more liturgical thinks, *This church is dead! Jesus Christ is alive! Come on, you all, get with it!*

I talk to hundreds of preachers every year. I know it is this issue—the format and style of the weekly worship service—that is the most divisive in American churches today. Churches are split and pastors are run out of town because someone tried to suggest changes in the style and routine of the worship service. This controversy over styles causes more division than all other possible issues—doctrine, philosophy of ministry, character of the leaders, finances—combined. And it is primarily a misunderstanding about two legitimate and biblical sides of worship.

I've heard people on both ends of the spectrum complain about worship services that are not their preferred styles, as if the other style is less "spiritual":

"It's just not worshipful to use drums."

"I wish they'd liven up and get rid of that old organ. We're acting like God is dead."

"There's too much entertainment going on here—like we were in a bar or something."

"I wish they would loosen up and experience the joy of the Lord. We're saved, you know!"

Authentic worship of God is characterized by *both* a spirit of awe and a spirit of joy. Sometimes we should feel the power and presence of God so much that we could hear a pin drop in the silence as we remember God's command, "Be still, and know that I am God." Sometimes we should be so overwhelmed with God's grace that we shout for joy.

GENUINE WORSHIP INSPIRES THE WORSHIPER

The primary purpose of worship is to honor God, but corporate worship should also uplift and encourage believers. David said, "I was glad when they said unto me, Let us go into the house of the LORD" (Ps. 122:1 KJV). When we genuinely worship God, the by-product is inspiration and empowerment. God ordained worship not just because he deserves it, but also because we have an instinctive need to worship. The Christian group Truth used to sing, "We get lifted up when we praise his name." Though he is the audience and the focus of our worship, it is we—the worshipers—who receive the most benefit from worship.

William Hendricks wrote a fascinating book called *Exit Interviews: Revealing Stories of Why People Are Leaving the Church.* As you might expect, people often said they were leaving church because it was "boring," but notice how they defined boring. Hendricks wrote:

"Perhaps the most common complaint was that worship services were boring. It was not just that these gatherings were not interesting; they were not worshipful. They did little to help people meet God. However, I did not hear this as a call for more entertainment, but for more participation."[1]

The most important benefit of a worship service is an awareness of the presence of God. That's more important than a captivating drama, an impressive soloist, or even a relevant message. I've heard it said that when interaction with God is absent, church loses much of its appeal. People come to church because they expect to find God there.

Blaise Pascal, the famous seventeenth-century physicist, said, "There is a God-shaped hole in every heart that only God can fill." Anne Sullivan approached her deaf and blind student Helen Keller one day and said, "Helen, today I'm going to teach you about God." Though Helen had never heard of God, she responded in her sign language, "Good. I've been thinking about him for a long time." Human beings instinctively worship because that is what God created them to do. When we do what we were created to do, we are inspired.

There's something inspirational and encouraging about singing praise songs with hundreds of believers. There's something cleansing about taking communion and praying for forgiveness and renewal while surrounded by believers who are doing the same. There's something uplifting about hearing the truth of God's Word proclaimed boldly to an assembly of listeners. There's something moving about seeing people respond to the invitation to accept Jesus Christ. That's why you ought to attend weekly worship even when you don't feel like going. Your presence might be an encouragement to another believer who has come to be uplifted. And you need to be edified too!

The writer of Hebrews communicated that idea when he commanded, "Let us consider how we may spur one another on toward love and good deeds. Let us not give up meeting together, as some are in the habit of doing, but let us encourage one another—and all the more as you see the Day approaching" (Heb. 10:24–25).

Have you ever gone to church when you didn't feel like going? Occasionally—not very often, but occasionally—I don't feel like going to church. And sometimes—rarely, but sometimes—I don't feel like preaching. I recently joked with our congregation that once in a great while I feel like getting up and staring at them like they stare at me. After I said that I crossed my arms and scowled at them. Then I yawned …and went back to scowling. Then I looked at my watch!

But even when I don't feel like it, I go to church anyway because God has commanded me not to forsake the assembly. And I sing the songs anyway because God has commanded me to make a joyful noise. And I preach anyway because God has commanded me to preach in season and out of season. And you know what I've discovered? When I do, I feel so much better. I am lifted up by worshiping God in the assembly of believers.

FOUR LEGITIMATE EXPECTATIONS FROM WORSHIP

Do Christians have a right to expect something when they attend worship services? I think so. The prophet Isaiah's experience in the divine "throne room" that I mentioned earlier leads me to believe there are four things we should expect from an authentic worship experience.

1. A Sense of God's Presence

When we gather for worship, we should expect to sense the awesome presence of God. "I saw the Lord seated on a throne, high and exalted, and the train of his robe filled the temple" (Isa. 6:1). God is everywhere and is not confined to buildings made with hands. But when we worship we should be convinced that "Surely the presence of the Lord is in this place!" Worship should be neither sheer boredom nor surface entertainment. It should convey a deep respect for the holiness, the majesty, the joy, the power of the Almighty God in our midst.

2. A Conviction of Our Sinfulness

When we gather for worship, we should experience a conviction of our own sinfulness. "Woe to me!" Isaiah cried. "I am ruined! For I am a man of unclean lips, and I live among a people of unclean lips, and my eyes have seen the King, the LORD Almighty" (Isa. 6:5). It may seem strange, but the closer we get to God, the more we're aware of our own sinfulness. The brighter the light, the more the wrinkles show. That's why the apostle Paul—probably the world's greatest Christian—said he felt like the worst of sinners (Rom. 7; 1 Tim. 1:15). When a person brags about his own goodness, it's a telltale sign that he hasn't been near the purity of God lately.

Paul Eshleman, the man responsible for distributing millions of copies of the *Jesus* film around the world, tells about the time that the film was shown at a refugee camp in Mozambique, on the southeast coast of Africa. Although most of the people had never heard the gospel, they fell in love with Jesus through the film. When he was arrested, beaten, and led away to be crucified, they began to weep and wail, and many rushed toward the screen. Their cries and the dust they stirred made it impossible to finish the film, so the projector was turned off. For more than thirty minutes, the townspeople were on their knees weeping and confessing their sins.

Each of the film crew members and counselors relayed how they would try to approach one of the villagers to pray with them, but the Spirit of God was so real that the counselors themselves were falling to their knees, confessing their own sins and glorifying God. "The sense of God's presence—his power and his holiness—was so great," the counselors told Eshleman, "that no one could do anything but confess sins."[2] When you experience the presence of God, you cannot help but recognize your own sinful state.

3. A Joyful Reminder of God's Grace

When we gather for worship, we should also receive a cleansing of sin and release from guilt. Isaiah wrote, "Then one of the seraphs flew to me with a live coal in his hand, which he had taken with tongs from the altar. With it he touched my mouth and said, 'See, this has touched your lips; your guilt is taken away and your sin atoned for'" (Isa. 6:6–7). A church service should motivate us to repent of sin, but it must not stop there. We should leave rejoicing in the knowledge that if we have submitted to Christ, "the blood of Jesus…purifies us from all sin" (1 John 1:7).

Paul Eshleman said that eventually, after more than thirty minutes, the *Jesus* film crew turned the movie back on so the people could know the end of the story. You know the end. It does not end in death on a cross, but in the resurrection of Jesus Christ. When the townspeople saw how the story ended, Eshleman said, "The crowd exploded as if a dam had burst. Everyone began cheering and dancing and hugging one another and jumping up and down."[3] When the invitation was given for people to accept Christ, nearly everyone in the crowd wanted to respond! The following Sunday five hundred new believers showed up at the forty-member church in the refugee camp!

When we experience the presence of God in worship, we should leave rejoicing. Though we have recognized our sinful state, we have been reminded of God's grace. Jesus paid the price for our sins and then conquered the grave.

4. The Inspiration to Serve

When we gather for worship, we should also be inspired to serve. "Then I heard the voice of the Lord saying, 'Whom shall I send? And who will go for us?' And I said, 'Here am I. Send me!'" (Isa. 6:8). Instead of an instinct to criticize, the worshiper should leave with an incentive to share the truth with the lost and to minister to the hurting in the world. "Enter to Worship—Depart to Serve" was a familiar and fitting statement on church bulletin boards years ago.

Sometimes when the worshiper departs to complain, the problem is with the worshiper. But, frankly, sometimes it's the worship. One Christian related that one of his biggest childhood disappointments came one day when he saw a huge tent in a field and thought a circus was in town. He excitedly walked in the tent only to discover it was a revival meeting. Then he added, "One of the biggest disappointments of my adult life came one day when I went to church expecting a revival and discovered it was just a circus."

When someone comes to church seeking God, he should leave a different creature because he has been in the presence of God. Peter Marshall once prayed before the U.S. Senate, "Lord, we thank you that we can come to you just as we are. But remind us that we dare not leave as we came."

EVANGELISM IS A BY-PRODUCT OF AUTHENTIC WORSHIP

It was said of the Jerusalem church, "[They were] praising God and enjoying the favor of all the people. And the Lord added to their number daily those who were being saved" (Acts 2:47). Evangelism is the natural by-product of authentic worship. When outsiders see Christians genuinely worshiping, they are attracted. The Holy Spirit works through worship to draw the seeker to Christ.

Sally Morgenthaler, in her excellent book *Worship Evangelism*, wrote:

> Worship is the most powerful tool we have for satisfying the hunger of famished, injured souls, for breaking down spiritual strongholds of pride and unbelief and for ushering in the gift of true joy. How can we refuse to use it? Our whole culture, saved and unsaved, is starving for an extraordinary glimpse of God.... Worship is not just for the spiritually mature. It is for

the spiritually hungry and that includes more people than we realize.[4]

Jesus said, "But I, when I am lifted up from the earth, will draw all men to myself"(John 12:32). When Jesus Christ is exalted, people are attracted. Later in Sally Morgenthaler's book, she quotes several pastors and worship leaders who have learned this truth about the evangelistic nature of worship. Here are some of their comments:

> The most powerful thing non-Christians can see is people worshiping. Worship shows people who God is.... I can't tell you how many times non-Christians have said, "I don't know what this is—something's going on inside!" like God's knocking on their heart's door! He's breaking down the walls. That's the anointing, and I'm afraid we may be taking it out of our services![5]

> What I thought seekers were looking for was not what they were looking for at all. I thought they were looking for services where you barely talk about God and you water everything down. But I found they were looking for just the opposite—a very personal God in a safe, honest environment.[6]

> The bottom line is, people are hungry for spiritual things. Ultimately, even the world wants the church to be the church and to own up to who we really are.... Everything else—they can get that anywhere. They can pay thirty bucks to go see Letterman or whatever. But what people want today is God. They want to feel God, to know God.... There is no substitute for the presence of God, for the anointing. There's none! Absolutely none. When God is making manifest His presence, I've seen the hardest people break down and weep before Him. They say, "I knew there was something to this."[7]

Christians have tried all kinds of methods—polished entertainment, special classes, slick pamphlets, emotional sermons—to win people to Christ. But the best method of evangelism may be the magnetic attraction of genuine worship.

How to Create an Atmosphere of Worship

Obviously, a sovereign God can make his presence known at any time and any place. He doesn't need our manipulative gimmicks. Yet his Spirit can guide us to remove obstacles to experiencing his presence. Here are some hints for facilitating authentic worship that I have found helpful.

Choose the Right Worship Leaders

Choose a worship leader based on personal character, not musical ability. We asked Greg Allen to keep leading worship even when he couldn't sing because he has the personal character, humility, and talent to lead people to worship. Greg's character shines through when he leads in a way that few others do because he is genuinely concerned about leading people to God.

Greg said of his voice problems, "Before the surgery started in Christmas of 1994, I never talked about worship at all. I talked about music. I never really got into having in-depth, biblical, studious thoughts about worship, because I could sing and I loved talking about music. I made the mistake of equating music with worship. When I couldn't sing any longer, I was forced to realize that music and worship are not synonymous. I began to realize that there are people sitting in the congregation who don't even like music. I began to pray, 'God, what can I say as a worship leader, or what can we do in formulating a worship service, that will engage their minds, spirits, emotions, and hearts, even though they don't like music?' It was easier for me to do that when I wasn't able to sing, because it kept me from focusing too much on music instead of worship."

On several occasions we have asked people to discontinue leading worship or playing in the worship band because of character issues. If a person cannot communicate a sense of humility in the way they sing, play an instrument, dress, or talk, they won't be allowed to sing, play, or help in the leading of worship. In other words, if you look like you're stuck on yourself, you won't be allowed on the platform.

We've also asked volunteers in the worship department on several occasions to take a sabbatical while working through personal problems. If a person doesn't have his personal life in order, he shouldn't be in front of hundreds of people trying to lead them to worship a holy God.

About twice a year the worship department meets with all their volunteers—all band members, vocal team members, and technical crew—for a private time of worship and teaching. The worship ministers teach the volunteers about the purpose of worship, explaining again that worship is not just an hour on Sunday morning but a lifestyle. They remind the volunteers about the example they must set if they are going to be leading people in worship. This means that their personal lives must be consistent, and that everything they do—even down to the way they dress on the platform, the way they stand, and how much they move their hips—must be a reflection of their desire to worship God.

Be Prepared and Intentional with Every Part of the Service

If God is the audience in worship, he deserves our best performance! Every part of the worship service should be planned, rehearsed, and intentional. You may ask, "How can the Holy Spirit lead if we're that planned?" The Holy Spirit can lead in preparation. God knows the future, and he can guide our plans. I believe God expects us to use the abilities he has given us to prepare for the future. Certainly he has the power to interrupt plans; but instead of making worship too stilted, I believe preparation has the opposite effect—worship becomes more inspiring.

Choose the right worship songs. Choose songs that are in a comfortable key, with lyrics that can be understood and a melody that relates to the culture. The lyrics should not only be understandable, but they should be doctrinally significant.

Let me again recommend Sally Morgenthaler's book, *Worship Evangelism*, because she does an excellent job of explaining why choosing the right songs is so important. She uses an acronym to say that every song should "PASS" the song selection test by having four characteristics:

> *Personal.* Songs should relate in some way to people's everyday lives and involve their whole being, including their emotions.

> *Attractive.* They hold people's attention.

> *Straightforward.* Both Seeker Bob and Saintly Bill should be able to understand and latch on to the songs quickly.

> *Substantive.* Songs should have a thoroughly biblical message that is faithful to the whole counsel of Scripture.[8]

Remember both sides of worship—reverence and joy. Every worship service should have moments of joy and moments of quiet reverence. Some worship leaders think that if they're going to be "cutting edge," they can't sing a slow song. But even rock concerts have a few slow songs! Don't equate "contemporary" with "fast"!

At Southeast, we celebrate the Lord's Supper every week. Besides the more obvious benefits that come from the weekly observance of Christ's sacrifice, we also receive the benefit of having a built-in quiet time each service. Surrounding the partaking of communion will almost always be several slow songs as we reflect on Christ's love for us.

Most churches in America would be wise to allow for a variety of expressions in their worship services, especially considering the varied backgrounds of those who may be gathered for worship on any particular weekend. Episcopalians and Catholics are accustomed to kneeling and saying "Amen" at the end of prayers. Charismatics are used to clapping and raising their hands when they sing.

In my independent church background, it was considered drawing too much attention to yourself to raise your hands in worship. But when my grandson comes to me and holds up his hands for me to pick him up, I don't say, "Put your hands down, you little charismatic!" The Bible commands us to lift up holy hands to God. If someone gently lifts up his hands when he sings in church, maybe he's not trying to draw attention to himself or flaunt his spirituality. Maybe he's just lifting holy hands to God and asking God to lift him up.

Practice and pray before you begin. Each weekend our worship team gathers two hours before the first service. They practice each part of the service, making sure each chorus, transition, and special music selection are well-rehearsed. If there is a drama, the drama team also must be there and rehearse at the right time in the dress rehearsal. There have been times during the rehearsal that features of the service —a special music selection, chorus, or drama—have been cut entirely because presenters weren't prepared or because it wasn't a proper fit with the rest of the service.

Then everyone involved in the service gathers before the hour begins and prays together. The band members, technical crew, worship team, drama department, and choir members gather in the rehearsal room. They will sing a chorus or two in praise to God, then bow in prayer, asking God to set their hearts right and to bless the hour of worship.

Begin and end on time. Some cultures don't have to concern themselves with starting on time, but in our culture it's a vital part of gaining people's respect. I can't tell you how many people have thanked us for being the first church they ever attended that began on time. In our culture, if you are meeting someone for an appointment and he shows up fifteen minutes late, he is considered to be taking advantage of your most prized possession—your time. To gain the respect of newcomers, you must begin exactly when you say you will begin.

I'm also an advocate of ending on time. We have a service that lasts between sixty-five and seventy minutes each week, including the thirty-minute sermon. People who come to our service each week know exactly when we will begin and about how long the service will last. Whether or not our culture should be so time-conscious is not the point. People *are* time conscious, and we must respect their most valued possession if we are going to reach them. Once they learn they don't have to glance at their watches and worry about how long the service will last, they can better concentrate on worshiping God.

Introduce the service by inviting people to worship. I'm writing this chapter at Christmastime. A few weeks ago, Greg Allen came out onto the platform at the beginning of the service and said, "Good morning, everybody. Merry Christmas. Would you raise your hand if you have finished all your Christmas shopping?" About a third of the people raised their hands. Greg smiled and said, "That's unbelievable. I can't identify with you people. I've just begun. But you know, that just means for you who raised your hands that you have no reason to be distracted at all today. You can totally focus on worshiping God.

"But you know what? The rest of us don't have any excuse either. God deserves our full attention. Let's pray for God to take away all the distractions so that we can focus on him today." With that, he prayed a short prayer and began leading us in several songs of praise to God.

That introduction was simple, but it didn't come easily. Greg prepared his words ahead of time and rehearsed them. He knew how long it would take him to introduce that thought and to begin singing. It wasn't profound, but it was a great reminder to everyone present that we had come for one purpose: to worship God.

Sometimes Greg will be much more "theological" in his introduction. A week later we began by singing one verse of "O Come, O Come Immanuel." After the first verse Greg said, "Those words don't mean as much to us as they would have to the Jewish people two millennia ago. You have to remember that they had been praying for centuries, 'God, send your Messiah, your Savior into the world.' And God had not answered that prayer yet. So when they sang, 'Ransom captive Israel,' they were saying, 'Send somebody to pay the price for captive Israel. We're caught captive in our sin and can't get out. Please rescue us.' So as we sing these next few songs together, think about what it might have been like to live before the coming of Christ. These songs tell the story of the prayers of centuries and then of God answering those prayers."

We sang the rest of "O Come, O Come Immanuel" and then "Come, Thou Long Expected Jesus." After that we sang "Lord, I Lift Your Name on High," because the chorus says, "He came from heaven to earth to show the way.... "[9] Then we returned to the refrain of the first song, "Rejoice, rejoice, Immanuel shall come to thee, O Israel."

For ten minutes we went from one song to the next with no talking between. But the songs were meaningful to us, and we did more than sing—we worshiped God—all because Greg had taken just a moment to introduce the song set in a powerful way.

Be creative but predictable. Everybody likes predictability and nobody likes change because change creates insecurity and anxiety. But if you never introduce any creative changes, your services will become too predictable, routine, and uninspiring. For many churches, planning the weekly worship service consists of getting out a hymn book, trying to decide which numbers haven't been used in a while, and changing the numbers from last week's bulletin for this week's service. If that's your idea of change, you're destined for a dead worship service!

Change needs to be implemented slowly so people can digest it without too much unrest. But change needs to be implemented. Don't get in the habit of doing the same old thing every week. Find ways to introduce fresh and creative ideas into your worship service—not so that people will think you are clever or talented, but so that people will be motivated in a new way to "love the old, old story." Don't ask yourself what clever thing you can do this week to get in trouble or be more entertaining. Ask yourself, "What creative thing can we do this week to inspire people to worship God and be transformed by his presence?"

Be Authentic

Don't manufacture emotion. Sometimes people will approach me after a service and say something like, "That was an outstanding service —a three-hanky," meaning they cried three times. I'm glad they were moved by the service, but I have to be careful not to make it my goal to see that everyone cries at least once each week. Don't think that the more emotional a worship service is, the better it is. Emotionalism does not equal authentic worship. Worshiping God is sometimes very emotional. Sometimes it is not emotional at all. In fact, the most important element of worship is not what happens while we're singing to God on Sunday morning, but what happens while we're living for God throughout the week. Our spiritual act of worship is to "offer [our] bodies as living sacrifices" (Rom. 12:1). God is not so much pleased with an emotional worship service as he is with an obedient life. Consider these Scriptures:

> Does the LORD delight in burnt offerings and sacrifices as much as in obeying the voice of the LORD? To obey is better than sacrifice, and to heed is better than the fat of rams. (1 Sam. 15:22)

> These people honor me with their lips, but their hearts are far from me. They worship me in vain; their teachings are but rules taught by men. (Matt. 15:8–9)

It's possible to experience all kinds of emotion in a service—tears, laughter, motivation, and inspiration—and never worship God. In fact, you can get all those things at a Rotary meeting. When Isaiah and others in the Bible were met with the presence of God, they were convicted of their sinfulness, motivated to repent, and overwhelmed with gratitude for God's grace. Emotion may have accompanied those experiences, but they weren't *just* emotional.

A deep sense of emotion will often be the natural response of those experiencing authentic worship, but it should never be the *goal* of worship. The goal is to glorify God, not to manufacture emotion. If you try to manufacture it, perceptive people will see right through it and will be turned off.

Make sure testimonies are authentic and reverent. When people want to share their personal testimony in our church, we require that they first submit a written draft of what they plan to say. That helps us assure that a person doesn't get up in front of several thousand people unprepared and say something that would embarrass himself or take more time than we planned. It also gives us the opportunity to boost their confidence with encouragement and make sure that what they plan to say is doctrinally sound.

There is one other benefit—and this is hard to explain—but have you ever heard someone's testimony and had a hard time believing it? Sometimes people get carried away talking about their sinful past in terms that are too graphic, or they talk about their life with God in such wonderful terms that it doesn't seem real. Or people can say things that are too crass or irreverent and make others feel uncomfortable. The things that we say from the pulpit—whether the one doing the talking is the preacher, the worship leader, or someone giving a testimony—should be authentic, dignified, and reverent.

Avoid speaking with a "preacher's tone." Why is it that we speak in modern English when we talk, then revert to King James language when we pray—as though God is stuck in the year 1611? "Our gracious Heavenly Father, we thank thee for these thy many blessings, and we beseech thee to continually pour out these bounties upon us thy children. In the name of thy blessed Son Jesus we pray, Amen."

When someone who has never been to church hears a prayer like that, he thinks, *What did he just say?* And we preachers are famous not only for our flowery language but for our preacher's tone as well. We lower our voice and become very "pastoral."

Our choir director, Dale Mowery, came to our church from a more "high-church" background. When he first came, he was in the habit of praying with a deep, resonating voice that sounded very liturgical. It was a beautiful sound, but very "churchy." We encouraged him to speak in a more conversational tone, because we're convinced that in our culture, it is more believable than the high-church sound. We teased Dale about how difficult a time he had breaking the habit and how we wondered if he spoke that way at home to his wife! But with practice he has become an excellent communicator with a much more believable sound to his voice.

One word of caution: A preacher or worship leader can also go to the opposite extreme in an attempt to become conversational. Don't become so informal and flippant that you no longer maintain a sense of reverence for what you are doing. Leading people in worship is a high calling that must be handled with dignity.

Don't manipulate people. A few years ago my brother John Russell, who is the preacher at an outstanding congregation in northern Kentucky, was visiting another church while on vacation. The worship leader, attempting to warm up the congregation, said, "Turn around to the person behind you and say, 'I love you.'" Sitting in front of my brother was a very attractive young lady. She turned around and said to him, "I love you." John's wife, Susan, grabbed him by the arm and said, "We love you too!"

Different sized groups have different dynamics. Leaders sometimes think that in order to warm up the service, they need to get people to do what they would only feel comfortable doing if they really knew the people around them or were in a much smaller setting. Most people feel comfortable turning to the people around them, shaking hands, and saying hello. But it becomes awkward to rub some stranger's shoulders and say a cute phrase like "You look like Jesus today," or "I love you in the Lord." The fact that people feel uncomfortable doing such things, or going through a "Repeat after me" routine, doesn't mean they're unspiritual. It means that to them, such behavior is inauthentic. Nobody likes to be manipulated or forced into doing something that's uncomfortable.

If you're a worship leader, you need to realize that not only are the new people hoping you won't make them do something "weird," but many longtime Christians are hoping not to have to do it too. You can say they ought to get out of their comfort zone, but just as they shouldn't cast judgment on you if you want to raise your hands in worship, neither should you cast judgment on them if they want to be more subdued. Worship is not defined by how many people raise their hands or dance in your service, but how many people have an encounter with God. Encountering God may sometimes be uncomfortable, but it can't be forced. Avoid saying and doing things that can smack of manipulation.

Avoid churchy language. Patricia Klein wrote a humorous book called *Growing Up Born Again,* in which she named a lot of phrases that people who grew up going to church could immediately recognize: *sword drill...and all God's people said Amen...unspoken request...go to the Lord* (translation: pray)*...I feel led...rededicate your life.*[10]

If we are not careful, those of us who have grown up attending church can become so familiar with church jargon that we forget there are people in our midst every week who have no idea what we mean by terms such as *baptism, the Lord's Supper, offering, hymns, greeting time, fellowship, bulletins.* And there are some phrases that may be understood by someone new to the church but that can come across as inauthentic if we're not careful: *I just want to be a blessing to you all today...It's a God-thing!...Isn't God just so wonderful?...Can I hear an amen?...We just need to lift them up in prayer.*

Don't drag out the invitation. We still have an invitation at the end of every weekend worship service. If no one comes forward during the first couple of verses of a song, we quickly finish singing and move on to the next part of the service. We do not manipulate people into walking down the aisles. I'm convinced that if you have to beg them to join, you'll have to beg them to stay. You're better off letting the Holy Spirit slowly work on people's hearts until they're ready to commit on their own. Then when they do commit, since it won't be a decision based on emotion or coercion, their commitment will be deeper.

At the close of our service, the person making announcements says, "The invitation to come to Christ is never over. If you thought about coming forward today but didn't, and you want to talk to someone about your relationship with God, you can come to this side of the platform and a decision counselor will meet you there." Since we began offering that reminder, scores of people have quietly approached decision counselors after the service to accept Christ and be baptized. (I talk more about our decision counselors in chapter 10.)

CHOOSE A MUSIC STYLE SUITED TO YOUR WORSHIPERS

I've tried to communicate in this chapter that a church's primary focus should be on the worship of God, which can be done through any style of music. Music is a vehicle. Are you convinced that your service will be more "worshipful" if you sing all contemporary songs? Then you've missed the point entirely. If you think an all-hymns service is a more worshipful service, again you've missed the point.

After you have chosen a worship leader who understands this point, and you're ready to lead your congregation in worship, then consider musical styles. Choose the style or styles of music that will help people worship the best. Find the musical styles that will reach the greatest number of people in your culture.

When I say "culture," that's including, but not limited to, your congregation. If you are focused solely on using a style of music that reaches your congregation, you may be severely limiting opportunities for evangelism because your congregation may not be a good reflection of your surrounding culture. For example, suppose you're located in a community where the median age is thirty-two and the average age of your congregation is sixty. You're going to have a hard time evangelizing if all you ever sing is what the majority of your congregation wants to hear.

But you can go to the opposite extreme. If no one in your congregation is inspired to worship because the music you're using doesn't relate to them, you're probably not leading them in worship. They won't be inspired to serve or evangelize.

Suppose my family and I decided to move to Africa to start a church and at first we were the only ones there. We might sing some African-style songs in hopes that some visitors would walk in and be inspired by the music. But for our own sakes, we'd need to have times when we sang some songs to which we could relate and that made us feel inspired to worship God.

That church of sixty-year-olds in the thirty-something neighborhood should sing a few new songs to reach the younger people, as well as the old hymns that reach the average member of the congregation. And they should do both with the ultimate motive in mind: to worship God.

To create an atmosphere of both reverence and joy, and to try to reach as many people in our culture as possible with the message of the gospel, at Southeast we have chosen to have what we call a "blended" style of music in our worship services. At each service we sing several of the old familiar hymns and several of the new, contemporary choruses. We treat them virtually the same, using the same instrumentation for both and projecting the words on the screen for both. Sometimes our worship leader, Greg Allen, will take time to explain the meaning of an old hymn that may contain some words we don't use today. But usually the hymns and choruses are treated the same, and we attempt to make as smooth a transition as possible from one to the other.

While I prefer the blended, I have to remember that we shouldn't limit the worship experience to my favorite style. There are churches who are completely contemporary, and others who have kept a traditional style, who help people connect with God without ever implementing this concept of blended styles. But I'm convinced that every church in our culture would do well to consider some level of combination in their style of service—singing some new songs and some old hymns on a regular basis. There are good reasons we all need to learn new songs and good reasons to teach the old hymns as well.

Why Sing Contemporary Songs?

God is honored by variety and freshness. If you don't think God loves variety, look at his creation. There are different kinds of stars and planets. There are different kinds of trees and flowers. There are different kinds of lakes and mountains. There are different kinds of people! But we call it the "*uni*-verse." There is diversity, yet it is unified in glorifying the Creator. If God loves variety and creativity, it only makes sense that he would be pleased with new and creative songs intended to bring him praise.

God commanded us to sing a new song. Six times in Psalms and twice in Revelation, the phrase "a new song" is mentioned. We are commanded to sing to the Lord "a new song" (Pss. 33:3; 40:3; 96:1; 98:1; 144:9; 149:1), and we are told that heaven will include the singing of new songs (Rev. 5:9; 14:3). If you don't like singing new songs, you're going to have a hard time enjoying heaven!

Many people—especially young people and new Christians—relate better to the new songs. A few years ago my friend Wayne Smith was the guest preacher at a West-Coast church that had just begun singing a lot of contemporary songs. Wayne asked one of the older, longtime members of the church if he liked the new songs. "I hate them," the elderly man said. "But I sure do like the fact that so many young people are coming here and hearing about Christ."

If the only songs we sing are songs that the older people like, then how do we expect the younger people to feel inspired? Ben Merold, who preaches at Harvester Christian Church in St. Charles, Missouri, is seventy-three years old. His church is vibrant and growing. He told me that if there isn't at least one song every week that he doesn't like, the worship committee isn't doing its job! When people at Southeast come up to me and tell me they didn't like the style of a certain musical selection, I try to gently remind them, "It's not all for you. I don't like some of it either!"

I've learned something recently about the need for contemporary music in our churches. I used to think that eventually the "contemporary music" debate would die out. Pretty soon we'd have a new set of songs that everybody knew, they'd have a contemporary sound, everybody would be singing them, and the argument would be over. But I've come to realize that we will always be singing new songs. Eventually the old ones don't inspire us to worship anymore. We become too familiar with them, and they sound old-fashioned, so we need to write new choruses. I can either fight against the new songs all my life or give in and just fight for an occasional old hymn!

Why Sing Old Hymns?

I'm equally convinced that the Body of Christ in America would benefit significantly by staying in tune with the great hymns of the faith. We should teach our young people the best of the old hymns. When I say "old hymns," I'm not talking about songs that were written fifty years ago and are now outdated. I'm talking about the songs—many of them written hundreds of years ago—that are still sung in churches today because they have such depth of meaning and have stood the test of time. I'm talking about songs like "Joyful, Joyful We Adore Thee," "A Mighty Fortress," "What a Friend We Have in Jesus," "When I Survey the Wondrous Cross," "Holy, Holy, Holy," "Come Thou Fount of Every Blessing," "Rock of Ages," "Amazing Grace," and "Great Is Thy Faithfulness."

Many of the ancient hymns are full of doctrine. Songs that have withstood hundreds of years of time usually do so because their lyrics have somehow connected with people. Your favorite song today may be one of the new choruses, but only time will tell which of those choruses becomes a classic hymn. Much of that will be determined not so much by the music as by the depth of the lyrics. When Martin Luther wrote "A Mighty Fortress," he put the words to a popular bar tune. Today we still sing that song because the words are so powerful.

The hymns keep us tied to other Christians—past and present. If my sons, who grew up attending church, can't stand beside their grandmother at her church and sing some of the old hymns with her because they've never heard them, that would be a shame. They need to learn some of the older songs so they can understand and identify with the older generation of Christians around them.

I have also learned from speaking at many different churches that if the church I'm visiting only sings new choruses, I may not know most of their songs. Whether it is a church across town or hundreds of miles away doesn't matter. The choruses they pick to sing each week won't be the same choruses we are singing. There are hundreds of modern-day choruses. There is no way your people can learn all of them. Your congregation won't sing all the same songs we do. So if you never teach them some of the old hymns, they're likely to not have anything in common with Christians in other congregations. When we gather for revivals, meetings, or conventions, we are united by our worship of God. Yet there are very few songs that we all know outside of the ancient hymns of the church. If we never sing those songs in our local churches, we're hampering opportunities for unity with other Christians.

Greg Allen and our worship team recently went to a revival meeting in a town just outside of Louisville. The worship director who was hosting them said to Greg, "I want you to do all your contemporary stuff." He was trying to implement contemporary music in this old, traditional church, and he wanted Greg to show them how it could really be done.

Greg didn't do "all our contemporary stuff." He told the worship leader, a good friend of his, "We're not coming here to do music. We're coming here to lead people in worship." The first set of songs was almost entirely hymns that Greg knew would be familiar to the congregation. A couple of the hymns were jazzed up a bit, but the tune and words were familiar to everyone. Greg created an inspiring atmosphere, and people worshiped God.

Then Greg chose a few choruses that he felt confident most of the people there knew. He then taught them one or two new songs. He never assumed they already knew the songs, but took the time to teach the lyrics and tune. It was a wonderful, uplifting night. The old hymns provided a point of unity between the visiting worship leader and the congregation, while the new choruses added just the right touch of freshness and life.

The hymns are familiar to many of our guests. Many church leaders are so wrapped up in reaching the culture with modern music that they never stop to think about what might be familiar to a visitor. A first-time visitor in our church has most likely never heard any of the choruses we sing. But chances are good that he has heard one or two of the hymns we will sing.

You might be surprised at the number of people in your culture who have heard a lot of the old hymns, even if they didn't grow up going to church. Many people who have never attended church have heard "Amazing Grace" and "Just As I Am." They're familiar with many of the Christmas songs like "Away in a Manger," "Joy to the World," and "Silent Night." And they've heard the patriotic hymns like "America the Beautiful."

There are also nominal Christians who grew attending church and singing the old songs but who have drifted away and now are seeking to come back. When they walk into your church, they probably don't want it to be exactly like the church they left, but they will feel more comfortable if they've heard a few of the songs you're singing. When unchurched people or nominal Christians visit our church, I want them to be pleasantly surprised by hearing some music with a contemporary sound. But I'm also hoping that they hear one or two songs that they recognize and might want to sing along with. They are more likely to recognize an old hymn than one of our new choruses.

Trying to Balance Musical Styles

Balancing styles of music is never easy, even for a church our size. A few months ago Dale Mowery, our choir director, brought together several very talented brass musicians and formed a Big Band group. They learned to play several Christian songs with a Big Band sound. Greg Allen thought the congregation would love the group because Big Band is popular right now in many contemporary circles, and of course the older people would love it because it was popular in their day, right? Wrong.

Greg decided to have the Big Band playing as a prelude. He thought people wouldn't mind the more jazzy music as they were entering the building since the service hadn't begun yet. The band played three or four songs, and then played one during the service. You wouldn't believe the criticism we received! (Well, if you've tried something new in your church lately, maybe you would believe it.)

Many of the young people loved it. But young people who hate the Big Band sound didn't like it at all. It's popular right now, but apparently not that popular! And some of the older people we thought would like the Big Band sound didn't like it because they said it was the sound they'd heard in bars when they were younger, and the music stirred negative memories. (We thought it would have the opposite effect!) I didn't know so many of our older people had been in the bars when they were younger, but I found out! We decided next time we wouldn't introduce a brand-new style of music so abruptly.

Almost everybody has strong opinions about different styles of music. You know what your favorite style is, and you know what kind of music you dislike. We do not select to entertain people, but we do want them to be inspired to worship God. Some people love Handel and Bach, and a beautiful rendition of a classical hymn will move them to tears. They'll leave saying, "That was wonderful. I felt so close to God today." They were inspired. But most people will be yawning by the end of the second classical number and will leave uninspired.

You can arrogantly claim that others should love your style of music, or you can humbly admit that not everyone has the same tastes that you have. This may be a revelation to some people, but it's true: Your preference of musical styles has nothing to do with your level of spirituality!

I like Southern Gospel music. Some people hate Southern Gospel music. You might like classical, jazz, rock, country, or something more on the fringes. If you're going to reach as many people as possible with the gospel, pay attention to the style of music that is the most popular in your culture, and stay away from the fringes.

Hard rock music is not the most popular style of music in America today, so don't immediately equate "contemporary" with "hard rock" or the newest style of music. Do you know what the most popular style of music is today? Country music. For the last several years, it has outper-formed "Pop Rock" in popularity. In many parts of America, young people are crazy about country music. One of the most contemporary things you can do in those sections of the country is sing a country-sounding song. That's why in our church we're singing more Southern Gospel and country-sounding songs today than we did a few years ago—and I love it! But if you are a forty-year-old worship leader and think the best way to reach your culture is to sing rock music like you listened to in the seventies, you may not be paying attention to the culture.

One word of caution: I think most people expect the church's music to be slightly tamer than the popular music. Music that is too much on the cutting edge will reach a few select young people who like that style, just as classical music reaches only a small group of people. But too much of the fringe music will make many people uneasy.

It will always be a challenge to keep a good balance of musical styles. It's true that people are more likely to be inspired by music they like. So while we try to find styles that help people worship, we must constantly remind the members of our congregation that not every song is for them, that the purpose is worship, not entertainment, and that we are striving to glorify God in all we do.

Greg Allen has a fourth polyp on his vocal cords. He's tired of going through surgeries and voice rest, so he's going to live with it this time and hope he is able to continue singing. His range is severely restricted, and he can't sing as well as he used to. But he's still the best worship leader I've ever seen. In fact, we're all convinced that his voice problems have made him a far better worship leader because of the changes that have occurred in his heart.

Greg said, "Maybe God allowed all these voice problems to happen to me because he knew our church was going to reach a lot of people, and he was more interested in people worshiping him than singing a bunch of songs. So he said, 'Allen, let's take you through some voice stuff to get your heart ready.' I love talking about my voice problems because it gives me another occasion to remember how incredible God is. He uses cracked vessels as long as they're clean. That's what he's pointed out to me. I'm a cracked vessel with a polyp on the vocal cords. I have one again, you know. Another polyp. But we're going to live with it this time. So I guess I'll just try to lead with a pure heart."

- ❖ Personal Character

- ❖ Leadership Capability

- ❖ Practical Suggestions on Leadership

- ❖ Developing Your Own Leadership Qualities

The elders
who direct the
affairs of the church
well are worthy of
double honor.
—1 TIMOTHY 5:17

As a prisoner
for the Lord,
then, I urge you
to live a life worthy
of the calling you
have received.
—EPHESIANS 4:1

You're the example,
not the exception.
—BOB RUSSELL

3

LEADERSHIP:
Develop Christ-Centered Leaders
Who Lead by Example

John Foster, a retired executive, has served as the chairman of our board of elders for the past six years. He is a man deeply respected by all who know him. On the front door of his house is a sign that reads, "As for me and my house, we will serve the Lord." If you knew what goes on inside that house, you'd say that sign is true.

John's wife is a popular teacher in our women's Bible studies and has been a counselor and confidante to many young women. John's home has been a loving, free hotel to dozens of missionaries and hundreds of spiritually needy people. I've often seen John drop to his knees in prayer, and it's obvious that he has been there many times. However, most of the people at Southeast wouldn't even recognize John Foster because he is seldom in front of the congregation. He just has a love for our church and a heart to exalt Christ, and he doesn't care who gets the credit.

In a recent elders' meeting, we listened to a report on the status of operations after our first year in the new building. Every category in the report was far above our expectations. Our attendance growth was higher than we had projected, offerings were better than we had hoped, and costs were less than we had anticipated. John Foster said, "Men, we're not this good." Following his lead, we all went to our knees and offered prayers of thanksgiving for the blessings God had poured out upon us.

That story sheds light on another reason why God has chosen to bless Southeast Christian Church in a powerful way. We have a remarkable group of leaders who strive to honor God and give him glory. When I'm asked to analyze why our church has grown so dramatically, I say there is one overriding reason God has blessed our congregation: excellent leadership. The elders and staff have consistently been an example of what godly leadership is all about.

I've visited a lot of churches and listened to a lot of people talk about their congregations, and I've observed that there is a desperate need for good leadership in most churches. A Christian publishing company recently concluded that the greatest need in Christian churches in America is the need for leadership. There is a leadership void in our churches. There is a hunger for dedicated, charismatic personalities who can inspire others to follow.

Leadership is a complex subject that is impossible to cover in one chapter. But I want to share some of my thoughts on two essential components of leadership: personal character and leadership capability. If you want to recruit and develop good leaders in your church, or if you want to be a good leader yourself, consider both of these aspects of leadership.

PERSONAL CHARACTER

A few years ago a group of us who are privileged to lead large congregations decided to begin gathering annually for the purpose of fellowship and inspiration. We knew we would enjoy the opportunity to share ideas and encourage one another. But each of the past three years, there has been at least one minister who didn't return. In every case, it was because of a serious moral failure in the person's life. They all had the talent you might think is necessary to lead a large congregation—charisma, intelligence, decisiveness, persuasiveness—but something had happened to their character, and their ministries collapsed.

Often we're looking for gimmicks, programs, and ideas that will make our church grow, while God is looking for consecration and genuine commitment among the church's leaders. When Paul listed the qualifications for church leadership in 1 Timothy 3 and Titus 1, almost all of the requirements focused on the person's character—he must be above reproach, faithful to his wife, temperate, self-controlled, not greedy, and so forth. Leadership begins with who we are, not what we do. A lack of integrity among the leaders quenches the flow of the Holy Spirit and removes God's hand of blessing from the church.

When Ananias and Sapphira lied about the amount they were donating to the church, Peter accused them of lying to the Holy Spirit, and they both dropped dead (Acts 5). Why would God bring about such strict punishment? Because this was the first breech of integrity in the young church, and God was making it clear that the New Testament church was to be pure. God's people were to be a holy people. God was demonstrating that sin in the church would quench the Spirit.

Years ago our church hit a plateau. The services were dead. There was no growth. Something seemed to be missing. We tried different activities and implemented some creative ideas, but we just couldn't seem to get the church moving again. I sat in the office after services one Sunday and thought, *Something is wrong. I can't feel the moving of God's Spirit among us.* Two weeks later, we discovered that one of our key leaders had been having an affair for the past year.

It was not easy for the elders to determine how to handle the situation. The leader was asked to step down from his position while he tried to get his life back in order. We encouraged him to stay out of the ministry for a while until he could reestablish some integrity and trustworthiness. We prayed for him and did our best to minister to his family. Finally, upon our suggestion, they left the church and moved to another town where they could get a fresh start.

I was concerned that the crisis might have devastating consequences in our church. But almost immediately after the situation was resolved, the church exploded in an outpouring of God's Spirit and a renewed sense of joy among the people.

For God's hand of blessing to be upon your church, there must be a degree of holiness among the leaders. God doesn't require perfection, but he does require sincerity and effort. The leaders must demonstrate for the people how to live like Jesus Christ.

I believe that three character qualities should distinguish every leader in your congregation.

1. Purity

Our associate preacher, Dave Stone, keeps in constant view reminders of the consequences that would result should he have a moral breakdown. He has pictures of his wife and three children all over the walls of his office. He also keeps on his desk an article about a minister in our town who had an affair and ruined his ministry—not an article that ran in our local paper, but in USA Today. He wants to remember that not only are there four people he loves whose lives would be forever scarred, and thousands in our church who would be disappointed, there's also a world of people who would hear and mock.

It was said of King David that his affair with Bathsheba gave "the enemies of God an occasion to blaspheme." When we fail to live lives of purity, the world mocks.

Every year at our staff retreat, I give basically the same speech. The staff calls it "the purity speech." I remind them what a great thing we have going at Southeast Christian Church and how much God has blessed us. Then I remind them how they could ruin it if they don't keep their lives clean. If they have an affair or get involved in gambling or a drug addiction, it could not only ruin their families but also really mess up what God is doing at Southeast. I tell them, "If you are right now living in a way that you know is not the way the Lord would want you to live, then please do us all a favor and resign. Step aside because God is doing a great work here and you don't want to be the one to get in the way."

A couple of years ago after that speech, one staff member later confessed he felt as if I were talking straight to him. He knew he wasn't living a consistent life, and he felt guilty. He was involved in pornography and was flirting with an immoral relationship. Just as the Lord singled out Achan (see Joshua 7), this young man felt singled out; and within a couple of months, he resigned. When he confessed, there was severe damage to his family and ministry, and many people were wounded by his actions. But had he continued working on our staff, it could have been even worse.

In the classic work *Mutiny on the Bounty*, the tribunal determining the fate of Captain Christian concluded, "If decency does not abide in the captain of the ship, then it is not on board." God will not tolerate duplicity and secret sin among the leaders of his church. If you are not living a life of purity, either God's Spirit will not bless your congregation, or he will move you out of the way.

2. Sincerity

I certainly don't mean to communicate that you have to be perfect to be a minister (It's a good thing!), or even act perfect. In fact, when ministers pretend to be perfect, they actually do harm to the Body of Christ. Jesus condemned the Pharisees for acting pious and spiritual and then not practicing what they preached (Matt. 23:3). Nobody respects a hypocrite.

Steve Brown of Key Life Ministries said that a woman once approached him after his sermon and told him, "I've heard other preachers say they weren't perfect, but you're the first one I've believed!" I'm not sure that's a compliment, but it does prove Steve Brown's sincerity!

Church leaders must maintain the difficult balance between authenticity and spirituality. If you appear to be perfect, people will see you as unreal and regard the Christian life as unattainable. But if you appear to be too sinful, people lose respect for you. They will see you as no better than the next guy, and they are uninspired. You should be transparent about your own failures and let people see your faults, but a church also has the right to expect its leaders to be a cut above the rest. Be real, but be an example that will motivate others to stretch in their spiritual walk.

3. Humility

The key to leading with both purity and sincerity is a spirit of genuine humility. I've already mentioned John Foster, our chairman of the board of elders, as an example of humility. Though he is a talented and capable leader, he stays behind the scenes and desires to exalt Christ instead of himself. That attitude is common in all of our elders, each of whom sacrifices several hours a week in anonymous service without demanding recognition. I'm sure most Southeast members couldn't name five of the twenty-three elders, but it doesn't matter to those humble leaders as long as Christ is praised.

Our church staff has the same desire to honor Christ. Three members of my leadership team have come from business backgrounds. They've taken dramatic pay cuts in their salaries—about 50 percent of what they were making in the business world—to be on the staff of our church. The other members of our leadership team come from ministry backgrounds. Talented ministers such as Ross Brodfuehrer and Brett DeYoung have been willing to labor in administrative roles behind the scenes so that Christ can continue to be honored at Southeast. I've seen them do whatever it takes to help the church succeed—from moving chairs, picking up litter, or stopping to help visitors find their way.

An agent for public speakers told me that our preaching associate, Dave Stone, could be booked four or five times a night as a motivational speaker, making more than two thousand dollars a night. Instead, he takes only a few speaking engagements because he wants to concentrate the majority of his time on his role as an associate minister. He doesn't mind playing second fiddle as long as Christ is exalted.

Sometimes people ask me, "How can you and Dave Stone get along so well? Aren't you threatened by this talented young man who is preaching in your pulpit once a month? Isn't it difficult to give up the pulpit that often?" Yes, it's difficult. People sometimes say to me, "I can't remember if it was you or Dave Stone who said in a sermon..." That's hard on my ego! But I'm willing to take the hits to my ego because of something more important. Dave and I love each other, and we get along like father and son because we both have the same goal—that Jesus Christ be exalted.

Paul commanded, "Do nothing out of selfish ambition or vain conceit, but in humility consider others better than yourselves. Each of you should look not only to your own interests, but also to the interests of others. Your attitude should be the same as that of Christ Jesus" (Phil. 2:3–5). We try to encourage that same attitude of humility among the staff and leaders. When we were meeting at our old building, there were so many parking problems that we began shuttling people on school buses from three or four off-site locations. The two hundred-plus elders, deacons, and staff members, who are usually the first to arrive, could take up a lot of valuable parking spaces, so we asked them to park in one of the shuttle lots and ride the school buses to church. My wife and I also rode the shuttle. When the choir sang, we asked all 150 of them to park off site too. It was one small way for the leaders to remember that we aren't doing this for our own egos, but to exalt Jesus Christ. None of us is too big to ride the bus to church!

[Editor's note: Senior minister Bob Russell's son Rusty asked John Foster, chairman of Southeast's board of elders, about the reason for the church's distinctive atmosphere. Without Bob Russell's knowledge, Foster said:

> In our church the senior minister is just another elder. At board meetings, he doesn't write the agenda, demand time, or demand things be done his way. He's just another one of the people around the table. Your dad doesn't have an ego that needs to be served. That allows for a lot of openness and objectivity. His lack of ego also allows the elders and staff to move about doing what they're supposed to be doing without having to look over their shoulder wondering how their actions are going to be perceived. It's easy to follow somebody you have trust in, whom you believe doesn't have any other agenda, and that only has the good of the organization at heart.

Rusty Russell continues:

> The first-century church was run by a plurality of elders, not just one pastor, and the New Testament writers talked about the "priesthood of all believers." We are all called to be ministers, and there should be no clergy-laity distinction in the church. When the church isn't run by one pastor, it's much easier to keep egos under control. The preacher naturally has a lot of unofficial authority, so he must regularly make a conscious effort to step down off the pedestal. For that reason, when our church began to grow at a rapid pace, Dad decided he needed to be up front less. That's when we hired a preaching associate—Dave Stone—and began to make plans for Dad's retirement. *If I truly want to exalt Christ and not my own ego,* Dad reasoned, *then I want Southeast Christian Church to continue reaching the lost long after I'm gone.*
>
> Dad has portrayed a humble attitude in the little things too. He doesn't have his own parking space, he doesn't wear a robe

when he preaches, and he doesn't ask people to call him Reverend or Pastor. When our local paper published an article about him a few years ago, they titled it "Just Plain Bob." That's been an inside joke at our church ever since. His name is no longer Bob, it's "Just Plain Bob."]

LEADERSHIP CAPABILITY

Many churches make the mistake of not realizing that *leadership capability* is a second key element to successful church leadership. If your church is led by people in your congregation who have personal integrity and are spiritually sensitive but have no leadership gifts or capabilities, you will have leadership problems. In Romans 12, Paul reminds us that only some Christians are gifted with leadership and that those are the people who should "govern diligently" (Rom. 12:8).

Henry Ford once said that to ask who should be the leader is like asking who should sing tenor in the quartet. The *tenor* should sing tenor, of course; and the person who is gifted to lead should lead.

Many books have been written about the qualities of good leadership. A good leader is decisive, organized, visionary, and inspiring. But good leadership *in the church* should be marked by some important distinctions that may not be necessary in other leadership positions.

Courageous Confrontation of Problems

A growing church is frequently the victim of vicious attacks from the adversary. Satan hates an alive church and does his best to destroy it. You can bet that just when things begin going well in your church, you will encounter serious spiritual opposition.

Over the years Southeast has been forced to confront several serious problems: One leader had an affair, two deacons became involved in a business partnership and threatened to sue each other, on a couple of occasions volunteers have flaunted immoral relationships, a new member was accused of murder. Such problems simply cannot be dealt with adequately without strong, though sensitive, leaders who do not shy away from confrontation.

John Wilson, longtime minister of the First Christian Church in Springfield, Ohio, suggested that when a church has problems, the leaders have to determine if it's measles or cancer. If it's measles, the problem will go away on its own; if it's cancer, it has to be eradicated. The temptation leaders face is to let all the problems slide, to be passive, and to hope they will go away.

Paul chastised the Corinthian leaders for not confronting immorality that was being flaunted in their fellowship (1 Cor. 5). He warned Timothy that false teaching was like "gangrene" (2 Tim. 2:17). And he personally confronted divisiveness in the Corinthian church (1 Cor. 1).

Distinctive leaders confront malignant problems scripturally, lovingly, and openly. Average leaders spend too much time speculating about people's reactions: *What will they say? Who will be offended? How many people will leave?* Superior leaders are primarily concerned with what God has instructed us to do in His Word. The one essential for stability in any organization is the assurance that someone is in charge in a time of crisis. Nothing destroys the cohesiveness of a body like the feeling that no one is doing anything about a serious problem.

A minister once came to visit me who was completely discouraged. A year earlier his youth minister, a young single man, had impregnated a girl in the youth group. The young man married the girl, but the congregation was divided over whether he should continue as youth minister. The preacher and the majority of elders believed he should be asked to resign. They were willing to forgive him, but his moral failure was not a good example for the young people to whom he was supposed to be ministering. The elders believed it would take time for the young man to reestablish credibility.

One elder, however, was the father of the young pregnant girl. He wanted his daughter to remain in town, so the principles for him got very cloudy. The minister told me the congregation was divided into the "forgiveness" camp and the "credibility" camp. Growth had been stymied, and people had left the church. The minister and youth minister barely spoke to one another. Such a situation will never be resolved until the leaders are in accord and decide to make some tough decisions.

Contrast that with a similar situation in another church. The senior pastor fell into immorality. He wrote a letter to the congregation asking for forgiveness and restoration. The elders determined he should be dismissed, especially since they had learned there had actually been a series of affairs. The minister had a serious character flaw. The elders acted immediately and with a united front. Although there were some criticisms and a few people left the church, the congregation as a whole rallied around the elders. The church has remained intact, and the Holy Spirit seems to be flowing through the congregation as they try to pick up the pieces and search for a new pastor.

An Attitude of Reasonable Flexibility

In Bible-believing churches, certain truths are absolute. Good leaders do not waver where the Bible speaks, as we discussed in chapter 2. Doctrines like the inspiration of Scripture, the deity of Christ, the plan of salvation, the resurrection, and the second coming are not debatable.

In matters of opinion, however, good leaders are flexible. Nothing stifles a church quite like legalism. Christian Schwarz studied over a thousand churches in thirty-two different countries. He discovered that despite the style or denominational background of the church, only 10 percent of the members of healthy churches said their church battled "traditionalism." But 50 *percent* of the people in low-quality, dying churches said they considered their church to be "tradition-bound."[1]

So many times leaders brag that they are "defending the faith" when in reality they are stubbornly guarding tradition. In matters of opinion, distinctive leaders are flexible. They aren't shackled by the seven deadliest words of the church: *We've never done it that way before*. Leaders maintain that nonessential matters are open for discussion without emotional reactions. Issues such as style of music, order of worship, paid nursery help, drums on the platform, selling tapes in the vestibule, and allowing non-ordained persons to administer communion and baptism are discussed objectively.

Good leaders are sensitive to the Body so as not to offend those with a weak conscience, but they aren't intimidated by a few vocal critics. They apply this rule: *Methods are many, principles are few; methods always change, principles never do*. Good leaders are receptive to change if it promises to benefit the Body.

I witnessed this principle in action a few years ago when our elders discussed what to do with some valuable items that had been donated to our church in connection with a special offering. People had lovingly sacrificed jewelry, furs, cars, guns, oriental rugs, motorcycles, etc. As responsible stewards, the elders had to determine the best way to liquidate those items.

Someone suggested having an auction. That was the most logical method, but should a church have an auction? Would it be misunderstood by the community? Would it set an unfavorable precedent? We couldn't find the word *auction* in the concordance of our Bibles. The bottom line was that the Bible didn't specify on such matters, so the church leaders could act according to what they concluded would be best for the Body. Out of sensitivity for those who might feel uncomfortable with an auction on church grounds, the elders chose an off-site property for the auction. It was conducted in good taste and resulted in positive publicity, good fellowship, and a fair price for the donated goods. Had the elders refused to do anything that *might* bring criticism, they couldn't possibly have made that stewardship decision.

Open Support of the Other Leaders

The New Testament commands us to respect and support our church leaders: "Now we ask you, brothers, to respect those who work hard among you, who are over you in the Lord and who admonish you. Hold them in the highest regard in love because of their work. Live in peace with each other" (1 Thess. 5:12–13). Cooperation among leaders is essential for a growing church. The preacher and other staff members have a responsibility to be submissive to the elders' oversight and to communicate openly with them. Good elders, on the other hand, are a source of encouragement to the staff. Backbiting, two-facedness, and ridicule can be devastating to a minister's confidence and his reputation with the congregation. Conversely, positive support from the elders can motivate staff members to reach their full potential.

We hear a lot about leadership, but very little about "follow-ship." Yet we are all called to be followers on occasion. Jesus said, "Follow me." A real test of character for all leaders is how they react when they're called upon to follow. I know of a church where the board chairman was an excellent leader of leaders, but when he ceased being the chairman, he made life miserable for the one who was. He was critical, moody, and divisive. He hadn't learned to follow very well. As a result he alienated others by his pride, and his leadership was not nearly as effective.

Even though I am the senior minister, I don't run Southeast Christian Church. That surprises a lot of people on the outside, and sometimes it takes our new members awhile to grasp that concept. As I mentioned earlier, the New Testament leads us to believe that the early local churches were governed by a plurality of elders. Church government was not a democracy where everyone in the congregation got a vote, nor was there one pastor who led autocratically. The church was a Christocracy. Christ was the Head of his Body. And the elders— a group of spiritual men with leadership ability—were appointed to

govern the Body according to what they believed to be Christ's leading. The preacher was a paid elder whose task was "preaching and
teaching." According to 1 Timothy 5:17, such an elder was "worthy of
double honor" and was to be paid generously, praise the Lord!

Therefore, we have decided at our church that the responsibility
for the oversight of the congregation should be shared by the twenty-
three men who are the elders of the church. I am considered one of
those twenty-three men, but I am not the *only* pastor. (In the New
Testament, the words *pastor* and *elder* are used interchangeably. Since
at Southeast we're attempting to restore those biblical definitions, we
view pastors and elders synonymously.)

I acknowledge the other elders' authority and try to be submissive.
They aren't rubber stamps either. They ask tough questions, make me
accountable in financial matters, and occasionally register objections.
But they are also very supportive and encouraging. The ministry can at
times be a very insecure and intimidating position. Since we are constantly plagued by a sense of inadequacy, good elders and deacons look
for opportunities to boost the preacher.

When I speak around the country, I'm often asked, "How have you
been able to stay at one church for thirty years?" In reply, I usually tell
of a time early in my ministry when I came to the elders with a problem. I'm not a complainer, but I was struggling with being overburdened in my job. I wasn't meeting the demands of the growing church
the way I felt I should, and I was feeling a great deal of pressure. So I
decided to tell the leaders exactly what my frustrations were. I wondered if they would respond cynically or dismiss me by saying something like, "Every job has its pressures," or "You're finding out what it's
like to work in the real world."

Instead, these church leaders were very understanding. When I finished, one man responded, "Bob is telling us the truth. We need to
make adjustments and help him out." They offered suggestions on areas
where I should cut back, and they helped me delegate some responsi-

bility. I can't remember all the adjustments that were made, but I'll never forget their spirit of support. Just knowing they believed in me and supported me created in me a renewed enthusiasm and love for the church. That's the primary reason I've been able to stay and enjoy the ministry at Southeast for so long.

Progressive Delegation of Responsibility

Excellent leaders watch out for the dangers of Boyle's Law: *If not controlled, work will flow to the most competent person until he is swamped.* When Moses became overburdened with counseling responsibilities (Ex. 18), his father-in-law wisely advised him to delegate the responsibilities by training several men to help him. When the church in Jerusalem grew to the extent that the twelve apostles began experiencing time pressures, they decided to select seven men to care for welfare needs so they could continue giving themselves to "prayer and the ministry of the word" (Acts 6:4).

As the preacher of a growing church, I've been forced to learn to relinquish secondary tasks so I can devote myself to preaching and teaching. I'm thankful that our elders encouraged me to delegate responsibility and didn't insist that I attend every subcommittee meeting or extracurricular function, call on every person in the hospital, or even preach every Sunday.

The elders not only encouraged me to delegate, they practiced what they preached. As the church grew, they realized it would be nearly impossible to continue to conduct business in the same way. Responsibilities were broken down to various committees. One officer —an elder or deacon—was selected to chair each committee. Where possible that selection was made according to the officer's interests and personal talents.

Each committee was then given its own budget. The authority to conduct the normal operation of that department was given to the committee. Each committee now functions in a sense as a separate board carrying on its own business and directing its own people. Our meetings became report meetings that sometimes lasted less than an hour! Elders' meetings last a little longer because there is discussion of spiritual concerns and important decisions affecting church policy. But even they are not the marathon meetings we had when the board was making all the decisions.

Small leaders will feel threatened by a loss of power and complain, "We're losing control! It's a loose ship we're running. Nobody knows what's going on!" But distinctive leaders trust their colleagues and rely on Christ to be the Head of the church. They realize that it's impossible to reach maximum growth potential without delegating responsibility.

The Succession Plan at Southeast

In a recent congregational survey, I was a little surprised at how many people asked the question about a succession plan at Southeast: "What happens when Bob Russell retires, is killed, or becomes disabled?" I just turned fifty-six, and Lord willing, I'd like to be around eight or nine more years. I'm as excited and challenged by what I'm doing as I've ever been. While I've tried to share the load, I'm having fun! But I noticed that Dr. James Dobson of Focus on the Family recently wrote a letter to all his supporters outlining a ten-year succession plan. That seemed wise to me, since it eliminates the question, "What's going to happen...?" So I began working on a succession plan for what happens after I retire.

It's understood in our church that if something happened to me, our preaching associate, Dave Stone, would be preaching the next service. I hope they'd mourn for me for thirty days, but we've tried not to build on one person. One of our members, Betty Willman, got tired of her friends saying, "Wait until Bob Russell retires! Your church will be in trouble then!" One day one of her friends asked, "What will Southeast do if Bob Russell is killed in an accident?"

She quickly responded, "Well, we'll bury the dude and go on!" Those who are involved at Southeast have learned that it doesn't revolve around one person.

I have watched closely and have yet to see a retired minister remain in the church he pastored for a long time and not be a burden to his successor. It's too great a temptation. That's why I recently submitted to the elders an eight-year succession plan. Someone said, "If you want to make God laugh, tell him your plans." Any plan has to be submitted with the qualifier, "Lord willing." Still, although God may alter any plan through dramatic circumstances or counsel, Jesus said, "No man builds a tower without first sitting down and calculating the cost." While we realize that God is in control, he does expect us to make provisions for the future.

At a recent elders' meeting, our leaders approved the following plan:

1. Dave Stone will become the senior minister at my retirement, sometime between my ages sixty-three and sixty-five. Dave is a man of integrity, intelligence, and extreme giftedness who over the past ten years has become familiar with our church's culture and has gained the respect of the congregation. He is an excellent communicator and an outstanding husband and father. He loves Southeast, and his heart and future plans are here. Dave is preaching one additional weekend each year. In the year 2000 he will preach twenty times, and I'll preach thirty. In 2001, he'll preach twenty-one times, and I'll preach twenty-nine, and so on for the next eight years or so.

2. During the next few years, we will be searching for a third preacher who will ease into the rotation. When I step aside, the new preacher will share the pulpit with Dave as he now shares it with me. It's our general feeling that since Dave's style of preaching is more motivational, the next member of the

preaching team should have an instructional style of preaching and be more of a Bible teacher.

3. Lord willing, when I step aside from this pulpit, I will continue to preach and teach elsewhere. With God's help I'm coping well at age fifty-six, but I don't think the pressures of a large church will wear well on a man moving toward seventy. My task over the next nine years will be to prepare Southeast for a future in which I will have no part. I admire Dean Smith, former basketball coach of the University of North Carolina, and John Wooden, former UCLA basketball coach. They retired at the top of their game. They didn't become a burden to their institutions, and they continued to be useful and supportive after their retirement. I want to retire in the same way.

When my friend Wayne Smith retired from the Southland Christian Church in Lexington, Kentucky, after forty years of ministry, everyone expected a period of decline and depression in the church. "It just won't be the same when Wayne leaves," people said. When Mike Breaux succeeded Wayne, the worship attendance jumped from four thousand to five thousand the first weekend! The next weekend they had 5,050 then fifty-one hundred the next. On the fourth weekend the attendance dropped back down to 5,050, and Wayne joked, "I knew they couldn't sustain it!" But they have. That great church is now averaging more than seven thousand in worship. That's in Lexington, Kentucky! That's amazing! That's a tribute to both preaching ministers. Mike Breaux said, "The reason we made a smooth transition was because of the foundation that was laid by Wayne Smith. He taught those people to love and grow."

If Southeast does better when I'm gone, that would be a tribute to the foundation I have helped to lay. If the church collapses when I leave, it would be an indication that we failed to build the foundation we should have, for no one should "lay any foundation other than the one already laid, which is Jesus Christ" (1 Cor. 3:11).

One of our deacons, Don Whitley, a gentle, soft-spoken man, had a conversation sometime ago with a man who obviously didn't think too highly of our church. The man said, "When that man dies, that church is going down the tubes."

Don quietly answered, " 'That man' died two thousand years ago and came back from the grave. You need to know that there is no man who runs the church. Its foundation is Jesus Christ."

That's why Southeast can continue to grow regardless of who fills the pulpit. Jesus said, "If I am lifted up, I will draw all men to me." I hope every Southeast member feels the same way Don Whitley does and will continue to lift up Jesus Christ after I am gone.

PRACTICAL SUGGESTIONS ON LEADERSHIP

No one can guarantee that your church's leaders will be people of character and ability. But a church can use some discernment and creativity to help assure quality leadership. Here are some practical ideas for developing a good staff, encouraging leadership among the elders, and improving your own leadership qualities.

Develop a Quality Ministry Staff

Hire the right person. I heard a minister say he didn't believe in Psalm 23. He said, "I've never had a staff that comforted me!" I've learned something as an overseer of ministers: Nothing will take more of your time and energy than hiring the wrong person. And nothing will help your ministry more than hiring the right person. Always hire the person with integrity. Don't let someone's talent override personal character flaws. It's easy to make that mistake, and it will haunt you. It's easier to train a person of character to do the job you want him or her to do than to turn a talented person into someone who is trustworthy.

The church staff shouldn't be a halfway house for character problems. Hire capable leaders, then let them lead.

Demand purity. At Southeast we have some ministry guidelines, especially in the area of male-female relationships, that would be good for any Christian to follow. (1) No repeated counseling sessions with a member of the opposite sex. (2) No traveling alone with a member of the opposite sex. (3) No lunch meetings with a member of the opposite sex. (4) Beware of "holy hugs" and careless touching. Those may seem like stringent rules, but I've read that leaders in the business world have begun implementing similar rules in their offices to cut down on office romances that steal company time, and especially to avoid sexual harassment claims.

The church is to be a place of healing, but the church staff is not a place for character-improvement projects. If you have a staff member who has a purity problem, he or she should not continue ministering. Demand a reasonable level of purity among the church leaders. When a moral problem with a staff member arises, act quickly and wisely. Do not make the mistake of sweeping it under the rug and hoping it will go away. Ask the advice of some trusted Christian leaders who are not close to the problem, and follow their advice. In almost every instance where there is a serious purity problem, it would be best for the staff member to get out of ministry for a while and attend another church where he or she can receive healing and discipleship. The only time I have seen people successfully return to ministry after experiencing a serious moral failure is when they have submitted to a period of discipleship and accountability, completely away from ministry responsibilities, lasting at least one year.

Deal with a poor worker wisely. Sometimes a person has a problem with laziness or another character flaw you didn't see in the interview. Suddenly it appears after they're hired. Don't flippantly fire someone. The church isn't like a business. If the problem is a moral issue, it must be dealt with immediately. But if a staff member simply has a lack of ability or a poor work ethic, be wise. Sometimes the cure is worse than the disease, and a weak staff member needs to be tolerated for a while. The harmony of the church has to be weighed against the ineptitude of a staff member.

After you have given a staff member adequate warning and plenty of opportunity to correct the problem, if the person doesn't have the character or talent to do the job and you decide to request a resignation, think first about the minister's future. If it is possible, allow the staff member to continue working at the church for several months while he looks for a new position. Many a good young minister has been hardened against ministry altogether because a church decided he was the wrong guy and fired him with no thought to his future. Maybe he's not the right fit for you but would make some other congregation a wonderful minister. Be gracious and give him every opportunity to leave with dignity.

Have an annual staff retreat. Our elders began sending the ministry staff on an annual retreat several years ago for three reasons: They wanted us to feel appreciated, they wanted us to learn to like each other, and they wanted us to have some time to consider God's plans for our future. So every summer our ministry staff spends three days together at a state park. We spend half the time in fun activities getting to know one another—we golf together, ride go-carts, ski, and play games. The rest of the time we spend developing goals for the coming year and working on future planning.

As preaching minister, I take one evening of the retreat to give the staff an annual "State of the Staff" address, wherein I give them my thoughts on where we are and where we're headed, as well as the annual "purity" speech I mentioned earlier. Another night we usually spend worshiping together, led by someone who is not one of our own staff members. Since many of the staff are almost constantly ministering to others, it's nice to have some time when we can be led in worship. For those three days, we spend a lot of time laughing, playing, and praying together. If you are a part of a church with a multiple paid staff, consider the benefits of a regular staff retreat.

Encourage family commitment. People in ministry have a tendency to neglect their family. Ministers usually love what they do and feel called to minister to people's needs. And ministry is never done; it's a twenty-four-hour-a-day commitment. But if you win dozens of people to Christ and your marriage falls apart or your kids fall away, then you have neglected your primary ministry and harmed your effectiveness for the future.

Paul said, "If anyone does not provide for his relatives, and especially for his immediate family, he has denied the faith and is worse than an unbeliever" (1 Tim. 5:8). I don't think he was just talking about financial provisions. We have a spiritual obligation to our family members as well. Husbands are commanded to love their wives as Christ loved the church (Eph. 5:25), wives are commanded to submit to and respect their husbands (vv. 22, 33), and fathers are to bring up their children "in the training and instruction of the Lord" (6:4). If the staff members at your church fail to obey these commands for husbands, wives, and parents—their first obligation—God cannot fully bless your congregation.

Encourage staff to take proper breaks for family time—one day a week (besides Sunday, which is never a day of rest for ministers), and be generous with vacation time each year. Our church encourages the ministry staff to go on a marriage retreat each year, which many of the staff *spouses* say is their favorite weekend of the year! Remind your staff members that family is a priority, and be understanding when they need family time.

Develop esprit de corps. One of our staff members, Don Waddell, is an ex-fighter pilot and retired air force colonel. Though he received a lot of leadership training before joining our staff, he now gives leadership seminars about what he has learned about leadership from working at Southeast Christian Church. In his seminars he talks about the esprit de corps he has observed among the Southeast staff. The ministers at Southeast get along with one another. We laugh a lot together and love to fellowship with each other. We have a common love for our church and our Lord, and we genuinely like each other.

I'm not a big fan of meetings. I'm convinced that not much gets accomplished in meetings and most of them are a waste of time. But I recognized long ago that one of the benefits—perhaps the greatest benefit—of our regular staff meetings was not work but fellowship. So we get together for regular staff meetings to take care of some necessary business items, but primarily to fellowship. Our preaching associate, Dave Stone, has a tremendous sense of humor, as do several other staff members. We have some traditions and inside jokes that are shared at staff meetings and help us develop that esprit de corps.

Just as children are impacted by the way their parents treat one another, so church members will be greatly affected by the way their ministers treat each other. So do what you can to develop a sense of harmony and camaraderie among the staff.

Encourage Leadership among the Elders

Uphold the biblical qualifications for elders. During a board meeting in my first ministry, one of the elders suddenly said, "What are we going to do about the [expletive deleted] air conditioning?" I knew I was not dealing with a deeply spiritual man. The qualifications for elders in 1 Timothy 3 and Titus 1 are primarily spiritual qualifications. The elder is to be self-controlled, faithful to his wife, gentle, not quarrelsome, etc.

But not all the qualifications have to do with the candidate's spiritual depth. The elder is also to be a person who is gifted to lead. He must be someone who manages his family well, because "if anyone does not know how to manage his own family, how can he take care of God's church?" (1 Tim. 3:5). He must also be "able to teach" (1 Tim. 3:2) and to discern false doctrine (Titus 1:9). So an elder should have biblical knowledge and wisdom, as well as character and leadership capabilities.

Robert Jones, former administrator of stewardship development at Johnson Bible College, has noted that the New Testament elder was supposed to do five things: preach (1 Tim. 5:17); teach (3:2); shepherd, giving special attention to the guiding and protecting of the flock (Acts 20:28); pray effectively, especially for the sick (James 5:14); and provide for the needy, with special attention to widows and orphans (Acts 4:35; James 1:27). In contrast, however, Professor Jones said that in the modern church we ask the elders to do five things: attend church Sunday morning, attend church Sunday night, attend church Wednesday night, give a generous offering, and attend board meetings. And we'll usually settle for three out of five!

An elder is to be an overseer—someone who can teach, shepherd, manage, and pray. He doesn't have to be able to perform each of these functions equally well, but he does need to show gifts in those areas before he is appointed. A person shouldn't be ordained as an elder simply because he's paid his dues for a number of years and you feel obligated to reward him with a leadership role. Just because someone attends church regularly, tithes, and is a nice person doesn't mean that he's qualified for leadership.

Select elders wisely. I'm often asked how we select elders at Southeast. Each of our elders had to endure an extensive interview process in order to become an elder. Almost all of our twenty-three elders first served as deacons. In the New Testament church, the deacons were apparently officers with special gifts of service. (The Greek word for deacon means "servant.") So in our church the deacons are officers who are in charge of service ministries—greeters, parking-lot attenders, ushers, servers, facilities volunteers, kitchen help, etc. Our candidates for elders come from those men because we are convinced that a person is most likely to develop the necessary qualities for eldership by performing the duties of deacon, where he is humbly serving in relative obscurity.

After a person is nominated to become an elder, he fills out an application form and has several interviews. He is encouraged to excuse himself from consideration at any time during the process if he feels he does not have the time to commit, is not ready to commit, or for any personal reason does not think he meets the qualifications outlined in the Scriptures for elders. After an extensive application process and one-on-one interviews, if the present elders believe the man to be qualified, he will be ordained as an elder. He will then serve a three-year term, after which he can be elected again. If at any time an elder is not upholding the biblical qualities of an elder, he will be confronted and asked to step down.

Encourage elders to get to know one another. If elders see each other only in meetings, they see the worst or the most intense side of each other. Your elders need to get to know and love one another. That happens much more naturally if they are spending time together on a casual basis. I take an annual golf trip with six or seven of our elders. We don't talk much about business on those trips. But business meetings are smoother after we've spent time together laughing, playing, and teasing with one another.

For the last year we've begun our monthly elders' meetings with a dinner. Sitting around the table eating, talking, and having fellowship together gives us an opportunity to become friends working toward a common goal, rather than a gathering of individual decision-makers bickering and playing power games. We also have an annual elders' retreat and several picnics during the course of the year. It has been extremely beneficial for us as an elder board to have a day or two together where we can fellowship, pray, and work. Not only is it another opportunity to get to know one another, it is also good to make the bigger decisions and set goals for the future without being pressured by the clock.

John Foster said that one of the things that has made his job as chairman of our board of elders a pleasant one has been the support of the other elders. He said, "My biggest supporters—more than anybody else—have been the other elders. They're my strongest fans. That's encouraging to me. I've always been convinced that the people who pray for me most, who really pull for me most, are the other elders."

Find tangible ways for the eldership to support the staff. At nearly every monthly elders' meeting, we invite staff members from a particular department to come to the meeting and share with us what is happening in their ministry. At 8 P.M. we stop what we are doing and welcome them into the meeting. We listen to their report, rejoice with them over what God is doing, encourage them, and ask them if they have any prayer requests. Then we lay hands on them and pray for them.

What a different atmosphere from the stereotypical "Departmental Report to the Board"! Staff members actually walk away lifted up instead of beaten down. Not only is each department given the feeling that the elders are supportive of them, the elders are given a different perspective from which to view each ministry.

Develop Your Own Leadership Qualities

If you are a church leader, here are some things you can do to develop quality leadership in your own life.

Live an authentic life. Years ago I lost my wedding ring. I was disappointed, but I put off replacing it, and my wife didn't say anything about it. The days turned into years. I grew so accustomed to not wearing a ring that I never even thought about it. Years later I found the ring, but it had been so long since I had worn it that I couldn't get it over my knuckle! About two years ago when we began using an Image Magnification System in our services, suddenly I was bigger than life when I preached. Not only could people see my facial expressions on the big screen, they could clearly see my hands. You can't imagine how many women began buzzing about why I didn't wear a ring!

Finally my wife and I decided I'd better get a wedding ring, so we had my original ring resized, and I began wearing it. Over the next few months I discovered just how many people knew I didn't wear a ring, because suddenly they were noticing that I *was* wearing one! Scores of people—mostly ladies in the church—commented about how glad they were that I had decided to wear a wedding ring. I guess in today's culture it just doesn't send the right message in some people's minds if you are married and aren't wearing a wedding ring. Had I known, I'd have done something about it much sooner!

A man once told me he listened to me preach on the radio every week. Although he liked what he heard, he was skeptical of preachers of large churches. He said, "I decided before I came to your church that I wanted to see where you lived. So I looked up your address in the phone book and drove by your house. You live in a nice house, but it's reasonable. So I came." That guy became a deacon in our church! I jokingly told him I was glad I had my two Jaguars parked in the garage where he couldn't see them! (No, I don't own any Jaguars!)

People are watching you. They know whether or not you're wearing your wedding ring, what kind of car you drive, where you live, how you treat your wife, where you eat out. A man came up to me recently after church and said, "You know, Bob, I noticed as you walked up the steps to preach that you have a frayed place in the heel of your socks just like I always get. I was encouraged to know that happens to you too!" They even know how frayed the heels of your socks are!

You can react one of three ways to that attention. You can withdraw and try to avoid people as much as possible; you can worry constantly about your image; or you can become such a person of integrity that your reputation takes care of itself. I love the old quote from St. Francis of Assissi: "Preach the gospel; if necessary, use words." Your life and the lives of the leaders of your congregation preach a much louder sermon than anything said from the pulpit. Albert Schweitzer said, "Example is not the best way of teaching—it's the only way of teaching." Paul said boldly, "Follow my example, as I follow the example of Christ" (1 Cor. 11:1).

People want to know if who you are is consistent with what you say. That's why Paul told Timothy, "Watch your life and doctrine closely. Persevere in them, because if you do, you will save both yourself and your hearers" (1 Tim. 4:16).

Take time off for spiritual development and rest. I heard about one preacher who said, "I never take a vacation because the devil never takes a vacation!" One of his church members said, "That's not the only way our preacher reminds me of the devil."

Years ago one of our elders suggested that someone who had been in ministry as long as I had been deserved a sabbatical. A lengthy time away from the church didn't appeal to me, but more vacation time did. So we worked out a plan where I would take a long summer break each year instead of a sabbatical. I now take five weeks of vacation every summer. I use them to spend time with my wife and family and to rejuvenate myself spiritually. I also do some future planning and brainstorming about sermon ideas and ministry opportunities. I always come back with some fresh thoughts and a renewed outlook on my ministry.

I also try to take one day a week as a day of rest. I'm not very good at slowing down, but I know I need a day off each week. Preachers should be hard workers, and many of them are. God commanded, "Whatever you do, work at it with all your heart, as working for the Lord, not for men" (Col. 3:23). But God also commanded us to take a day of rest. For most preachers, Sunday is anything but a day of rest. And neither is Saturday, which we often spend preparing for Sunday. I usually take Tuesdays off. Choose a day of the week as your regular day off, and be faithful in spending that day resting and renewing family relationships. Then take the vacation time that your church has offered you. Don't abuse the privileges that the church has given you, but be serious about spending time "sharpening the saw," revitalizing yourself physically and spiritually.

Be accountable to someone. Charles Swindoll took an informal poll of the ministers he counseled who had ruined their ministries because of a moral failure. Swindoll said that without exception the men were accountable to no one.[2] They had not one relationship in which they felt comfortable sharing the temptations they were enduring, not one friend close enough to say, "You're walking into dangerous territory."

Find someone you can truly trust and invite them to keep you accountable—perhaps another minister with whom you can speak openly or a close friend who has known you a long time. It may be awkward and risky, but it's better than risking the loss of your ministry, your family, and your reputation. Find a mentor or a friend who loves you enough to ask the difficult questions: *How is your marriage? Are you growing spiritually? Is the ministry going well? Is there anything you need to confess?*

It's also important that you live a transparent life so that those around you feel comfortable confronting you when they sense a problem. My ministry staff isn't afraid to keep me accountable. Gary Whitenack, our director of finance, will say to me, "Bob, I got your request for reimbursement for your convention expenses. We need all your receipts." It doesn't impress him that I've been preaching at this church for thirty-three years. Everyone is held to the same standard. And that's the way a good leader should expect it to be. We have a saying among our staff: You're to be the *example*, not the *exception*.

Love your family. Russ Blowers, the longtime minister of East Ninety-First Street Christian Church in Indianapolis, was once asked, "What was your greatest accomplishment in your forty-four years of ministry?" Russ's congregation had become one of the leading churches in Indiana. He had helped lead a successful Billy Graham crusade in Indianapolis. He had been the president of a large Christian convention. But he didn't mention any of those things. He said, "My greatest accomplishment is that I never had to go into my kids' room and try to find some way to apologize to them for being unfaithful to their mother."

I once heard a female member of Russ Blowers's church comment that it was nice to go to a church where the preacher was being an example of how to love your spouse. I honestly believe that one of the reasons that church grew was because Russ had his priorities right. He visibly and authentically loved his wife. Your spouse and your children are the most important sheep in your flock. You have the opportunity to personally grow in Christ and to set a wonderful example for your church by genuinely loving your closest neighbors—your family.

A couple of years ago, White House domestic policy adviser Bill Glalston resigned his post after receiving a letter from his ten-year-old son, Ezra. The letter read, "Baseball's not fun when there's no one there to applaud you." Mr. Glalston resigned so he could spend more time with his family. He told President Clinton, "You can replace me, and my son can't." People in ministry tend to think they have the most important job in the world. But there is a job that's more important—a role that only you can fill—and that's the role you have in your own family.

Stretch yourself. Leaders often become disenchanted and stagnant when they reach the pinnacle of success. Noah was instrumental in saving the human race from disaster, then he got drunk. David succeeded in making Israel a strong and prosperous nation, then he lounged around his ornate palace and committed adultery. I've seen people reach the pinnacle of success by the world's standards—successful career, fame, all the money they could want—and be bored because the challenges are over.

If you are stagnating spiritually, perhaps God is preparing your heart for a new challenge. Consider what it could be that God is leading you to do: start a new ministry in your church, go on a mission trip, start a building project, take a staff retreat, invite a guest speaker, enroll in seminary.

This is one of the reasons I take a mission trip every few years. I've been to Kenya, India, and Cuba in the last ten years. Going overseas gets me out of my comfort zone. It forces me to pray. I learn to depend on God more. (I've been in some shaky airplanes and on some wild bus trips!) After I've returned from a mission trip, my appreciation for my own country is deepened, I'm more thankful for the blessings I have, and I have some fresh illustrations for my sermons!

I love the story of Caleb, one of only two faithful spies from Israel who, along with Joshua, brought back a good report to the Israelites about the Promised Land. He and Joshua were the only two people God allowed to survive the forty years in the wilderness and see the Promised Land. Forty-five years later, when he was eighty-five years old and could have retired in peace in his new land, Caleb instead said to Joshua:

> Now then, just as the LORD promised, he has kept me alive for forty-five years since the time he said this to Moses, while Israel moved about in the desert. So here I am today, eighty-five years old! I am still as strong today as the day Moses sent me out; I'm just as vigorous to go out to battle now as I was then. Now give me this hill country that the LORD promised me that day. You yourself heard then that the Anakites were there and their cities were large and fortified, but, the LORD helping me, I will drive them out just as he said. (Josh.14:10–12)

Caleb didn't say, "I'm tired. I'm forty years older than everybody else. It's time for somebody else to do the work. Give me a nice house in the valley so I don't have to climb any stairs." He said, "I can still whip those young bucks. Give me this mountain. I'll conquer it." I hope I have that kind of energy when I'm eighty-five years old!

We just finished a ninety-million-dollar building project. During the four-year project, we hired Clark Esser to be the construction manager. Clark is eighty-one years old! But he has more energy and enthusiasm than most forty-year-olds I know. When we honored him in one of our services and called him up to the platform, he *ran* up the steps! Clark worked very hard for four years and did a magnificent job. If you ask him what he plans to do now that this project is over, he says he wants to find another project to conquer! I hope I have that kind of vision and enthusiasm when I'm eighty-one years old!

———————

Charlie Wooley, a longtime Southeast staff member, said that when he was a young man, several World War II veterans frequented his home to visit with his father, who was their special friend. Charlie heard them tell about a time that General Patton was leading a group of them when they came to a river. It was cold, it had been snowing, and the soldiers mumbled that it was impossible to cross the icy river with all of their gear. Patton listened briefly, then waded out into the water, swam across the river, climbed out on the other side, glared at them from the opposite bank for a moment, got back in, swam back, and said to the soldiers, "Do you think you can do it now?"

The church is in need of a few good men and women who will lead by example. The old movie *Viva Zapata* has a famous dramatic deathbed scene in which the elderly Zapata speaks his last words to his son. "Trouble is coming," he says. "Find a leader. If you can't find a leader, *be* a leader." That challenge motivated his son to become one of Mexico's greatest and most colorful leaders.

I don't know what trouble might lie ahead, but I do know the church needs quality leadership if it is going to fulfill its calling and win the battle. If you want your church to successfully tackle the challenges ahead, find a leader. If you can't find a leader, be a leader.

A third-grade Sunday-school teacher at our church asked her class to write notes of encouragement to me as their preacher. I appreciated all the notes, but I especially liked the one from Kenny Ward. It read, "To Bob Russell: You have to be brave to be able to stand in front of thousands of people. I am glad you're a preacher at this church, and I think you do a wonderful job. I am praying that one of these times you don't mess up."

Leading a church is a heavy responsibility. Whatever your responsibility in the church, pray for the leaders of Christ's Body—that they will be anointed of God, that they will lead with the power of the Holy Spirit, that they will be guarded from temptation…and that one of these times they don't mess up!

- ❖ Evangelism Demands Our Best Effort

- ❖ Observations about Excellence

- ❖ Negative Results of Striving for Excellence

- ❖ Some Practical Advice

4

EXCELLENCE:
Do Your Best
in Every Area of Service

O ur youth ministry staff loves to do things with excellence. Todd Clark, our senior-high minister, told us, "My personal obsession is to make all the conditions right so that God can give the growth. We've got to do everything we can to make the environment such that there is no hindrance to God's Word penetrating a kid's heart."

The high-school ministry decided that the fall semester of 1999 would be dedicated to talking about Jesus Christ—his character, his mission, and his ministry. They wanted to lead up to a decision day near the end of the semester. The week before the decision day, when the kids arrived at church, there was a giant, twenty-foot cross extending out from the stage into the auditorium. After they watched a movie called *The Crossing*, the youth were invited to take a piece of paper and write down all the sins they wanted to nail to the cross. "No sin is too big," they were told.

"Come and nail it to the cross, and *leave it there*. God can take them all away."

Hundreds of nails were made available, and fifteen or twenty hammers were placed around the cross. The worship leaders allowed twenty minutes for as many of the five hundred students who wished to come forward. It took the entire twenty minutes, since nearly all the students came and nailed sins to the cross.

Todd Clark told us that what he didn't anticipate was the moving environment that was created during those twenty minutes. While the students worshiped and sang, in the background you could hear the pounding of the nails. By the time Todd rose to speak, he was gripped with emotion. He told the kids he was working on a sermon for the next week called "The Boat." "There are three boats," he said, "and everybody in the room is going to find themselves in one of those three boats next week. Either you need to get in the boat for the first time (which means to accept Christ for the first time), you need to get back in the boat (to rededicate your life), or you need to help someone else get in the boat."

That next week they rented three huge lifeboats and brought them into the auditorium. The boat for those who were making first-time decisions for Christ was placed underneath the cross. Around the auditorium hung oars, life preservers, and other boating paraphernalia. When they came in, everyone was handed a card on which was written the three choices Todd had described the week before.

Todd walked out onto the stage in a full rain gear outfit, with a life preserver in his hand. He told the kids a dramatic story that I have shared near the end of this book about the efforts of one lone boat, the Carpathia, to rescue drowning passengers on the Titanic. Todd talked about how we are all drowning in our sin and need to be rescued. And he said, "I'm going to throw you a life preserver today. But I'm not going to throw you this [pointing to the tube in his hand]. I'm going to throw you this [pointing to the giant wooden cross still there from the week before]. I know it doesn't look like a life preserver, but I'm going to prove to you that it is."

For the rest of the message, Todd used a PowerPoint presentation to explain the basics of the gospel. Then they offered the invitation. For twenty minutes they sang worship songs and gave kids the opportunity to come and place their cards in one of the boats. Thirty adults were also stationed around the room to provide counseling for any students who sought guidance in their decision.

Nineteen kids put their cards in the boat under the cross. (The staff members divided up those cards after the service and contacted them immediately to talk about their relationship with Christ and arrange for their baptism.) More than one hundred rededicated their lives to Christ that day. Several hundred placed their cards in the third boat. The prerequisite for placing their card there was to write on the card someone's name that they wanted to lead to Christ. Copies of Todd's presentation were made available to those desiring to witness to someone for Christ, and more than three hundred were taken. They were encouraged to memorize the scriptures on the list and use the copy to help someone come to Christ.

It's exciting to witness that kind of impact on the lives of five hundred high-school kids. But it didn't happen by accident, and it wasn't prepared in a few hours the night before. That kind of event took hours of advanced planning and preparation by the youth staff and volunteers. But they were determined to do it with excellence.

The Bible commands, "And whatever you do, whether in word or deed, do it all in the name of the Lord Jesus, giving thanks to God the Father through him" (Col. 3:17). When we give our best, we honor Christ. Jewish worshipers were commanded in the Old Testament to sacrifice a lamb or an ox that was perfect, without spot or blemish. God required them to give the firstfruits of their crops—their best portion—

back to him. In the New Testament we have no such written require-ments, but since Jesus Christ gave his all for us, doesn't he merit our best in return?

EVANGELISM DEMANDS OUR BEST EFFORT

Experiences of Mediocrity

I've visited a lot of churches in America. The experience for a first-time visitor in many of those churches goes something like this: You drive into the parking lot of the church at 10:40 Sunday morning. You assume you're five minutes early because the sign says the service begins at 10:45. You'll soon discover that the sign still needs to be changed to show the new minister's name and that it definitely doesn't reflect the proper starting time of the service.

The grass was cut yesterday—good thing, because it was badly needed. You can tell because nobody raked, and the lawn looks more like a hayfield.

As you walk into the church, you're greeted with a melancholy "Good morning" and handed a bulletin. The bulletin has a line through it because the copier hasn't been serviced in a while. You head toward the sanctuary and take a seat. You wait for twenty long minutes because the service doesn't actually begin till around eleven o'clock.

At about 11:02 a piano player begins plunking out some chords on the piano. She's not very good, but she's been doing it for forty years, and nobody has the nerve to tell her it's time to step aside. Someone shuffles to the platform and says, "Please take your hymnals and turn to page 150. We'll sing all five stanzas of 'One Day.'" The song leader has no musical talent, but he's the only one courageous enough to get in front of this crowd and try.

After struggling through a couple of hymns, the song leader says, "Now we're going to have a special number by the girls' trio." One girl gets up from the back row and heads to the front. In the silence, everyone turns and watches her walk forward. About the time she gets to the second row, a girl sitting in the first row stands up and heads to the piano. The girl from the back row says, "Sheila is sick today, so there's only two of us. Bear with us because we haven't had much time to practice this." They sing "Give of Your Best to the Master." At the end of the song, someone says, "And all God's people said..." You feel like shouting, "We can do better than that!" But the crowd mumbles, "Amen."

After the song everyone watches the two return to their seats. When they are seated the song leader shuffles back to the platform and says, "Now we will take up the offering. Will the men designated to take up the offering please come forward." Three men get up from various parts of the sanctuary. One of them nods to a fourth man, who either forgot he was ushering or was needed in someone's absence. The fourth man, in a brief panic, drops his hymnal, gets up, and follows the other three to the front. One of the men prays methodically, "Our majestic heavenly Father, we thank thee for this day and all of thy bountiful blessings. Please bless the gift and the giver. In Jesus' most precious holy name we pray, amen." The piano player plunks out a few more chords as the offering plates are passed.

The service continues in equally haphazard fashion. If communion is served you struggle to watch how everyone else partakes so you can follow suit. When the sermon is delivered, you battle to stay awake during a message that is long on time and short on content. When the invitation is given, no one responds. When the benediction is over, you're relieved and head for the door as quickly as possible.

By the grace of God, people still come to know Jesus after enduring church services like that for most of their lives. But that kind of service, where people are giving less than their best, doesn't bring honor to Jesus Christ. And it's certainly not the most effective way to evangelize.

The Attraction of Excellence

Mediocrity breeds indifference, but quality attracts. That's true in every field, not just in the church. Have you ever been to Augusta National Golf Course or watched on television when the Masters Golf Tournament was being played there? I've been there. It's one of the most beautiful places I've ever seen. The administration at Augusta National has a commitment to excellence. The landscape is spectacular, and the grounds are immaculate. I've been told that on occasion the officials will rewrap some of the candy sold at the concession stands in green paper so that if someone litters, the trash won't be as visible on television. It is so beautiful that there is almost a surreal aura about the place. When the Masters is held there, it is advertised as "a tradition unlike any other—the Masters." Every golfer dreams of the chance to play at a course like that.

Have you ever been to see the stage play *Les Miserables*? I was inspired by the quality of music, acting, and staging when I saw the performance. For the next several days, I told everyone I saw how great it was—and that they needed to go see it.

I recently visited the Air Force Academy in Colorado Springs, Colorado. When you see the beauty of that setting at the base of Pike's Peak—the magnificent chapel, the well-kept grounds, the beautiful athletic facilities, the perfectly dressed personnel, the precision of the marching and drills—you can't help but be inspired. It makes you proud to be an American. You want to tell others about it.

Imagine how much easier evangelism would be if your church services were done with so much excellence that they inspired people to the extent that they couldn't help but tell their friends about their experience.

Someone has defined evangelism as one beggar telling another beggar where to find bread. Consider how many people came to know Jesus because someone said, "Come and see." Andrew said to his brother Peter, "We have found the Messiah," and he brought Peter to

Jesus (John 1:41–42). Philip also told his friend Nathanael they had found the Messiah. When Nathanael questioned whether anything good could come out of Nazareth, Philip said, "Come and see" (John 1:46). After Jesus spoke to the Samaritan woman at the well, she went back to town and said, "Come, see a man who told me everything I ever did. Could this be the Christ?" Many came to believe because of her simple invitation (John 4:29, 39). Thousands of people were brought to Jesus by their friends to be healed or just to hear his teaching.

A recent survey of Southeast members revealed that over 90 percent of our members—that's 90 percent of fourteen thousand people—have invited someone to come to church with them in the last year. Almost half of our members report that they came to Southeast at the invitation of a friend. That reason alone nearly outweighed all the other reasons combined—the radio ministry, curiosity about the building, spiritual hunger, the church's reputation.

But why have our people been so bold in inviting their friends and so effective in getting them to come? Because they are excited about what they've experienced and are confident that every week the grounds, the nursery, the greeting, the singing, and the preaching will be done with excellence.

When you come to church and the grass isn't cut, the paint is chipping off the walls, the bulletin boards have missionary letters tacked on top of each other dating back to 1973, the greeters are sloppily dressed, the children's class has no teacher, and the service is slipshod, not only is it unworthy of Jesus Christ, it also negates our efforts to evangelize. No one is inspired to say, "Come and see." But when something is done with excellence, people want to tell others about it.

When I first came to Southeast Christian Church in 1966, the people were meeting in the basement of a small house. But the basement was spic-and-span, the bulletin was printed without typos or grammatical errors, the people were friendly, and the worship was well planned and orderly. There was something attractive about them from the start, because they cared about what they were doing. And because of their efforts and the blessing of God, the church was already beginning to grow.

Observations about Excellence

Excellence Takes Hard Work

There is a big difference between doing a "pretty good job" on something and doing it with excellence. Excellence takes a lot more time.

We have a live band and about six backup vocalists in every service. Those musicians are so talented that they could arrive a few minutes before the service, look over the songs, and "wing it" without anyone noticing. Actually, however, they arrive two hours before the first service and practice every worship song and every special out on the stage with the sound system and Image Magnification System running, so they will be prepared. They rehearse the transition between songs, correct any glitches in the sound system, decide where to stand or sit during each part of the service, make sure they know the words to the songs, and iron out any miscues on the background harmony or instrumentation.

I usually spend about fifteen to twenty hours a week in sermon preparation. I've discovered that the difference between a good sermon and an excellent sermon is about *five hours!* I could be satisfied after fifteen hours with a pretty good sermon; but if I want it to be excellent, I've got to work harder. Excellence takes time and effort.

Several times our church has won a local "Beautification Award" for the most beautiful grounds of any business or organization in the community. The facilities department could be satisfied with doing a pretty good job on the grounds, but they strive for excellence. A few years ago our grounds crew decided that the grass in the islands of our parking lot didn't look right, so they decided to mulch each of the islands. They brought in tons of mulch and worked hard to make the islands look right. But for some reason weeds began shooting up through the mulch, and in a few weeks it looked awful. It was so bad that we dubbed the problem "mulch-gate" in staff meetings. The grounds crew, after recruiting dozens of volunteers to help the first time, could have thrown up their hands and said, "Forget it. We'll fix it next spring." But they didn't. They worked hard for hours fixing the problem.

The facilities staff and volunteers nearly performed a miracle getting our building ready for occupancy in 1998. We had sold our old building to another congregation and promised to be out by Christmas. That meant we were homeless unless we got the new building ready. One day several volunteers were cleaning the concrete floor to prepare for the seat installers who were to come the next day. They heard we hadn't planned to seal the floor. The volunteers insisted that if the floors weren't sealed, concrete dust would constantly be a problem in our worship center because we planned to carpet only the aisles and stage. They said, "We're building this beautiful building to the glory of God. It has to be done right."

They were right, of course, but we were in a time bind. So the team decided they would clean and seal the concrete floor of that ninety-one-hundred-seat worship center *that day!* Nancy Stanbury, Don Waddell, and a group of twenty volunteers worked past 1:00 A.M. to get the job finished. They spent much of the evening on their hands and knees, digging dust out of the holes where the seats were to be installed. Had we not told their secret, few people would know how hard they worked to make that building a place of excellence.

Excellence Is Evidenced in the Details

Our children's ministry requires hundreds of volunteers. They're doing well just to recruit enough people to get the job done by the first weekend of each semester. They could say, "We're just glad to have the eight hundred bodies we need to pull off this program." But they don't just want bodies. Because they want to do everything with excellence, they do background checks on each volunteer, they require references, and the references must respond to a questionnaire. They take the time to train the volunteers in teaching and classroom management, and they require them to arrive at least fifteen minutes before the service begins.

Don Waddell, our new-member minister, often asks the new members why they chose to become a part of Southeast. One lady told him, "We were looking for a new church home. We went to the children's department, and as we were signing in our child, they asked if our child had any food allergies. Our child is deathly allergic to peanuts. Of all the churches we've ever attended, you were the first to ever ask us that question."

Our Easter pageant attracts thousands of visitors every spring because it is done with excellence. Part of the reason it is so well done is that several people behind the scenes have paid attention to details. The costumes are authentic. The animals are real. The actors are told they can't wear glasses or nail polish during the performance because people in Jesus' day didn't wear glasses or nail polish. Several times throughout the play when the Roman soldiers are on the scene, other Roman soldiers stand throughout the auditorium—even in the upper balcony—so that everyone feels a little more a part of the play.

The ascension of Jesus at the end of our pageant is spectacular. In fact, the ascension was noted in the annual "Best Of" section of our local *Louisville Magazine*. They made a new category called "Best Use of Guy Wires in a Theatrical Production." Under the category the editors wrote, "Sorry, [Actors Theater of Louisville] and Peter Pan, but you've been outflown by Southeast Christian Church's Easter Pageant. Until you've seen Jesus ascend into heaven—or the third balcony, whichever comes first—you haven't seen real stagecraft."[1]

More than thirty-five thousand people saw our Easter pageant in 1999. Scores of people have credited the pageant as the major influence in bringing them to a saving relationship with Jesus Christ. Thousands of people who otherwise wouldn't come to church have come to see our pageant because it has a tradition of excellence. But the tradition has been established because people paid attention to the details.

At our last leadership conference, a preacher from the Atlanta area told me how much our conference has helped his church. He said, "We've grown in six years from one hundred to six hundred people! We've brought people from our church to your leadership conference every year. Our people go home so fired up just from being here. But you know what impressed our people the most? One little thing. The first year we were here, the nametag for one of our group members was misspelled. When your volunteer discovered it, she insisted on correcting it. She didn't cross it out and write over it. She went back and reprinted the whole thing. Our group was so impressed that your volunteer cared enough to go out of her way to serve like that."

Walt Werling is a member of our church who has gone to Cuba several times on mission trips. Before his first trip, he took an intensive, one-month Spanish course so he could know the language. He prepared a special sermon for the Cuban audience, and he memorized all the Scriptures he used in Spanish. The Cubans were impressed that he had taken the time to learn their language, and five people accepted Christ after his first sermon!

Excellence Takes Daily Diligence

Suppose you build a new house. When the house is finished, you plant a flower garden and landscape your yard. You might do all those things with excellence, then step back and say, "That's beautiful." But it's not long before your work begins to deteriorate. The walls need repainting, the grass has to be cut, the weeds must be pulled from the flower bed. You can't relax for long. If your home is going to maintain that look of excellence, the work must be ongoing. You can lose the edge really fast. The same thing is true in the church. You can begin a program with excellence, but it takes daily diligence to maintain that standard of excellence.

Mistakes are going to happen. When they do, it becomes the leaders' job to constantly hold people accountable and remind them why we are striving for excellence. Someone has to remind the maintenance committee about excellence when the parking lot isn't properly lighted on a dark night. Someone has to remind the worship team about excellence when the service doesn't start on time. If the publications department has a misspelled word in the bulletin or the children's department missed an opportunity to serve, someone has to remind them why we do things with excellence. That someone shouldn't be a church member who just likes to complain. It is the leader to whom those people are accountable who should constantly hold them to a standard of excellence. That takes daily diligence.

Longtime employees or volunteers should be given some space to make some corrections on their own, but carelessness shouldn't be tolerated. And I've learned over the years that new employees and volunteers need to be tactfully but clearly confronted the first time the standard of excellence is not achieved. They are more likely to step up their efforts when they realize the standard that is expected of them before they get into the habit of doing things haphazardly.

NEGATIVE RESULTS OF STRIVING FOR EXCELLENCE

Once you make a commitment to excellence, prepare for two negatives. First, there will be some *criticism* from those who interpret your commitment as arrogance. People who are committed to mediocrity resent excellence. They'll say, "You're too into performance. It's all just a show—a big moneymaker." But it's not about performance. Excellence is about utilizing your gifts to build up the Body. It's about giving Christ the firstfruits. It's about doing everything you can to win people to Jesus Christ.

Second, if you strive for excellence, be prepared for *disappointment.* Contrary to what others might think, being committed to excellence doesn't produce pride—it breeds humility, because there is a frequent sense of failure. You never really measure up to the picture of perfection that you have in your mind.

I can list several areas in our church where our staff agrees we are falling short right now: following up and training volunteers; the landscaping around our new building; traffic flow. I can remind myself of all the reasons we aren't measuring up to a standard of excellence in these areas—and many of them are valid and beyond our control—but it's still disappointing. I have to remember that we'll always be striving for perfection. We'll never reach that goal in this life.

Paul communicated his desire to keep striving to do his best. He wrote, "Brothers, I do not consider myself yet to have taken hold of it. But one thing I do: Forgetting what is behind and straining toward what is ahead, I press on toward the goal to win the prize for which God has called me heavenward in Christ Jesus" (Phil. 3:13–14).

SOME PRACTICAL ADVICE

Here's some practical advice for establishing a pattern of excellence in your ministry and in your church.

Set the Standard for Excellence Early

Often your first effort at a new task becomes the standard for later expectations. If you make all As in your first semester of college, you've established a standard. You won't be very satisfied with all Bs the next semester. If you make straight Cs the first semester, then Bs in the spring look pretty good. Someone said, "Mediocrity is excellence in the mind of the mediocre."

If you start teaching a new Sunday-school class, you'll probably work harder that first week than any other week. If you spend fifteen minutes preparing for the lesson, you'll survive the day even though the lesson won't be that great. You'll realize you can "get by" with fifteen minutes of preparation, and you'll be tempted to do that every week. You're not very likely to increase your preparation time in the future. But if you study for four hours that first week, people will be able to tell you worked hard. Everyone (including you) will expect the same standard the next week.

Determine that the first time you try something new at your church, it's going to be done the best it can be done.

Don't Trust Your Own Evaluation

A higher level of preparation means that the job will be done better, but it won't necessarily bring you more satisfaction. In fact, as I mentioned earlier, the more you prepare, the more likely you are to be *dissatisfied* with your work because you have higher expectations. Your level of expectation is directly linked to the amount of preparation you have done.

As I said, I usually study for fifteen to twenty hours in preparation for my sermons. Suppose one week I only studied for six hours. On a scale of one to ten, I'd expect the sermon to be about a five. If the sermon turned out to be a seven, I'd be satisfied—maybe even elated. I'd be convinced I had preached a great sermon! But suppose the following week I spent twenty hours in preparation. If I was sure the sermon was going to be a ten, then after delivering it I felt that it was only a nine, I'd be disappointed. The second sermon was much better and much closer to excellence, but I wasn't nearly as satisfied because I had raised my level of expectation. That's why you're not the best judge of your own work. Your evaluation is too closely tied to your level of preparation and expectation.

Be careful not to judge your own work too closely. You might be satisfied with it not because it was excellent but simply because it was better than you thought it would be! Or you might not be satisfied with something that was well done simply because your expectations were too high. So raise your level of expectation, but then be careful not to become depressed when things don't quite measure up. Don't judge the excellence of something by your own feelings of satisfaction.

Do Only That Which Can Be Done with Excellence

You cannot do everything that needs to be done. Even in a church as large as ours, with so many programs and opportunities, we are constantly forced to say no to good ideas that could potentially reach thousands of people. If we are convinced that the program won't help us with our primary mission or we don't feel we could yet do it with excellence, we won't do it. For example, many churches much smaller than ours have a television outreach, and people have encouraged us to start one. So far we've decided not to be on television—in part because we don't have the commitment necessary to do it with excellence.

You must often choose between a good ministry opportunity and a better ministry opportunity. Your first consideration should be the mission of the church, asking, "How will this opportunity help us reach our mission?" But also consider whether it is something you can do with excellence. If it isn't, then don't do it.

If an Activity Isn't Fruitful, Drop It

I've often seen a good idea succeed for a few years and then fizzle, but a few people keep it alive because they don't want to give up the tradition. Don't do something simply because you've always done it. Suppose you've done a Vacation Bible School, Living Christmas Tree, or Fall Carnival every year but it's not reaching very many people and most of the volunteers see it as drudgery. Consider not doing it next year. Some ideas have died and need to be buried.

Sometimes if you give an idea a decent burial, somebody more capable may resurrect it later and have more success. We dropped our youth choir for a while. We had tried for years to have a good teen choir, but as hard as we tried, the program was never very good—and not many kids wanted to join. Then Jim Burgen became our youth minister and wanted to revive the youth choir. And did he ever revive it! They suddenly had more than one hundred kids in the youth choir, and it was done with tremendous excellence. For several years they traveled to different churches in different states and had a wonderful ministry. Then that idea fizzled again, and Jim gave it a proper burial. Perhaps in the future it will be revived again, but in the meantime they're concentrating on other ministries.

Encourage Service in Areas of Giftedness

If a task is to be done with excellence, it needs to be accomplished by the person most gifted to do it. I've been given a gift to preach. If I sing a solo next Sunday morning, people will not walk away thinking the service has been done with excellence! And if I am put in charge of the grounds, every flower will die because I have a brown thumb instead of a green one. The church needs people who are doing things in areas in which they are gifted so they are done with excellence. If the singers are gifted musically, the teachers are gifted to teach, the nursery workers are gifted with a heart for children, the groundskeepers have green thumbs, and all of them do their best, then everything is going to take on a new level of excellence.

Sometimes using people in their areas of giftedness creates conflict because people don't always recognize their own level of talent. If you're a leader in the worship ministry, someone who can't carry a tune will come to you offering to sing a solo, because somebody in the past lied to him and told him he's a great singer.

I heard about one such young man who sang a solo at his church and did a terrible job. After the service, people were trying to express appreciation without lying. But one older man told him the truth. He shook the young man's hand and said, "Son, it's not your fault. You did the best you could. But whoever asked you to sing should be shot!" It's not easy to communicate the truth to people who think they're gifted when they're not. But in every sphere of service someone in leadership has to be decisive and bold. People deserve to be told the truth, tactfully, about their level of giftedness.

Such a conversation can be positive if done correctly. People who need to hear the truth need to have the proper amount of humility or their ego is bound to be wounded. But if they have an ego problem, you didn't want them leading the congregation anyway. Gently and lovingly explain your desire to help them evaluate their gifts and help the church do things with excellence. Channel them to another ministry where they can be more effective in helping the Body of Christ. Then, by God's grace, it can be a positive experience.

Strive for Excellence without Extravagance

When we made the plans for our new building, this was our goal—excellence without extravagance. Our architect, David Miller, and project chairman Jack Coffee worked hard to plan a building that would be durable and attractive, but practical and cost-efficient. The building has no expensive chandeliers and little indirect lighting. It's spacious, but not ornate. There are no expensive brass railings or stained-glass windows. We didn't use granite or marble anywhere. The exterior is made of preformed, colored concrete slabs that look attractive but aren't extravagant. Instead of installing expensive terrazzo floors, we used carpet or concrete floor finishes throughout the building. None of the stairwells is dry-walled, since they're not in prominent places. Instead, a concrete finishing process was used that makes them look attractive without much additional cost.

It's possible in nearly every area to perform tasks with excellence while keeping them cost-effective. Church members appreciate leaders' wise stewardship of the church's resources, even though they also appreciate seeing God's work done with class and excellence.

Have a Sense of Humor

Mike Graham, one of our associate ministers, was in charge of baptisms one day shortly after he began working with us. He hadn't performed many baptisms, and he got his wedding speech mixed up with his baptism speech. After taking someone's confession, instead of saying, "I now baptize you in the name of the Father, Son, and Holy Spirit," he said, "I now pronounce you…" He paused as he tried to find a way to recover. Then he just said, *"baptized!"* and lowered the person under the water. We teased Mike about it for weeks and still occasionally remind him of his goof. We joke that Mike hasn't performed many baptisms since then but he has picked up several weddings!

Paul said, "Aim for perfection…live in peace. And the God of love and peace will be with you" (2 Cor. 13:11). That's a hard balance to maintain—to aim for perfection but live in peace. When you aim for perfection, you're often disturbed because you fail to meet the goal. But one of the ways you can be sure to live in peace is to develop a healthy sense of humor and be able to laugh at your occasional failures.

One of our members, Perry Thomas, recently gave his testimony during a conference at our church. He said, "I had recently moved to Louisville from New York City. I was impressed that things [at Southeast] were done well, but as a struggling professional actor, I wondered if it was all an act. I wondered if Greg Allen [our worship leader] was really that sincere, or if that is just his 'sincere act.' Then I volunteered to usher for the Easter pageant—in part to get a little closer and investigate what was going on.

"The first night after I ushered, I went in to watch the performance. I cried through the whole thing because I was so moved. I couldn't believe how powerful the story was. I went home and got down on my knees and prayed, 'Lord, I'd do anything to be a part of something like that. I'd clean up after the camels if that's what it took.'

I was moved that night because a few people had decided to do something with excellence."

Last year Perry didn't have to clean up after the camels—he played the part of Peter, one of the lead roles! And as you can imagine, Perry played the part with excellence. Only God knows how many hearts have been touched or will be touched after watching the Easter pageant at Southeast—all because a few people like Perry are dedicated to doing things with excellence.

- ❖ A History of Walking by Faith

- ❖ Faith Requires Vision

- ❖ Faith Requires Courage

- ❖ Visionaries versus Administrators

- ❖ Results of Walking by Faith

5

FAITH:
Be Willing to Step Out with a Bold Faith and Take Risks

B ecky Edmondson has faith. She has spunk too. Becky Edmondson is the director of our two Crisis Pregnancy Centers. For eleven years the wonderful agents of mercy working at these centers have saved scores of babies and ministered to thousands of troubled young women.

In January of 1998, Becky Edmondson attended a seminar where Norma McCorvey was the guest speaker. Norma McCorvey was the Jane Roe of the 1974 *Roe v. Wade* Supreme Court decision that legalized abortion. But in her speech Norma McCorvey testified that while she was working as an assistant in an abortion clinic, she was befriended by Christians who had opened a Crisis Pregnancy Center next door. Eventually she gave her life to Christ and is now strongly pro-life.

After hearing Norma McCorvey's dramatic testimony, Becky Edmondson drove back to Louisville convicted. *We have two Crisis Pregnancy Centers, she* thought, *but neither is anywhere near the aborturaries in our town. We need to have a Crisis Pregnancy Center as close to the abortion clinic as possible.* When she arrived back in Louisville, she drove downtown to the site of one of the two largest abortion clinics in the state of Kentucky. As she drove, she prayed, "Lord, if it's your will that we open up a new center near this place on Broadway, please make a suitable space available."

When she drove down the street toward the abortion clinic, Becky couldn't believe her eyes. Right next door to the clinic was a house for sale! It wasn't just next door—the walls butted up against each other! Becky told her story to the board of directors of A Woman's Choice Crisis Pregnancy Center. Southeast agreed to give a percentage of our annual Thanksgiving offering to purchase and renovate the building, and within a few months a clean, attractive facility was opened. That little house right next door to the abortion clinic soon sported a large sign: "A Woman's Choice Resource Center."

The results have been dramatic. Many women have chosen to come into A Woman's Choice instead of going next door. Some young women seeking counsel or abortions have come into A Woman's Choice by mistake. The receptionist graciously informs them that the abortion clinic is next door, but then asks, "Would you like to see a free ultrasound of your baby while you're here?" Almost every woman who watches the heartbeat of her baby or takes home ultrasound pictures decides to keep the child. One woman who came into the center discovered she was pregnant with twins! She decided to keep them both and give them the gift of life.

The workers at the Crisis Pregnancy Center began to pray regularly for the workers next door and attempted to reach them with kindness. They laid their hands on the walls the center shared with the clinic and prayed that God would stop abortions in that place. Then in July of 1999, an amazing thing happened. The abortion clinic closed down! They no longer perform abortions. A local newspaper column lamented that there are now very few facilities in our town that perform this "service" for women in our area. The article speculated why the clinic had closed. One of the suggested reasons was that a Crisis Pregnancy Center had opened next door! The article didn't mention the power of prayer, but we are confident that the clinic shut its doors because God responded favorably to the faith of his people!

Becky Edmondson exemplifies what Hebrews 11:6 says: "And without faith it is impossible to please God, because anyone who comes to him must believe that he exists and that he rewards those who earnestly seek him." God always blesses those who trust him enough to follow his guidance even when it appears risky. Abraham packed up and moved, not knowing where he was going. Moses commanded Pharaoh to release the Israelites, not knowing what Pharaoh's reaction would be. Elijah called down fire from heaven though he had never seen it done before.

A History of Walking by Faith

The history of Southeast Christian Church is marked by a series of bold steps of faith. In 1962, fifty people left the familiar comforts of their routine to risk starting a new church on the outskirts of town in a growing area. Three years later the first minister, Joe Rex Kearns, resigned to help start another church. After several experienced ministers turned down the offer to succeed him, Southeast hired me to be their minister.

I was a twenty-two-year-old country boy fresh out of Bible college. That was risky! During my first year at Southeast, a seventy-five-year-old elder wanted to discuss in an elders' meeting what they were going to give me for Christmas. Since I was in the meeting, he said, "Men, have we decided about the X-M-A-S gift?" I guess he didn't think I was old enough to spell!

About that time, in 1967, the church hired an architect who designed the most contemporary, unusual-looking church building I had ever seen. It was completely concrete and entirely gray, with no stained-glass windows, no front entrance, and no steeple. Scoffers said it looked like a tobacco warehouse. Inside the building, the seating was on three sides with pews facing each other, the choir loft was way over to one side, and the baptistry was at ground level. Despite those who ridiculed the building, it won a statewide award for excellence in architectural design, and it got people's attention! It was different and risky, but the congregation walked by faith, and God blessed.

The church grew, and soon we needed additional space for classes and activities. There was considerable debate about whether we should add an educational wing or a gymnasium. The advance planning committee eventually recommended to the board that we build both buildings, which would cost $750,000. The planning committee chairman said, "We know that's twice what we intended to spend, and this would really stretch our church. But here's how we can do it." In forty-five minutes the elders and deacons voted to build both buildings. It was risky, but God blessed that decision. The church continued to grow—to five hundred members, then six hundred, then seven hundred.

Seven years later, in 1983, a relocation committee reported, "Twenty acres just down the street has become available. We can purchase it if we act now." It was risky, but we voted to purchase the land and relocate the entire congregation.

Another new building was built, and in 1987 we relocated just a few blocks away from the old site. By the time it was nearing completion, we were overflowing the old building so badly that some wondered if we might have built the new building too small. The first Sunday in the new building, we had two Sunday morning services. Soon we went to three, then four. We tried a 7:30 A.M. service but discovered it's hard to get people to come to church that early. (Not every risk we've taken has worked out!)

We eventually started a Saturday night worship service. We knew that decision would mean bearing some skepticism and criticism. But the New Testament doesn't command us to worship only on Sundays, and Paul said we didn't have to hold one day higher than another (Rom. 14:4–6). We had heard about the success of Saturday night services at other churches, so we decided to try it. Hundreds of people attended the first Saturday night service in 1992, and there were baptisms and other responses to the invitation. It seemed apparent that God was again blessing our faith.

In 1992, only four years after we moved into our new building, we listened to another future-planning-committee report. They said we needed to consider complete relocation again. With only twenty acres and a seating capacity of twenty-two-hundred in our sanctuary, we were rapidly approaching capacity in every way. Attendance was averaging over six thousand in five services, the parking lot was jammed, and we were running out of space in all of our facilities.

I could barely speak for trembling when I stood before the congregation and explained the findings of the planning committee. Then I said, "After much prayer and searching, the leadership has found nearly one hundred acres of ground that we want to purchase for relocation. The land will cost three million dollars." The congregation voted 94 percent in favor of relocation. We launched a program to raise twenty-six million dollars—one of the largest church capital campaigns in history—and by God's grace we exceeded the goal.

FAITH REQUIRES VISION

The great hockey player Wayne Gretzky was once asked why he was so successful on the ice. He answered, "I skate to where the puck is going to be." Do you have people in your church who are always looking to the future, one step ahead, skating to where the church is going to be?

Jesus was a vision caster. Consider some of his visionary phrases:

- "Lift up your eyes! The fields are white unto harvest."
- "If you have faith the size of a mustard seed, you can move this mountain."

- "Go into all the world and make disciples."

I recently listened to a tape of one of our Sunday night worship services in 1983. It was "youth night," and three high-school seniors had been asked to speak. One of the young men, Barry Wooley, shared in his message some of his thoughts about the future. To understand his comments you have to know that Southeast was averaging about a thousand in attendance at our Sunday worship services, and we had just taken what we thought was a bold step of faith to purchase land and build a "gigantic" sanctuary that would hold twenty-two hundred people. To show you where my faith was, I thought we only needed to build a sanctuary that would hold fifteen hundred, and that twenty-two hundred was going to be too large!

But that night Barry said, "I look forward to attending the Southeast Christian Church of the future—the one with *ten thousand* members." On the tape you can hear the congregation *laugh!* How small was our faith! And yet, when I think back to the context of that statement, I should say, how large was Barry's faith! The ten thousand he envisioned was *ten times* the number we were averaging then. Now we have more than ten thousand, and I think, *How small was our faith.*

But what would we do today if someone were to dream of the same ratio of growth? Imagine someone dreaming of a time when one hundred thousand people attend Southeast! We would laugh again! The natural reaction of the rational person is to scoff at the dreamer. But if your church is going to accomplish big things for God, it will only be because your leaders didn't scoff at the dreamers.

Every church needs a few people who have imagination and faith. The Bible says, "Where there is no vision, the people perish" (Prov. 29:18 KJV). Without visionaries, the church will stagnate and eventually die. Your church needs visionaries like Barry Wooley who will see the harvest fields and have the faith that can move mountains.

Here are some practical things you and your church's leaders can do to "lift up your eyes" and to encourage the visionaries among you to increase their faith.

Pray

I often quote an old poem:

> *Thou art coming to a king!*
> *Large petitions with thee bring,*
> *For His strength and power are such*
> *Thou canst never ask too much.* (Anonymous)

James put it very simply: "You do not have, because you do not ask God" (James 4:2). And his teaching reflects the teaching of Jesus: "I will do whatever you ask in my name, so that the Son may bring glory to the Father. You may ask me for anything in my name, and I will do it" (John 14:13–14).

Dwight Moody said, "The world is yet to see what God can do through a few people who are totally sold out to Him." Ask God to grant your leaders a vision for what can be done through a few faithful people, and the courage to accomplish it. Solomon said, "In his heart a man plans his course, but the LORD determines his steps.... There is no wisdom, no insight, no plan that can succeed against the LORD" (Prov. 16:9; 21:30).

Listen to Visionary People

My sermons are broadcast all over the world each week because of the vision of two men—Joe Fedele and George Drake. Joe Fedele is a local radio personality in Louisville. He came to me in 1981 and said, "Bob, I'd like to put you on the radio." I objected immediately. My plate was already full, and I wasn't interested in going to a studio to produce a radio program. "Oh no," Joe explained. "You won't have to do anything. I'll tape and edit your Sunday morning sermons and put them on the radio. You won't have to do anything more. Just preach!"

Joe secured radio time on a small local station, and *The Living Word* broadcast was begun. It was nothing but my thirty-minute sermon—no music, no interviews, no pleas for money—just preaching. For the most part, that's still the way the broadcast is run today.

Two years later, Liz Curtis Higgs, a popular radio personality from WHAS (Louisville's fifty-thousand-watt clear-channel AM station) informed our missions committee that an eight o'clock Sunday morning time slot had opened. "There must be thirty churches wanting that spot," she said. "But if we act quickly, I think we can get it for *The Living Word*. It's four hundred dollars a week."

I knew there was no way our leaders would bite off that much money each week. We were just beginning a relocation project, and we had vowed to tighten our belts. But a board meeting was called to discuss the issue. The elders filed into the meeting room after church asking, "What's this all about? More money for radio? Has the missions committee forgotten we're in a relocation project?"

George Drake, one of our deacons, was the spokesman for the missions committee. If you were looking for an influential visionary among our church members, you probably wouldn't pick George Drake. George is a quiet, unassuming teacher who rarely speaks in board meetings. But George has a heart for God and a passion for radio ministry. He also has a tremendous gift for imagining what can be done through God's faithful people.

George had caught a vision for what God could do through this expanded radio program and addressed the board with a dramatic proposal. It was early January, just a few weeks before the annual Super Bowl. He said, "Gentlemen, I want you to imagine the Super Bowl. Eighty thousand people are jammed into the arena awaiting the big moment. But this is not a football game. In the middle of the arena is a lone microphone. The crowd hushes, and Bob Russell steps up to the microphone. He begins preaching to eighty thousand people! Gentlemen, that's what can happen *every Sunday* at 8 A.M. for just four hundred dollars a week!"

Within minutes, after a few relevant questions, George's recommendation was approved unanimously, and *The Living Word* soon began weekly broadcasts on WHAS. The success of that weekly program became the catalyst for expansion of *The Living Word* in other markets. More than thirty stations and Internet sites are now broadcasting the program each week.

Instead of scoffing at the crazy ideas of the visionaries around you, seek their advice and listen wisely. God may be trying to lead you. Proverbs 20:18 says, "Make plans by seeking advice."

Attend Conferences That Lift Your Vision

Many churches and parachurch organizations offer conferences for church leaders. We host a leadership conference twice a year for ministers, lay leaders, and their spouses. Many times our own leaders have had their vision lifted by attending leadership conferences at Willow Creek Community Church in Chicago, Saddleback Church in California, and Belleview Baptist Church in Memphis, as well as other motivational conferences across the country.

Visit Churches Where People Walk by Faith

In 1974, I visited three large churches in California. Our congregation was growing fast, approaching five hundred members, and I was beginning to wonder what God wanted us to do next. I had always been skeptical of big churches. But that summer I visited Los Gatos Christian Church, where Marvin Rickard was the minister; First Evangelical Free Church in Fullerton, where Chuck Swindoll was ministering; and Eastside Christian Church (also in Fullerton), where Ben Merold was preaching.

I was impressed. Those people were bringing their Bibles to church and studying God's Word. They were excited about what God was doing in their church and in their own personal lives. The worship services were inspirational, and the sermons were meaningful. The greeters were friendly, and the bulletins were organized. The choirs sang with more expression than ours did, and without music books! I saw big things and small things that those churches were doing to attract people to Christ, and I said, "We can do that!" Just believing it was possible was so helpful to my own vision.

Have Regular Brainstorming Sessions

Create regular times where visionaries are encouraged to dream without opposition. A ground rule in those meetings should be that no idea is too crazy. Some ideas will seem silly and some unachievable, but listen anyway and don't scoff. Such sessions create energy and get the creative juices flowing in the minds of the visionaries among you.

Write a Mission Statement

Other writers have adequately explained why an organization benefits from a mission statement and how to write one, so I won't belabor the point. A mission statement helps keep the balance between the visionary and the administrator by reminding you of your primary focus. The visionary can point to it and remind the administrator that there are more important things than money, and the administrator can point to it when the visionary's ideas stray from the primary mission.

You can borrow someone else's mission statement, but often the process an organization goes through to develop its own mission statement is as beneficial as the mission statement itself. We've made a lot of changes at Southeast over the years, but we've stayed true to our mission: *We exist to evangelize the lost, edify the saved, minister to those in need, and be a conscience in the community.* I like that simple mission statement because it captures our purpose, it's brief and easy to understand, and it's easy to communicate to the congregation. In a recent survey, over 90 percent of our members said they understood and agreed with the mission of the church.

FAITH REQUIRES COURAGE

Just catching the vision isn't enough. In their book *In Search of Excellence*, Peters and Waterman list the number one principle of excellence as being "a bias for action." They contend that for an organization to perform with excellence, there must be a preference for doing something—anything—rather than sending a question through cycles and cycles of analysis and committee reports.[1] So many people are afraid to act. Maybe they're lazy, or afraid of criticism, or afraid of making the wrong decision. Instead, they do nothing.

A leader must have the ability to make confident, prompt decisions and to act upon those decisions. Nothing destroys leadership like indecisiveness. If your church is going to walk by faith, *there must be a bias for action among the leaders.* Many of the disciples may have dreamed of walking on the water, but only one took action. A lot of good ideas are floated in board meetings without anything ever being done. They're discussed but not acted on. The idea gets tabled or channeled to a committee. When the opportunity presents itself, there comes a time for decision and action.

At my first ministry the average age of the congregation was seventy-five. I was twenty-one years old. There was one adult Sunday-school class, and the preacher traditionally taught it. During the week I would call on some young people in the community and invite them to our church. Soon I found a young couple who was interested in coming —then soon another couple, and then a third. I was so excited to have three hot prospects for the church! I figured any Sunday that one of those couples was going to walk into the sanctuary, and I wondered what they would think if they attended and had no peers in the church.

Then I looked up one Sunday morning and all three couples, though they didn't know each other, had decided to visit that same day! I got up and announced that the next Sunday there would be a new "Young Couples Class" meeting in the choir loft! That was before I knew about things like "Elders' Approval" and "We've Never Done It

That Way Before." I quickly found out about those things, but I—and the class—survived.

There comes a point when you must take action. Lee Iaccoca said, "A good leader makes the decision when 95 percent of the information is in." If you wait until you're 100 percent sure, it will be too late. You need leaders in your church who will make the decision to act before they're 100 percent sure. That's called faith.

During our twenty-six-million-dollar capital campaign and the relocation project that followed, the elders made two decisions that to me illustrated their courageous desire to walk by faith even in the middle of such huge change. The first was their decision to increase missions giving during our capital campaign. (I'll talk about this more in the chapter on stewardship.)

The second example was their decision to launch the *Southeast Outlook*, our weekly newspaper. We had always distributed a small newsletter like many churches do, but so little information could really be communicated there. I was convinced we could do something much bigger, with more excellence. I envisioned a weekly newspaper—complete with articles, pictures, and information about every ministry. When Ninie O'Hara, a lady who had run two small-town newspapers, began attending our church, I knew we had the right person. I asked Ninie if she thought a weekly newspaper could be done, and she was ecstatic. She had already caught the vision herself and dreamed of running a paper for Southeast.

Ninie said that for the paper to be done right and to be self-sufficient, it had to have advertising too. *Advertising?* In a church newspaper? I wasn't sure the elders would go for that. But they did. In the middle of this capital campaign, they were so convinced that the weekly newspaper was a good idea that they funded the start-up of a new, separate not-for-profit organization to publish the *Southeast Outlook*. Within a few years the *Southeast Outlook* has reached a circulation of more than fifteen thousand. It has not only become the members' choice for information and a great outreach to the community, it has also become financially self-sufficient!

VISIONARIES VERSUS ADMINISTRATORS

There are two kinds of leaders on most boards—the visionary and the administrator. The administrator is practical, organized, and thorough. He's a stabilizing force in the church. CPAs, corporate executives, managers, and school administrators usually fit this mold. The administrator is solid and dependable—like Thomas in the Bible who said to his fellow disciples, "Let's go up to Jerusalem with Jesus that we may die with him."

The visionary, on the other hand, has fresh ideas. He's idealistic, upbeat, positive, with a strong faith in God. The visionary is constantly challenging the church to stretch, always pushing the envelope. Entrepreneurs and salesmen are often in this category. Peter was this kind of leader. "Let me walk on the water with you, Jesus," he said. And at the transfiguration he blurted out, "Let's build three tabernacles right here."

These two leaders—the visionary and the administrator—can get on each other's nerves. The visionary makes the administrator nervous because he's seldom concerned with the cost. "Have faith," he'll say. "God will provide." But there are a lot of loose ends, and the administrator knows who always has to clean up the loose ends!

Likewise, the administrator exasperates the visionary. "He's always concerned about money," the visionary will moan. In the eyes of the visionary, the administrator appears to lack faith, is always negative, and is holding the church back.

In the church, as in any organization, both kinds of leaders are necessary. Without the visionary, the church becomes predictable and fails to reach its potential. Without the administrator, there is no one to organize and follow through with the visionary's plan.

A church full of visionary leaders with no administrator can quickly become like the man Jesus mentioned who planned to build a tower without counting the cost. Leith Anderson, in his book *A Church for the 21st Century*, says that a successful church can't do everything. It has to say no to some things.[2] Without the administrator, the church wouldn't say no to anything.

Through the years we've had to turn down a lot of great ideas. We've declined the opportunity to have our own Christian school, to plant more churches, and to be on television, for example. Those are great ministry opportunities, and we support other organizations who are doing them; but for reasons that are sometimes complicated, our leaders who are more bent toward administration have advised us not to get into those things right now.

I had what I thought was a great idea when we first moved into our new building. We were very concerned about the long walk many people would have to take from the parking lots to the church because the lots were so large. I wanted the church to purchase two dozen golf carts to shuttle six or eight people each from the back corners of the lots. It would be quicker and less of a hassle than getting on a bus, I thought. And you wouldn't have to hire professional drivers to drive the carts around. Our teenagers would be lining up to volunteer to be cart drivers!

Several administrators quickly enlightened me, and eventually I realized it was a terrible idea. Picture a teenager driving an open golf cart full of people dressed up for church on a cold, rainy day!

Although it may be unwise to let the visionary run the church alone, *the strong tendency in most churches is to let the administrator have the most influence.* He sounds practical. He warns of failure. He promises security if we just keep the status quo. He knows all the horror stories of those churches that tried it and later regretted it. The visionary can eventually get smothered and become discouraged. Even the natural visionary has to work at maintaining enthusiasm and faith because it's human nature to get discouraged. Visionaries can easily become disheartened and fade into the shadows as the administrator confidently leads the church into mediocrity. If your church is going to step out in faith, you must have visionaries among your leaders, and the visionaries must be encouraged to keep dreaming.

At the point of action, the visionary and the administrator must work together. Both are needed. The visionary has a sense of timing, momentum, and available resources. "The time is now," the visionary will say. "The momentum is in our favor, and we have the people and the funds to do this." If the church is to make any progress, the administrator has to be willing to go along at some points, to take the risk, and step out in faith. But then it is usually the administrator who takes the action, organizes the work, and sees that commitments are fulfilled so that the vision is successfully realized.

One of my concerns as we neared completion of our new facility was that we would stagnate. It would be tempting to focus solely on administration as we worked to assimilate the new members and get used to the new building, and we could begin to rest on our laurels. Someone has said, "Death comes when memories of the past supersede the vision for the future." I knew we needed to find some new goals that would stretch us and continue to increase our faith.

In April of 1999, four months after we relocated, one of our elders, Matt Chalfant, presented a vision he had for a camp and retreat center. A beautiful campsite was available within a forty-five-minute drive from the church. Some said it was too soon after the move. But Matt was enthusiastic and well organized, and he had already made a personal financial sacrifice to make the camp a possibility. He convinced the board of elders. We stepped out in faith, purchased the camp, and in our first year of camp we had outstanding results. Almost five hundred campers attended camp in the summer, and there were fifteen baptisms.

Since then, several retreats have been held at the camp, and plans are underway to add a fifty-room lodge to the center. I envision the camp hosting events for adults as well as summer Christian service camps that will bring young people closer to Christ. Spiritual renewal retreats will inspire people to walk more closely with Christ, marriage retreats will strengthen and save marriages, and leadership retreats will help people develop a vision for what God can do in the future.

RESULTS OF WALKING BY FAITH

I've witnessed some dramatic steps of faith in my thirty-three years of ministry, and I've observed that the church that walks by faith realizes four distinct benefits.

Walking by Faith Generates Enthusiasm

Jim Collins, in his book *Built to Last*, reveals that successful organizations consistently develop what he calls BHAGs. They're pronounced *bee-hags*, and the letters stand for Big Hairy Audacious Goals.[3] At Southeast we've adapted that idea—we talk about Big *Holy* Audacious Goals! We want to try something big—something huge and audacious—so that we can show the world that we serve a big God. Bill Beauchamp, who served as our chairman of the board for more than a decade, once said something that became a Southeast slogan: *Let's try something so big that if God isn't in it, we will fail.*

Big goals create excitement. Our hearts beat faster as we wonder together what the future might hold. We begin to wonder aloud, *Can we do this?* Or better still, *Can God do it through us?* The enthusiasm mounts as we near the goal. Everyone wants to be a part of accomplishing something that's never been done before.

Last year a leader in our church had a vision for mission involvement. We decided to start a program called "2000 in 2000" designed to encourage two thousand church members to commit to serving in a local mission or going on a short-term mission trip in the year 2000. That was a huge goal! We have fourteen thousand members, but that's including young people, college students, busy moms and dads, the elderly, and almost three thousand people who haven't even been a part of our congregation for more than a year! Asking for two thousand people to sacrifice their most prized possession—their time—is a BHAG!

Yet as I'm writing this, more than fourteen hundred people have already committed to being among the two thousand, and the entire church is buzzing about the project. People are excited about what God will do in the future because a few visionary people decided to walk by faith!

Walking by Faith Stimulates Prayer

Jesus said, "I tell you the truth, if you have faith as small as a mustard seed, you can say to this mountain, 'Move from here to there' and it will move. Nothing will be impossible for you" (Matt. 17:20). If your goal is to move a molehill, you won't have much incentive to pray. You can do that with human effort. But mountainous goals will motivate you to go to your knees and seek an outpouring of God's grace.

When we set a goal of raising twenty-six million dollars above our regular giving, we were told it was the largest goal of any church in history. One man with a financial background said, "If we accomplish that goal, it will be the biggest miracle I've ever seen." That audacious goal stimulated prayer. We met in homes by the hundreds and prayed. Church leaders knelt and prayed. We had a round-the-clock, forty-eight-hour prayer vigil. We knew that raising that kind of money would take a tremendous outpouring of God's goodness. God answered those prayers, and we raised well over the twenty-six million dollars we needed. A bold faith produces big challenges; big challenges stimulate prayer; and prayer results in miracles.

Walking by Faith Motivates Sacrifice

People respond to an inspiring challenge. I've seen people sacrifice hours of their time and thousands of dollars to help the church reach its goals.

I mentioned earlier that in 1983, a relocation committee reported that a twenty-acre tract of land just down the street had become available and that we could purchase it if we acted immediately. I didn't tell you the rest of the story. The committee said, "In order to purchase those twenty acres, we need $215,000 in two months."

After the board voted to purchase the land, we had to decide how to finance it. One of our elders said, "Let's come to next month's board meeting with a cash offering and pay for it ourselves out of this leadership body. Then we'll use that offering as an incentive to encourage the congregation to give one million dollars in the fall toward the new building. I've done some calculating, and there are fifty-five elders, deacons, and staff members in this room. That boils down to thirty-five hundred dollars per family next month. Are there any questions?" There were a few timid questions. Then we voted—and the idea passed! We walked out of the meeting saying to one another, "What did we just do?"

That month we had to ask ourselves whether the church was first in our lives or we were just "playing church." The chairman of the board got a few calls of concern. "I'm just a schoolteacher and don't make that kind of money," one would say. "I'm retired and living on a fixed income," another would say. But then we began to hear reports of people canceling vacations, selling second cars, dipping into their savings accounts. At least three families borrowed ten thousand dollars each from the bank to contribute to the project.

Walking by Faith Produces Harmony

When we came to the meeting the next month, the tension was thick. No one really knew what the others had done—how much they had sacrificed. One elder, Jack Coffee, came to the meeting wearing dark sun glasses, carrying a tin cup, and walking with a cane! He wanted people to know he'd really sacrificed!

We collected the offering, and the tally committee went off to count it. When they returned with the news, we hadn't raised

$215,000—we'd raised $255,000! The room exploded with joyous celebration. Everyone exchanged high-fives and embraces. We knelt together and thanked God for his blessing.

When the "Amen" was said, someone said, "I'll be outside polishing shoes."

Bob Carpenter asked, "What shoes? You obviously didn't sacrifice enough if you still have shoes!"

What a joyful occasion that was. The leaders had risked their own future for the church because of their faith in God. A few months later, inspired by the leaders' faith, the congregation gave over a million dollars toward the new building. The spirit of harmony among the leadership permeated the entire church. The new building was built, and we moved into it in 1987.

Soldiers in the barracks will bicker and fight with one another. But soldiers on the battlefield stand united because they need each other. One of the reasons Christians often bicker among themselves is that there is no challenging goal that binds them together. A church that is arguing over traditions has forgotten its vision. But a challenging purpose can help people put differences aside and join forces for the advancement of Christ's Kingdom. (We'll talk more in the next chapter about the need for harmony in the church.)

What is God waiting to do through your congregation? Like Becky Edmondson, Matt Chalfant, and George Drake, do you have a vision of what God can do through his people? Are you willing to try something so big that if God isn't in it, it will fail?

Jesus said, "With man this is impossible, but with God all things are possible" (Matt. 19:26). May God give you a vision for what can be done through a few people who are willing to walk by faith.

❖ The Importance of a United Leadership

❖ God Blesses Harmonious Churches

❖ Threats to Harmony

❖ Steps to Harmony

6

HARMONY:
Maintain a Spirit of Harmony

Early in my ministry at Southeast, a conflict developed within leadership. The elders asked the associate to resign. He refused to do so and decided to take the matter before the full board. At that time, the full board of elders and deacons had the authority to override the elders (which was a bad structure that we later changed). The associate sent to all the deacons a ten-page letter relating some of the disagreements and detailing his conversations with some of the elders and with me.

At the monthly elders and deacons' meeting, there was sharp division within leadership. When it became obvious to the associate that he didn't have the necessary votes to remain, he resigned in anger. Then he wrote a letter to the entire congregation detailing his disagreements, promising he would be outside the church on Sunday morning offering the ten-page document he had prepared! And he kept his promise.

For the next two months, the associate continued to lead a Sunday-school class in his home and stirred up further dissension. Each week after his class, he and the class members would drive to church and sit in the first three rows of the sanctuary, scowling at me!

While this conflict was going on, a church in another town invited me to become their preacher. The offer was really attractive. I reasoned that I was part of the problem for the conflict at Southeast and here was my way out of the trouble.

In the midst of the problem, I came home one day to find my five-year-old son jumping up and down for joy, pointing to the living room. There sat a brand-new, large, color television set to replace our tiny old black-and-white model. The elders had pooled their own money to get that gift for me. The chairman of the board called me that night. He said, "We know you've received an offer to go elsewhere. We're not trying to bribe you. We just wanted you to know that we appreciate you and hope you'll stay with us through this difficulty. We're unanimously behind you."

THE IMPORTANCE OF A UNITED LEADERSHIP

Maybe the elders didn't handle this situation perfectly, but they handled it with a united front. One of the reasons the church survived through that difficulty was that the elders were united. All the elders agreed that they needed to ask the associate to resign, and they stayed with that decision in spite of the criticisms they received.

Before that crisis, things were going really well at the church, which had about 350 members at the time. We were really concerned about how this issue would affect the church. I remember many sleepless nights when I paced the floor, wondering if we would ever make it through. The associate had been my close friend. Suddenly an entire group of influential people in the congregation didn't like me and were not supportive of what we were doing in the church. That was hard to swallow. I was twenty-seven years old! It was a difficult time, but it seasoned me as a minister and a person. And remarkably, by the grace of God, we survived that challenging time and grew in spite of the conflict.

In each chapter of this book, we've tried to put examples of how we've implemented these principles at Southeast. This chapter is an exception since, except for the preceding case, it is void of any recent examples of our church overcoming threats to harmony. It's not because there haven't been any. We've had our problems: doctrinal differences, egos out of control, personality conflicts, and disregard for the leadership. But it's awkward for me to talk about those situations because in most cases harmony has been restored and relationships have been mended. To deal with them in print would be to open old wounds; so to practice what I'm preaching, I'm avoiding controversy by not mentioning specific examples! We've learned from our own battles how to deal with divisiveness and ensure that the delicate balance of harmony is maintained in the church.

GOD BLESSES HARMONIOUS CHURCHES

I once preached a revival for a church that was split right down the center aisle. The people on one side of the aisle hated the people on the other side, and vice versa. They didn't even speak to those who sat on the other side. I asked about the problem and discovered that it all started with the church softball team. One of the elders was the team's coach, and he refused to play the son of another elder in an important game. After heated words were exchanged between the two elders, they wouldn't speak to each other. Everybody in the congregation began to choose sides, and a war of silence ensued. Needless to say, there wasn't much revival there—and there won't be until there is harmony among the leaders.

I doubt that God ever blesses a bickering church. God loves the church. The Bible says God hates the one who sows discord among the Body (Prov. 6:19). It's a dangerous thing to wound or divide the Body of Christ. But when there is harmony, the Holy Spirit flows and God blesses the church. It is said of the early church that they were all *together* in one place when the outpouring of God's Spirit came (Acts 2). Later in the same chapter, when the practices of the early church are described, three times in two verses the writer, Luke, mentions their togetherness: "All the believers were together" (v. 44); "Every day they continued to meet together.... They broke bread in their homes and ate together" (v. 46).

In Jesus' prayer to his Father the night before he was crucified, he prayed for his disciples. Then he prayed for all of us who would come to believe in him through their message. And he prayed for one specific thing among us so that the world would know God had truly sent his Son. What was the one thing needed to prove the deity of Christ? The ability to perform miracles? Powerful preaching? Great music? No, Jesus prayed for harmony—"that all of them may be one, Father, just as you are in me and I am in you. May they also be in us so that the world may believe that you have sent me" (John 17:21).

The disciples had frequently bickered among themselves. In fact, on the night of the Last Supper, there was contention among them about who was going to be the most important in the Kingdom. Just as a loving father hates to see his children arguing among themselves, it grieved Jesus that his disciples were being contentious. So he prayed that his followers—not just his inner circle of disciples, but all who would come after them—would live harmoniously with each other.

Jesus wanted his followers to get along so that their testimony would be believable. It's a farce for the church to tell the world we have the solution to strife—"come experience the peace that passes understanding"—when we are fighting among ourselves. Jesus said that a house divided against itself cannot stand (Luke 11:17). Paul said, "If you keep on biting and devouring each other, watch out or you will be destroyed by each other" (Gal. 5:15).

I heard about a church years ago that began bickering over the use of a musical instrument. Half the congregation wanted to use a piano, an instrument that was gaining popularity in the culture, in their church services. The other half felt it was a tool of the devil. Sharp disagreement resulted in hard feelings on both sides. One Sunday when the people came to worship, there was a new piano on the stage; and to the horror of half the congregation, it was played during the congregational singing. The half that disapproved walked out of the building in protest. The next Sunday everyone was back, but the piano was missing. Those who bought it couldn't find it. They looked for months as accusations flew back and forth about the thievery. Six months later the piano was found. It had been hidden in the baptistry all along!

Division negates evangelism. When the church fights, the baptistry isn't used very often. If your church is to grow, there must be a sense of harmony among the leaders and congregation. The leaders have to communicate and be truthful with people. The congregation has to be supportive and encouraging of the leaders. We are blessed with unity at Southeast, but we make every effort to maintain it because unity can be fragile.

THREATS TO HARMONY

There are four primary threats to church unity. Here they are, in what I've observed to be reverse order, from the least common threat to the most common.

False Teaching

A popular false teaching that is threatening church unity today is a liberal theology that disregards biblical principles. The preacher begins to say things like, "I know the Bible says that God created each individual species, but we're more enlightened than that now," or "Yes, the Bible condemns homosexuality, but that was back when the writers didn't understand genetics and psychology."

Paul warned the Ephesian elders, "I know that after I leave, savage wolves will come in among you and will not spare the flock. Even from your own number men will arise and distort the truth in order to draw away disciples after them. So be on your guard!" (Acts 20:29–31).

If false teachers aren't confronted early, they will distort the truth and divide the flock. The early church was often threatened by false teachers. Acts 15 notes that "Some men came down from Judea to Antioch and were teaching the brothers: 'Unless you are circumcised, according to the custom taught by Moses, you cannot be saved.' This brought Paul and Barnabas into sharp dispute and debate with them" (vv. 1–2).

This false doctrine, expounded by the legalists, brought a heated exchange among the leaders that threatened to divide the early church. They determined to have an open discussion about this issue to resolve it immediately. "So Paul and Barnabas were appointed, along with some other believers, to go up to Jerusalem to see the apostles and elders about this question" (v. 2).

The church in Antioch wisely sought the apostles in Jerusalem for guidance and mediation. There was a long debate, but a compromise was finally reached. The Gentiles didn't have to become Jews, but they should refrain from certain pagan practices like sexual immorality. They were also told to refrain from eating certain types of meats, apparently in deference to the Jews who lived among them and worshiped with them, so that the Jewish believers wouldn't be offended and unity could be more easily accomplished. Often when there are disagreements, the party who is in the right needs to make some concessions, without compromising the truth, in order for harmony to be maintained.

Later when the letter containing the infant church's new guidelines was delivered to the church in Antioch, "The people read it and were glad for its encouraging message" (Acts 15:31). Harmony was restored and the church continued to grow.

Legalistic Spirit

Liberals want to change everything, but the legalists refuse to change *anything*. The legalist has no tolerance for disagreement. Every proposed change is seen as a threat to stability and will be vehemently opposed. In the church, the legalist often has a difficult time discerning between the *method* and the *message*. Any proposed change of *method* is seen as liberalizing the *message*.

The legalist imagines he is standing for truth, when he is usually guarding his precious traditions. I've heard legalists comment that certain churches had "gone liberal" because they had begun singing praise choruses in their worship service (with drums!) or they had drama or built a gymnasium or had a few people in the service who raised their hands when they sang. The legalist insists that you do it his way, or else you must be doctrinally in error.

I know of a preacher who tried to lead his congregation in building a multipurpose facility to enhance fellowship and outreach. Some of the leaders insisted that organized recreation on church property was not spiritual. They debated for a long time whether it was the Lord's will for them to have a basketball court on the church grounds. They finally arrived at the conclusion that it was acceptable to have one basket, but not two! Having two baskets was liberal in the minds of the legalists because that would indicate that the church was promoting competition and games. Their decision had nothing to do with their original purpose—to enhance fellowship and outreach—or even finances. It had everything to do with the legalistic spirit of some of the leaders.

At another church, one leader objected to having a fellowship hall in the church building where the congregation could eat together. Finally he agreed to approve it if they'd build it across the street!

You can understand why such legalism threatens harmony. In Romans 14, Paul confronted the legalists of his day who insisted it was wrong to eat meat if it had been sacrificed to idols. Apparently some of the pagan merchants would sacrifice their goods to their gods before selling them in the market. So it was possible—even likely—that the meat that was sold in the market had been part of a pagan religious ceremony. Some Christians felt very uneasy about eating meat that had been sacrificed to idols and thus "supporting" that pagan practice.

Paul asked his readers not to make too big a deal out of minor matters. Don't divide over your opinions. Don't insist that everyone see it just like you do. If you think it's wrong to eat meat sacrificed to idols, he said, then don't eat that meat and violate your own conscience. (If you think it's wrong to watch PG-13 movies, buy AT&T stock, visit Disney World, or worship on Saturday nights, then don't violate your own conscience.) But Paul went on to say that we shouldn't condemn others in the church who don't see it our way. Those things aren't worthy causes for division.

What do you do with the legalist who refuses to change? Paul says that if someone in your midst thinks a certain practice is sinful, even though you have freedom in Christ, don't flaunt it. Try to make concessions and respect their traditions. Try your best not to divide the Body of Christ. (See all of Romans 14, especially verse 15). Paul concludes, "Let us therefore make every effort to do what leads to peace and to mutual edification. Do not destroy the work of God for the sake of food. All food is clean, but it is wrong for a man to eat anything that causes someone else to stumble. It is better not to eat meat or drink wine or to do anything else that will cause your brother to fall" (vv. 19–21).

However, it is wrong to allow the legalist to dictate the direction of the church. In that same chapter, Paul also said, "Do not allow what you consider good to be spoken of as evil" (v. 16). It is wrong for the legalist to bind the church in slavery to traditions by claiming that certain activities or styles of music are sinful when they clearly are not. In another passage Paul said, "It is for freedom that Christ has set us free. Stand firm, then, and do not let yourselves be burdened again by a yoke of slavery" (Gal. 5:1). People who feel that it would be a sin to raise their hands in church shouldn't be required or manipulated into doing so. But neither should they be allowed to judge another person who may choose to worship in a different way.

The challenge is to find a way to accommodate the legalists without allowing them to run the church. To do that successfully, remember these principles:

1. *Understand people's natural resistance to change.* The style of music in our congregation is primarily contemporary. If we began this week to change that style to a classical, liturgical style of worship, we would have mutiny. Young and old alike would be shaken, confused, and angry, because change is uncomfortable to people. "What happened to *my* church?" they'd ask. Unless you realize this principle, you will never successfully implement change without rebellion.

2. *Determine if the issue is scriptural or traditional.* Often legalists will claim a scriptural reason for wanting to keep the status quo, when in reality they are tradition-bound. When we decided to begin a Saturday night service, a wonderful little old lady in our church came up to Greg and said, "The Bible says we are to worship on the *Sabbath*," and then she just walked away. She didn't give Greg a chance to tell her that the Sabbath *is* Saturday! But before you flippantly brush off people as legalistic, be sure they don't have a scriptural point. Be sure you stand on solid biblical ground when you implement a change.

3. *Change slowly but consistently.* If you want to begin singing choruses instead of all hymns in your church, you can throw out the hymnals tomorrow and sing all choruses next week—but you'll have a rebellion. Or you can sing the same number of hymns then sing one chorus at the end of your service, and you have introduced a slight change that might be well received. Someone said we usually overestimate what we can do in a year and underestimate what can be done in five years. Implementing change takes time. Adopt a long-range plan and be patient.

4. Realistically count the cost. Are there one or two families who are bound to legalism and traditionalism who might get offended by your actions? Then make the decision to act anyway and live with the criticism. Will your decision divide the church in half? Then unless you are standing on biblical principles, you're probably changing too fast and need to compromise. Don't allow your own spiritual pride and desire to "do great things for God" to become a stumbling block by causing division in the church.

Criticism

One of the easiest ways to divide the Body of Christ is to constantly be critical of the church's leaders. Some people have razor-sharp tongues that are cutting, caustic, and sarcastic. They usually have no idea how much damage their criticism does. They think it's their nature to be negative. They're convinced they have the "spiritual gift" of criticism! But their attitude is divisive. The Bible says, "Consider what a great forest is set on fire by a small spark. The tongue also is a fire, a world of evil among the parts of the body. It corrupts the whole person, sets the whole course of his life on fire, and is itself set on fire by hell" (James 3:5–6).

Constant, vicious criticism is lethal. It dampens enthusiasm, stifles creativity, discourages the leadership, and quenches the spirit of the church.

Conflict often develops because church leaders pay too much attention to the criticisms. If every critical word devastates you, then part of the problem is that you're too sensitive. To keep the peace, a good leader must know when to confront criticism and when to ignore it. Don't make a bigger issue of the criticism than it deserves. If you respond to every criticism, then the critic runs the church. His opinion may be the minority view, or it may be directly against the will of God for you to follow the critic's advice. Bill Cosby said, "I don't know what the secret to success is, but I'll tell you the key to failure: trying to please everybody."

Some criticism is inevitable. There may be some legalists in your church who, for reasons of pride and stubbornness, will be critical whenever you want to make the slightest change. Even Jesus Christ couldn't keep everybody happy. In fact, he warned against those who worked too hard to please everyone. A good leader learns that it's impossible to please everybody all the time. In fact, there are some people who won't be pleased *any* of the time! Learn to take criticism seriously but not personally. If you are too flippant when people are critical, you will be seen as arrogant. But if you are too thin-skinned, you'll be miserable, and nothing will ever be accomplished.

I was once complaining to my friend Steve Chapman about someone who had been critical of me. He said, "Well, at least you got that 'Woe' off your back." I asked him to explain. He said, "Jesus said, 'Woe unto you when all men speak well of you.' Now that's one 'Woe' you don't have to worry about!"

Steve Brown, the well-known Bible teacher from Key Life Ministries, reminds us of the old Aesop's fable about an old man and his grandson who made their way into town with a donkey. The grandfather put the boy on the donkey until he heard people say, "Look at that selfish child making that old man walk!" The grandfather couldn't stand to have people criticize his grandson, so he asked the boy to walk while he rode. Then he heard people say, "Look at that selfish old man riding and making the poor little boy walk." So he got off and they both walked. Then he heard people say, "Look at those stupid two people. They've got a donkey and they're not even using it." So both the man and the boy rode the donkey together. Then they heard people say, "Look at those cruel people abusing that poor animal! They're going to break his back with that load!" They finally walked into town carrying the donkey!

If you're carrying a donkey, it's time you realized that there is no way you can please everybody. Learn to ignore unfounded criticisms, or those criticisms will stifle the Spirit of God and divide the Body of Christ.

Uncontrolled Ego

It's been said that EGO stands for Edging God Out. The number one cause of division in churches today is pride. People become proud of their influence and status, so much so that when you threaten their little seat of power, they will come out fighting. They will pretend they have the church's best interests at heart, but the real issue is a matter of *who's in charge.*

In many churches, you have to endure a lot of hurdles to accomplish anything, so much so that by the time you implement a new program, it's already obsolete. Often those red-tape hurdles are put there to protect someone's turf.

In the business world, little perks usually come with increased influence. An employee might be given his own office, a faster computer with Internet access, his own expense account, a key to a special room, or access to a company car. Those little benefits become status symbols. If you want to create havoc in the company, just remove one little privilege. It could even be something that employee hasn't used in years. But that doesn't matter, because it's an issue of pride.

That same carnal mind-set can divide a church. Sometimes people come to regard their little area of service not as a ministry but as a source of ego gratification. You'll hear them say:

- I've served as treasurer of this Sunday-school class for ten years now, and nothing should be purchased without my prior approval.

- I've sung a solo in the Christmas program every year since I was a teenager—now suddenly I'm not needed.

- I've always served as a greeter for the first service, in the main lobby, because I like to see the same people every week. Now they've moved me to the second service, west lobby, and I don't see the same people. I'm concerned that some of those people who don't see me may leave the church!

- I used to be asked to lead singing on occasion, but I haven't been asked since we moved into the new building. I guess I'm not good enough anymore.

A preacher in a rural area who had a very successful ministry was asked why so many country churches were stagnant. He said that in many small churches, there are one or two families that for generations have controlled the church. Their influence in the church becomes a matter of pride and power for them. They resist any new leader or new idea because it threatens their little empire.

STEPS TO HARMONY

My sons used to fight with each other a lot. I guess that's normal among children, but it really bothered me that they didn't always get along. I remember my lowest day as a father. When my two sons were teenagers, they got into a fistfight. I heard them shouting and banging around in their room, and I bolted upstairs to break up a nasty fight. (I know you probably can't imagine such a thing in a preacher's home. You thought we spent most of our time sitting in a circle reading the Bible and praying.) I don't expect children to be perfect, but I was so disappointed in my sons for fighting. Why couldn't they get along?

Our heavenly Father feels the same way about us. It grieves the heart of God when his children bicker and fight with each other. One of the best ways to honor the Father is to make every effort to see that his children get along with each other.

If you've ever been in a fighting church, you'll never want to be there again. One man who was in a church battered by division—so much so that they'd had three preachers in as many years—said to me,

"I notice one of your slogans is, 'Speaking the truth in love.' We don't have a church slogan, but if we did it would be, 'If you want to fight, go to First Christian!'"

Keep Your Ego under Control

Although this issue is treated above, I want to repeat it here by applying it specifically to church leaders. If there's one primary reason that our church has maintained harmony, it is that we have church leaders who have kept their egos under control. Unity requires humility. The leaders of your church need to adopt this attitude: It doesn't matter who gets the credit as long as the job gets done. That takes gentleness, patience, and effort. You have to avoid harsh words and angry tones.

One of the reasons our church has grown so large is that we've never split. And one reason we've stayed together is that we've asked people to check their egos at the door.

Be Flexible

If pride and stubbornness are the greatest threats to harmony, then humility and flexibility are the greatest ways to maintain peace. If you are going to demand that you always get your way and that nothing ever changes, then you will be miserable and make everyone around you miserable. Be flexible.

When we moved into our new building, I knew there would be a time of adjustment. There were rooms that still weren't carpeted, offices that still weren't completed, signs that still weren't erected. I challenged our staff to adopt an attitude of flexibility. Someone introduced a "tenth beatitude": *Blessed are the flexible, for they shall not be bent out of shape.* Our staff remained flexible, and everyone got along great even though conditions weren't ideal at first.

One of our staff members, Don Waddell, says in the leadership seminars he conducts that one of the greatest characteristics of the people at Southeast is their ability to adapt to change. The older people don't demand, "We're not going to do it that way because we've never done it that way before." Their flexible attitude is one of the biggest reasons we've been able to maintain such a spirit of harmony in the church.

A leader from a church in another town visited us a few years ago when we were in the middle of plans to relocate. He said, "I've admired your relocation project. Our church needs to do the same thing. We have one thousand members in a downtown location. We have no parking and are having three services. We found some property, and the leaders recommended to the congregation that we relocate. But the vote was 51 percent to move and 49 percent to stay, with about thirty abstentions. We were devastated. We can't relocate without better consensus. We're probably going to stagnate and decline where we are."

He asked what percentage of our congregation voted in favor of relocating. I said it was over 94 percent. He asked, "How were you able to get your senior citizens behind it? Our senior citizens are so resistant to change. They've been in the building for years and don't want to move." I was happy to tell him that our older people were leading the way on our relocation project. (The fact that in the old building their classroom was located in the middle of our most congested hallway didn't hurt!)

John Faust, our senior-adults minister, recalled a conversation he had with one of our favorite senior citizens—Emory Cockerham—when we were raising funds and making plans to move to a new building. Emory said, "I may never worship in that building, but I'm sure going to support it because it represents so much for the younger generation."

John told us, "That was to me a great example of harmony and the right attitude—looking to the next generation, passing the baton of faith to the younger people." We're all very thankful that Emory did get to worship in our new building for a few months before he died in 1999.

Develop a Sense of Humor

Maintaining harmony often requires a sense of humor. "A cheerful heart is good medicine" (Prov. 17:22). I have a unique relationship with Dave Stone, our preaching associate. We get along great even though we share the same pulpit. We both have to swallow our pride at times and exalt Christ.

One Wednesday night before a service began, we were both standing behind the platform near the baptismal changing rooms when a woman came up to us and said, "I'm glad to meet you both. I've been coming for six months and haven't met either of you. It's good to see you laughing with each other and getting along so well. I'm back here because my fifteen-year-old son is getting baptized." Then she looked at Dave and said, "Dave, he loves your preaching. He thinks you're the funniest thing. Dave, would you come and meet my son? It would really mean a lot to him." She grabbed Dave by the arm and walked away, leaving me standing there alone!

Dave later asked me if that bothered me. I said, "No, I used to preach on a sophomore level too!"

One man who had never been to our church but listened to my sermons on the radio once commented to me about how realistic our laugh track was. I said, "We don't have a laugh track." He couldn't believe a group of church people could really laugh like that!

An extensive survey of churches revealed that growing, healthy churches were more likely to be characterized as congregations that laughed together. Almost 70 percent of those in healthy churches agreed with the statement, "There is a lot of laughter in our church." Only a third of those in stagnant churches could make that claim. Christian Schwarz summarized those findings by saying, "The question of whether there is much laughter in a church has a strong correlation to the quality of a church and its growth. Interestingly enough, aspects like this find little mention in church growth literature."[1]

The church that frequently laughs together is more likely to be healthy because it is more likely to be harmonious. A healthy, genuine sense of humor can smooth over hurt feelings, relax tense moods, and make bitter pills of confrontation easier to swallow. One of our elders once expressed his displeasure in a board meeting over our decision to occasionally move the Lord's Supper to the end of one of the worship services. He felt that it was compromising the importance of communion, which had always been in the middle of the service. "The Lord's Supper should be in the center of the worship service, because the Bible says the Lord's Supper is to be the center of worship," he said.

"Where does the Bible say that?" someone asked.

He paused, then said, "Well, if it doesn't, it should!" He laughed, then everybody laughed, and the meeting moved on without further discussion.

Respect the Leaders

The Bible commands, "Obey your leaders and submit to their authority. They keep watch over you as men who must give an account. Obey them so that their work will be a joy, not a burden, for that would be of no advantage to you" (Heb. 13:17). When members of the church criticize the leadership—when they second-guess, ridicule, politic, recruit opposition, and circulate petitions—they make the work of the leaders a burden, and they wound the church.

We have two "silos" of leadership in our organizational structure. The *elders* are twenty-three lay volunteers who are appointed to oversee the church and set its tone and culture, and the *paid staff* now consists of over two hundred ministers and employees who seek to daily implement the philosophy set by the overseers.

The elders have generously supported and loved the staff. The staff has been submissive and accountable to the elders, and there's been little backbiting or jostling for power. In order to have harmony in the church, these two groups must trust one another, and the congregation must respect their mutual leadership.

The staff and congregation must submit to the elders' authority. I don't think God intended the church to be a democracy in which the congregation votes on every issue. Nor is it to be an autocracy, with the pastor or priest running everything. The church is to be a Christocracy in which Jesus Christ is the Chief Shepherd. And according to the New Testament model, under Jesus is to be a group of shepherds— called elders, overseers, or pastors—who lead the flock according to what they believe to be the will of Christ, the Chief Shepherd. (In our church, I'm considered to be one of the twenty-three elders; in 1 Timothy 5:17–18, Paul says it's acceptable for me to get paid for being a preaching elder, praise the Lord!)

The elders are to lovingly lead the church, and the congregation is to wisely follow. That doesn't mean you should blindly follow the elders. You shouldn't blindly follow any human leader. You should examine God's Word personally and hold the leaders accountable. Paul said, "Follow me as I follow Christ." But as long as the shepherds are consistent with Scripture, the flock is to respect their guidance.

Southeast has not only been blessed with Christ-centered leaders, we've also had humble, cooperative followers. Although our congregation includes many talented people who are leaders in the secular world, they have respected the leaders of our church primarily because our leaders have proven themselves trustworthy. The leaders are students of God's Word, live lives of integrity, and make prayerful, wise decisions that have the church's best interests at heart. They've made mistakes, but it's been amazing how God has guided the primary direction of the church even when the decisions were difficult.

The most dramatic example of the church's cooperation with the leadership is one I've already mentioned—the congregational vote of 94 percent in favor of the elders' decision to relocate, even though we had been in the new building less than five years. That dramatic vote demonstrated a healthy trust in the leadership of the church. Even the 6 percent who voted no graciously supported the congregation's decision. They could have questioned and criticized the elders at every juncture throughout the relocation project, but instead they submitted to the elders' leadership and maintained a spirit of harmony.

The elders must trust the staff's leadership. Although the ministers should submit to the authority of the elders, a wise body of elders will trust the ministerial staff and give them as much free rein as possible to lead the congregation. If the ministers always think the board of elders is looking over their shoulder, their leadership and creativity will be hampered. They'll be acting out of fear of the elders' reaction rather than their passion for ministering to people.

About a year ago we disbanded the personnel committee that was made up of a few elders and staff members and decided to turn over that hiring process completely to the staff. Because of our growth, we knew we'd be hiring more staff members in the coming year than in any other year in our history, so that was a big decision and took a lot of trust! But the elders said, "We trust the staff to make these decisions. They know what they're looking for better than we do."

That not only took trust, it took humility on the part of the elders. Rarely will a person or group of people in authority willingly give up portions of that authority for the good of the organization. But if the elders cannot trust the staff to lead the congregation, then the staff will never be free to serve to their full potential.

Avoid Controversy If Possible

Paul wrote, "Avoid foolish controversies and genealogies and arguments and quarrels about the law, because these are unprofitable and useless" (Titus 3:9). A third-grade boy wrote an essay on pins in which he illustrated the importance of avoidance. "Pins save thousands of lives every year," he wrote.

His teacher said, "Pins perform a lot of functions, but how do they save thousands of lives?"

The boy replied, "By not swallowing them!"

Prevention is always the best cure. There are many problems that can be avoided if we're wise. Of course, we should observe that Paul instructed Titus to avoid "foolish" controversy. Not all controversy is foolish. Some issues are critical and have to be discussed. But stupid arguments and useless quarrels should be avoided. Some controversies in Christian circles have no solution and only take up endless hours of unproductive time.

People can talk for hours about different views of prophecy—the premillennial versus amillennial debate. No one can prove the other wrong, despite what some of them on both sides think! Theologians can talk for hours about the difference between God's sovereignty and man's free will. You can spend an entire Sunday-school class discussing whether God created the world in six twenty-four-hour segments. Many of us think we're spiritual because we can argue about such religious questions, and we're convinced we've got the answers. In fact, you might be a little uneasy right now after reading the beginning of this paragraph because I hinted that you can't prove your side of one of those debates! Remember that it's one thing to be able to discuss theology, but it's quite another thing to be able to live like Christ—to be kind at home or diligent at work or forgiving of the one who wronged you.

Paul said we ought to avoid those controversies for two reasons. First, *they accomplish nothing.* Paul called them "unprofitable and useless." When you're finished arguing, your time has been wasted. What virtue is there in spending your time in a deep theological discussion that has been rehashed dozens of times while the simple tasks of the Christian life are going undone?

In 1917, when the Russian revolution was rocking the streets of Petrograd, leaders of the Russian Orthodox Church were in session just blocks away from the fighting, having a heated debate over what color vestments the priests should wear! You can get so caught up in the trivial issues that you become blinded to the real needs of people and the true purpose of the church.

The second reason to avoid such controversies is that *they are potentially divisive*. The Greek word for "arguments" in Titus 3:9 is translated "strife" in other passages. When people get involved in studying such controversies, they lose perspective and become increasingly intense. Their egos get involved, and when they meet someone who doesn't see it their way, they immediately start debating and strife results. I read years ago of a man who shot and killed another after a disagreement over an interpretation of the Bible! It's amazing how people can lose perspective and fight over trivial matters. Do your best to avoid such controversies in your church.

Confront Divisive People When Necessary

Paul told Titus, "Warn a divisive person once, and then warn him a second time. After that, have nothing to do with him" (Titus 3:10). A divisive person is someone who is threatening the harmony of the church, not just someone who disagrees with you! But there are times when a person's contentious spirit, false teaching, or immoral lifestyle threatens to divide the Body of Christ. Such a person must be confronted.

Let's say Churchgoing Chuck comes to you and tells you about Arguing Alice and her contentious spirit. What should you do?

Personal confrontation. First you should direct Chuck to speak personally with Alice about his concerns, in accordance with Jesus' words in Matthew 18:15–17. If Alice won't listen, then Chuck should take two or three witnesses. Then if she still doesn't listen, bring it to the church leaders.

Warnings from the church leaders. Suppose the matter is grave enough that it does indeed threaten the body, and Alice refuses to repent after being confronted. What should the church leaders do?

According to Paul's words in Titus 3, they should gently but firmly warn her that she is being divisive and is in jeopardy of being excommunicated from the church.

Excommunication. Paul says that Alice should be given two warnings, after which—if she doesn't repent—the church should have nothing to do with her.

Repentance and restoration. Even if she is dismissed from the fellowship, the ultimate goal for Alice is repentance and restoration. In 1 and 2 Corinthians, Paul writes about a man who apparently was dismissed from the fellowship for his immoral behavior (1 Cor. 5), but then repented. Paul commanded in his second letter that they restore the penitent man (2 Cor. 2:6–8).

In another letter Paul wrote, "Brothers, if someone is caught in a sin, you who are spiritual should restore him gently. But watch yourself, or you also may be tempted" (Gal. 6:1). You must be willing to take such dramatic action not only because it is truly the loving thing to do for that individual, but also because the harmony of the church is so crucial. Putting up with a divisive person in the church to avoid problems is like putting up with a cancerous tumor without operating to avoid the pain of surgery. You must operate so that you can continue to be alive and healthy. If your church is to continue winning souls and transforming lives, you must maintain harmony. That occasionally means that a difficult operation must be undertaken by the leaders.

I can count on both hands the number of times our elders have gone to individuals over our twenty-seven-year history and warned someone about divisiveness. I can think of only two times when disciplinary action went to the second warning or someone was removed from the church. In both of those cases, the result was repentance and restoration.

Churches today are very hesitant about any church discipline at all. Ours is an era in which everyone wants to be free to live as he pleases. "No one tells me what to do" is a common response to any attempt at church discipline. The threat of legal action makes church leaders hesitant to practice any kind of confrontation or discipline, but the church will inevitably suffer if appropriate discipline is ignored.

Practice Servanthood

The best way to maintain harmony in the church is to get the congregation to think more of others than they do of themselves. As I mentioned earlier, the greatest threat to harmony is wounded egos. The best way to overcome pride and develop a spirit of humility is to practice servanthood whenever possible.

There was fighting in the upper room. The disciples were bickering among themselves about who was the most important. They were battling over who would have the most power in the coming Kingdom. They were so egotistical that no one dared stoop to wash the feet of the others. But Jesus took a basin of water and washed their feet, saying, "The greatest among you must be the servant of all. As I have washed your feet, so you also should wash one another's feet" (John 13).

I've never met a contentious servant. When people devote themselves to doing good, they don't have time for criticism. When people serve others, they become positive and cooperative.

One of the reasons the older people in our congregation don't complain is because they're too busy serving. For years the Friendship ABF (Adult Bible Fellowship) class, a group of senior citizens, came every Monday morning to clean the worship area. It would take several hours for them to clean out the trash in every row, straighten the pew Bibles, and vacuum the carpet. Now the group has grown older, and the building is much too large for them to handle alone, so there are others helping with that task. But for years they have been a picture of loyalty and servanthood at Southeast.

Many of our senior citizens are still involved in cleaning the worship center and volunteering elsewhere—serving in other parts of the facilities ministry, greeting during the week in the welcome center, teaching a class, volunteering in the activities ministry, or working in the nursery. They are true servants; and servants are cooperative, supportive people who have their egos under control. When people are serving like that, your chances of maintaining harmony are greatly increased.

Be Quick to Forgive

Leadership Journal asked me to write about "my biggest leadership mistake and what I learned from it." I wrote an article titled "The Day I Forgot the Wedding!"

> On Saturday afternoon I had gone to watch my son play baseball. When I returned my wife said in a panicky tone, "We've been trying to find you for an hour and a half. You were supposed to do a wedding this afternoon. Did you forget?"
>
> My heart sank to my feet.
>
> Immediately the rationalizations formed: it was a small wedding, the rehearsal took place several days before the ceremony, I had another wedding that day, it was on a Saturday— my usual day off. But the bottom line was, I forgot the most important event in the life of a couple in our church. There was no valid excuse.
>
> I felt like such a loser. How could I have possibly made such a stupid mistake?
>
> I learned that the wedding had been delayed for a few minutes and an associate minister had substituted for me so that the ceremony could proceed. But I knew I needed to apologize, so I quickly changed into a suit and drove an eternal ten minutes to the church building, knowing the couple would probably be getting their pictures taken or maybe even having their reception by now.
>
> On my way, my carnal nature dreamed up a dozen lies: "I had a flat tire"…"I got stopped by a train"… "I had a vision of a 700-foot-high Jesus and was in a trance." It was the longest, most sickening ten-minute drive of my life.
>
> When I walked into the sanctuary, the couple was posing

for pictures. When the bride saw me, she burst out, "Oh, Bob, I'm so glad you're all right! We were afraid you were in an accident or something! What happened?"

I shook my head and muttered, "I'm sorry. I forgot. I have no excuse. I just blew it. I'm so sorry."

To their credit, the bride and groom were gracious and forgiving. But I have never really forgiven myself. It's still embarrassing.[2]

In the article I went on to say that I learned a lot from that experience. I turned over my calendar to my secretary rather than trying to handle all my appointments myself, and I reordered my life so that I wouldn't be as likely to run out of margins.

But one of the most valuable lessons I learned from that experience was that our elders were willing to forgive. They didn't chastise me or threaten to fire me if it happened again. They helped me delegate responsibility, supported me in spite of my failures, encouraged me, and forgave me. No leader is perfect, and a good leader learns to forgive occasional blunders.

My sons get along much better today than they did as teenagers. There's one big reason: *maturity*. It's a joy to see your family mature, to get to the point where they enjoy being with one another, laughing together, and loving each other. As we mature in Christ, we should become more harmonious, not more contentious. A divisive, dogmatic spirit is not a mark of maturity but of immaturity. The Bible says that *peace* is a fruit of the Spirit (Gal. 5:22). If it grieves the Father when we fight, it must bring joy to his heart when we maintain harmony in the church.

❖ Why Should Every Member Be a Minister?

❖ How to Involve as Many Members as Possible

7

PARTICIPATION:
Expect the Congregation to Participate in Every Ministry

Three or four times a year, our high-school ministry puts on a giant program for the high-school students so that they can have a place to come for good, clean fun and an opportunity to introduce their unchurched friends to the youth group. The youth ministry's goal for such an event is to "create common ground." Todd Clark, our senior-high youth minister, told us, "We see common ground as a place where a student feels comfortable and we can maintain our integrity." On December 31, 1999, the ministry threw a giant party in the youth and activities center. More than one thousand high-school kids showed up.

It took the youth ministry six weeks to plan for the party and three days to set up for it. When the kids arrived they were given the red-carpet treatment. There was a huge red carpet (thirty-two by twenty-five feet!) outside the door. Two sets of bleachers lined the sides of the carpet, and a thirty-foot truss of lights glared down on the entryway. Volunteers were taking pictures of the kids as they walked in, and two wooden statues made to look like paparazzis were equipped with cameras that constantly flashed.

Inside were dozens of entertainment opportunities: games in the gym, video games in a couple of the classrooms, a picture booth, an electric bronco, and a karaoke room. In the main auditorium, three live bands shared the platform throughout the evening, a pizza buffet was offered, and all the kids gathered at midnight for a balloon drop. Then as soon as midnight sounded, they began "the first worship service of the new millennium." For thirty minutes, a thousand kids stayed in that auditorium and sang praises to God.

To pull off that event, they had to be organized, and they were dependent on scores of volunteers. Todd Clark knew that if they didn't have at least seventy-five volunteers, they would have to shut the doors at a certain number of kids and turn the rest away. Not wanting to turn anyone away, they worked hard to recruit enough volunteers. They sent out letters and made phone calls. More than one hundred Southeast members volunteered to help, and the event was a success.

If you read the chapter on excellence, you know how successful the youth ministry has been at doing things with excellence and winning young people to Christ. If they weren't willing to work hard to recruit volunteers, and if the members of Southeast didn't see themselves as an integral part of each ministry, there is no way the youth ministry could have that kind of impact.

Few things are more exciting than to see hundreds of people willingly give of their time and energy to see that the church's ministry continues. Few things are more frustrating than to be burdened with the majority of the work of ministry yourself. When I was the pastor of a small church, I did everything. I opened the door on Sunday morning, turned on the lights, filled the baptistry, washed the baptismal robes, picked up the hymnals, printed and folded the bulletin, preached Sunday morning and Sunday night, taught a Sunday-school class and a Wednesday night Bible study, led the youth group, attended class functions, was an ex-officio member of every committee, coached the softball team, and drove the church bus! When I would hear about large churches, I would think, *That minister must be more talented or have more time and energy than I do. How does he drive all those church buses?*

WHY SHOULD EVERY MEMBER BE A MINISTER?

One of the keys to advancing the gospel is for the church to be made up of individuals who consider it their task to do the work of the ministry, rather than having a congregation of people who expect the paid staff to minister to them. According to the New Testament, the purpose of church leadership is not to do all the work of the church, but to equip the church to minister to one another. Paul wrote, "It was he who gave some to be apostles, some to be prophets, some to be evangelists, and some to be pastors and teachers, *to prepare God's people for works of service*, so that the body of Christ may be built up" (Eph. 4:11–12, author's emphasis). It's the task of the leaders to train God's people for ministry.

Under the Old Testament Law, the Jews understood that there were certain things that only the priest could do. Only the priests could offer certain sacrifices and perform certain rituals. And only the High Priest could enter the Holy of Holies. But at Jesus' death the veil of the Temple was torn, symbolizing that all worshipers may now enter into the very presence of God. No longer is there to be a distinction between clergy and laity. All God's people are to be ministers; we are all priests. The New Testament says, "You also, like living stones, are being built into a spiritual house to be a holy priesthood, offering spiritual sacrifices acceptable to God through Jesus Christ.... You are a chosen people, a royal priesthood, a holy nation, a people belonging to God, that you may declare the praises of him who called you out of darkness into his wonderful light" (1 Pet. 2:5, 9).

John added that Jesus Christ "loves us and has freed us from our sins by his blood, and has made us to be a kingdom and priests to serve his God and Father" (Rev. 1:5–6). The purpose of each Christian is to be a priest—to serve God.

Involvement Maximizes Your Church's Potential

In a small church, the preacher and a handful of volunteers usually do most of the work themselves, and they directly oversee the rest of it. The leaders are often exhausted and near the point of burnout. If you don't learn to motivate others effectively and to hand the responsibility to them, you might be able to oversee as many as two hundred people. That's why many churches never grow beyond 150 or two hundred people.

Before I was hired at Southeast, the church went for more than a year without any paid staff at all. During that year they still had a weekly church paper, a weekly bulletin, and the normal weekly activities. They initiated a fund-raiser and conducted a groundbreaking service for their new building. The church even grew in attendance during that year! From the beginning of the church, the members have been involved in ministry.

When I saw the church as a pyramid, with one person at the top meeting everyone's needs and doing all the work, my vision was limited. I couldn't see how one guy could do it all. I was right—one person *can't* do it all. When you have that style of ministry, your pyramid can only grow so large.

But now I see the church as a circle where we minister to each other. Inside the circle is a series of smaller circles, each one representing a different ministry. You grow the church not by adding people to the bottom of the pyramid and forcing the top guy to minister to more people, but by adding more circles of ministry inside the encompassing circle of your church.

When our church was small, I visited every member who was in the hospital. I loved to hear people say to me, "Bob, you were really good to me when I was in the hospital. I'll never forget it." Now I seldom go to the hospital. When I do, it's usually because a staff member or church leader is ill. At Southeast, that group alone numbers about four hundred people. The only time I visit other members is when they are near death's door. I joke with our members, "You don't want to see me coming when you're in the hospital. That's not usually good news."

Now when I see people in the hall, they'll say, "Hey, I was in the hospital recently for about a week." I'll cringe, afraid they're going to criticize me for not coming to visit them. But then they'll say, "The church was really good to me."

Which is better—for a member to say, "Bob, you were really good to me," or "Bob, the church was really good to me"? When the church becomes a circle instead of a pyramid, Christ gets the glory instead of the guy at the top of the pyramid.

I went on a mission trip to India a couple of years ago. When I returned, Ann Holdaway, one of our members, wrote me this note:

> It is very obvious that you have been an example to Southeast leaders to follow Christ. You have trained and nurtured a legacy of leaders (Christ-followers) who also will train a legacy of leaders.... And the church goes on. You were greatly missed while you were away in India, but the leaders you entrusted for our care stepped up to bat and made a home run. You should be very proud of them.

As a church begins to grow, there's a temptation to hire more staff to do the work of ministry. But this practice runs the risk of reducing the congregation to an audience. The ministers assume that if they make it as easy as possible for the new members, then the church will continue to grow. But if that happens, it actually has a negative effect. If the members of the congregation begin to sense that they are not needed, then growth will be stifled.

Thom Rainer, after studying hundreds of churches, wrote a book called *High Expectations*. He discovered that one of the secrets in healthy churches that were successfully assimilating new members was that it expected *more* out of its members, not less. He wrote:

> Repeatedly we heard about effective assimilation methodologies that worked only if the ministries carried with them high expectations of those involved. Such is the primary conclusion and thesis of this study. *Effective assimilation churches have one primary characteristic that sets them apart from churches that do not keep their members in active involvement. Effective assimilation churches had high expectations of all of their members.*[1]

Involvement Enhances Each Person's Spiritual Growth

Dwight Day had been in a dysfunctional church in his youth. The leaders had disillusioned him by their exploitation of the people. He had lost his faith altogether and hadn't been in a church for years. But he came to Southeast, found the Lord again, and found peace as well. I walked into the sanctuary one day and saw Dwight scrubbing grape-juice stains off the pews. Dwight is a pilot for United Parcel Service and makes enough money that he could hire someone to come in and do that job for him if he wanted. But he volunteers to come in regularly to clean communion stains.

"I can't thank you enough for doing this!" I said.

"After what this church has done for me," Dwight replied, "it's the least I can do. It's a privilege." This sophisticated pilot wasn't too important to clean the pews.

Nothing helps you grow as a Christian like service. If you want to be stretched, visit a nursing home, teach a class of six-year-olds, go on a short-term mission trip, or volunteer to do a humbling job like cleaning stains in the sanctuary. If your church is not providing opportunities for your members to serve, you are stifling their spiritual growth.

At Southeast we've made a concerted effort to involve volunteers in every facet of the work of the church so that people can continue to grow and stretch. Staff people are hired primarily to recruit, train, and empower members of the congregation to do the work of ministry. That's why less than 40 percent of our budget is spent on staff—a much smaller percentage than most churches. Not only do you stretch your members by involving them in ministry, you save the church money too!

When one of our staff is working too hard, I've observed that it's often because they're doing too much of the work and not recruiting enough help. I'll say, "I'm glad you're working hard, but we didn't hire you to do that. We hired you to train others to do that job."

When someone suggests that their ministry is overburdened and we should consider hiring more staff, the first question we ask is, "Have you explored all the volunteer options?" We're not against hiring more staff, but we want to continue to make every effort to get the members involved in serving at every level of ministry, because one of the best ways to see each member grow in Christ is to get them exercising their spiritual gifts and serving Christ. That's probably one of the reasons that in a recent survey over 98 percent of our members said they had grown spiritually since becoming a part of Southeast.

How to Involve as Many Members as Possible

There's no perfect formula for getting your members involved in ministry. Even though our church has more than thirty-five hundred volunteers—more than one thousand in the children's ministry alone—I still believe we could do even better in this area. We have room to improve. But we've learned a lot about volunteer recruitment over the years, and here are some suggestions from what we've learned.

Offer a Spiritual Gifts Class

Paul said, "We have different gifts, according to the grace given us." He went on to list some of those gifts and how we should use them: "If a man's gift is prophesying, let him use it in proportion to his faith. If it is serving, let him serve; if it is teaching, let him teach; if it is encouraging, let him encourage; if it is contributing to the needs of others, let him give generously; if it is leadership, let him govern diligently; if it is showing mercy, let him do it cheerfully" (Rom. 12:6–8).

Remind your people that they grow not only through learning the Word of God and fellowship with others, but also by using their spiritual gifts. Rick Warren, pastor of Saddleback Community Church and author of *The Purpose Driven Church*, says, "God gave me a gift, not for me but for you, and God gave you a gift, not for you but for me. If you don't use your gift, you're depriving me; if I don't use my gift, I'm robbing you."

We have a four-hour course we offer several times a year, taught by our new-member minister, Les Hughes, called "Discovering Your Spiritual Gifts." Not only does Les discuss the spiritual gifts as listed in the New Testament, he also has class members take a personality profile, write about their spiritual journey, answer questions about their spiritual passion, and take a test to discover their own spiritual gifts.

There are two natural reasons to involve people in their area of giftedness.

The ministry will be more effective. Whom would you rather have teaching your five-year-old—the person who loves kids and has the spiritual gift of teaching or the person who begrudgingly agreed to do it because someone laid a guilt trip on him? Whom would you rather have taking care of the grounds at your church—the person who loves gardening and has a green thumb or someone like me with no such talent? Would you rather have as your song leader the only person brave enough to get up there or the person who is gifted at music? Your church is going to be much more effective at ministering to people and saving the lost if the members are involved in areas of service that match their spiritual giftedness.

The chance for burnout is greatly reduced. People who are working in the area of their gifts and passions are going to be more successful and enjoy their work more. They're much less likely to get burned out. When we are doing a task we hate, we get easily tired, count the days until it's over, and are relieved when we can quit. When we are doing a task we love, we're energized, the time flies by, and we hate to see it end.

Bill Weedman has been preaching for our children's worship for years. Bill is a police officer and a karate instructor. He's a tough guy. (We don't have many discipline problems in children's church!) But he loves the kids, and the kids love him. He works hard on the sermons he delivers to the children, and he's effective. Often when a child wants to be baptized, he'll ask Bill to do the baptism. Once, when I was getting ready to baptize a man, Bill Weedman was going to baptize a child in the same service. In the baptismal changing room, Bill removed his coat, revealing a gun in its holster. The eyes of the man I was getting ready to baptize widened as he stared at that gun. Bill quipped, "We have a no back-out policy about baptisms here!"

Why do you think Bill Weedman has been so effective at preaching to the young people, and why has he kept doing it for years? Because he's gifted to do it, and he has a passion for it. Train your people to minister in the area of their giftedness.

Have an Annual Volunteer Recruitment Event

Every June we spend two or three weeks building up to a Volunteer Recruitment Day. In our church paper we reprint the Spiritual Gifts Test that Les Hughes offers in his class. We also list and describe dozens of service opportunities. In the weeks leading up to the special day, we preach sermons on the topic of service. On Recruitment Day we have a special prayer time, after which we encourage everyone to fill out a card for a one-year service commitment. Every ministry is then responsible for contacting, enlisting, and training the volunteers throughout the summer to get ready for the fall kickoff. This approach has several obvious benefits.

1. People realize the need. When every ministry is recruiting at the same time, it's easy to see how many different people are needed to enable the church to carry out its ministries effectively. I've heard people in other churches lament that 80 percent of the work is done by 20 percent of the people and that "We're all overworked and overburdened. We do all the work ourselves." When each ministry need is presented at the same time, it's easy to see how many volunteers are needed, and people are more likely to respond to the need.

2. *Volunteers can choose the ministry that best utilizes their gifts.* When they see all the areas of service opportunities at one time, they can more easily choose a ministry suited to their gifts. A potential volunteer who can see all the options is then less likely to sign up for the youth ministry only to discover they were better suited for the welcome center.

3. *Volunteers are more likely to commit to a one-year task.* Church leaders often make the mistake of recruiting someone for a challenging task and then expecting them to perform it indefinitely. The minister gets up and says, "Sally Smith has resigned as our fourth-grade teacher after fifteen years of faithful service. We desperately need a fourth-grade teacher by next week. Will someone please volunteer?" Everyone hearing the announcement is thinking, *Fifteen years of teaching fourth grade! No way!* But if you say, "I need someone to make a one-year commitment to the fourth-graders," then someone is much more likely to volunteer—ideally someone who has taken the Spiritual Gifts Test and scored high on *teaching* and *wisdom*!

Even the volunteers at Southeast who have been doing the same task for years are asked to recommit each year. Then they know they're still needed and feel more appreciated. They're less likely to feel taken for granted if they know they can release themselves from the responsibility at the end of the year.

4. *The entire congregation gets involved.* An annual recruitment drive unites the congregation in an effort to accomplish something, much like a fund drive or attendance drive. Also the information about each department reaches the entire congregation. A grandmother who

seldom pays attention to what is happening in the nursery because she no longer has children there may suddenly be made aware of a need for nursery workers and willingly volunteer. Or a new member with a background in technology may learn of a need in the publications department and be happy to serve.

Offer Different Levels of Responsibility

Not everyone is qualified to teach a class, coach a ball team, or sing in the choir. But almost everyone can clean stains off the pews. Make sure there are a variety of responsibilities and different commitment levels available from which volunteers can choose. The person who is a new member with little knowledge of the church needs some opportunities to serve. And so does the person who just became a part of your church after moving from another state where he was an elder and Sunday-school teacher. But they don't want the same opportunities. They need to serve where they can be successful and where their gifts can best be utilized.

In almost every department there are different levels of opportunities. Eugene DePorter, our activities minister, says that in his department there are some positions that anybody can fill, such as concession-stand workers, ball-field groundskeepers, or equipment cleaners. Then there are other positions for which they must recruit skilled volunteers, such as people to lead weightroom orientation meetings or coaches of basketball and soccer teams.

Recruit Qualified People for Leadership

For the first few years that our activities ministry ran its own basketball league, they asked for volunteers to coach the teams. The volunteers were often unqualified and uncommitted. Eugene DePorter told us, "We were getting coaches that shouldn't be coaching. We made the mistake of first signing up the kids, then going after the coaches. We would look and see that we had x number of kids. That meant we needed y number of teams, so we asked for y number of volunteers to coach. We didn't have y number of quality coaches, so the league suffered."

Finally they reevaluated their purpose. "Let's decide what our objectives are," they told each other. From that came a set of goals and objectives just for the activities ministry. The goals included things like "Introducing others to the church," "Introducing others to Christ," and "Providing a friendly competition in a Christian environment." Eugene said that almost overnight their ministry went from being program driven to being ministry driven.

They then attempted to recruit people to be coaches who not only had some knowledge of the sport but also understood the objectives of the league and would work to accomplish those goals. Once they determined how many coaches they could recruit, that dictated how many teams they would have. After every slot was filled, they shut down registration and politely told people they'd have to wait till next season. They had fewer teams for the next few years, but the league was much better and it grew from there.

Some positions take a certain skill level and personality that require a little extra effort to find. The temptation is to do the job yourself or hand it over to the first person who volunteers. It takes more work in the beginning to find a qualified volunteer and train him to do the task, but it's an investment of time that will reap huge dividends later.

I know of a church where one preacher served faithfully and effectively for years. The church was growing and doing well. But after the preacher resigned to take another position, the chairman of the board stood before the congregation and asked, "Is there anyone who wants to volunteer to be on the pulpit committee to find the next minister?" Because of his unwise decision, several unqualified people volunteered for the committee, and they made a poor choice for the next minister. That congregation has suffered ever since. Some tasks are too important to leave to the first person who volunteers.

Release the Responsibility

Once a qualified person is in place, the key to successfully delegating the task is to *delegate the responsibility*. After you've explained the task and trained the volunteers effectively, let them go. Do not hover over them to make sure they perform it just the way you want. A quality volunteer will often do the job *better* than you would have done it, if you give him complete responsibility.

Our drama team is currently run entirely by volunteers. They report to the worship ministry, but they have very little oversight. The volunteer leader organizes the entire ministry. They write their own skits, plan their own practices, and make their own arrangements for costuming and sets. They do an excellent job because they own the ministry themselves.

When reliable volunteers oversee a ministry, the volunteers are often more forceful as leaders than the staff people are. They take ownership of that ministry, and they have less to lose than the paid staff does. They accept fewer excuses and are more confrontational. They'll say to an irresponsible worker, "Hey, you signed up for this. Are you going to do it? We expect you to be here. That's what this church is all about—faithful service."

It's often difficult for ministers and staff to release responsibility and allow volunteers to take the lead. We're conditioned to do it ourselves, and we get ego boosts from performing certain tasks. We're not sure others will do it as well. But a leader who wants to increase his effectiveness must learn how to work himself out of certain tasks—even the most important ones.

The senior minister sets the tone for successful delegation in the way he delegates to his staff. I don't hover over the staff. I set the agenda, they know what I expect from them, and then I release them to do the task. For example, the worship team is responsible for the first half-hour of the worship service. They choose the choruses we will sing, the testimonies to be delivered, the order of the service, whether or not there will be a drama. More than 90 percent of the time, I'm not involved at all in that first half-hour. I often walk into the service at the beginning and have only a vague idea of what will happen leading up to my sermon. I trust the people who are in charge. I know they will be more creative and intense if they own their program. If they're constantly trying to please me, I'll stifle them. I want them operating out of their own passion for ministry and desire to please the Lord, not out of fear of my response. They know, however, that if they don't use their freedom responsibly, I'm not afraid to confront them.

I have the same relationship with those in the activities ministry. I don't visit the church gym very often. I'm a big supporter of Eugene DePorter, our activities minister, and I think he does an outstanding job. I disagree with a few things they do. (I've always wished they would add lights to the softball fields.) But Eugene contends that playing under the lights means playing too late in the evening, and those late games separate families. When the dads are playing softball in the early evening, the wives and children come out, too, and there's a family atmosphere around the stands and playground area. But if the games are late at night, the dads are coming out by themselves and leaving mom and kids at home alone. Eugene decided that a better investment of funds would be to add another field. Then more games could be played at the same times in the evenings and all day Saturday, when our popular Little League baseball games are held.

You know, Eugene may be right about that decision. I'm glad I didn't campaign for lights on the fields, because he probably would have given in to my wishes, and it wouldn't have been the best decision. I've learned to make concessions in such situations because often the minister in charge of that department has more knowledge about the situation and has thought through the issues more than I imagine. I also want Eugene's heart and soul to be in that ministry, and that won't happen if he always has to be concerned about what I think and whether I'll agree with his decisions.

Occasionally I'll get a letter from a church member saying something like, "I was denied the right to coach a young boys' ball team. I think I was treated unfairly. Will you please intervene?" Or, "I tried out for a solo part and was denied the right to sing. I've sung professionally for years. Is there something they're not telling me? Will you please talk to the people in your worship ministry?" Almost never do I step into that situation. I have to stand by the decisions that the leaders under me have made, or I'll be taking back responsibilities I've delegated to them, and they'll feel undermined. So I've learned to say, "I trust that leader, and if he thinks you shouldn't sing, I'm sure he's got a good reason."

Encourage the Workers

Keep your volunteers and staff members motivated by genuine encouragement. Everyone loves to be encouraged—that's why we have cheerleaders at sporting events. I played basketball in high school for the Conneaut Valley Indians. Before the beginning of every ball game, our cheerleaders would run out to the middle of the floor and sit Indian-style in a circle. They would begin pounding on the floor in rhythm and start this cheer:

> Boom,boom,boom,boom,
> Boom,boom,boom,boom,
> Send them to their
> Doom, doom, doom, doom!

Nothing would fire us up like that cheer! Everybody needs to be motivated sometimes, and a good leader knows how to be a cheerleader for his workers.

Talk about them positively. One of the ways I encourage our volunteers is by mentioning them frequently in sermons (and books!) as positive examples of people using their gifts to glorify God. You can also write encouraging notes, give them a pat on the back, mention them in your church newsletter, or brag about them in staff meetings.

An excellent opportunity for encouragement comes when you introduce one of your workers to others. If I'm giving someone a tour of our building, I'll run into several staff members and volunteers. I'll try to remember to say things like, "This is Nita Johnson; she's invaluable in this library. This is Linda Brandon; we run a tight ship in our nursery because of Linda's organizational skills. This is Larry Taylor; he's a faithful volunteer in our facilities ministry—I think he's here at the church building more than I am!"

Be sure your encouragement is genuine. Four qualifiers will make your encouragement genuine and effective.

1. *Encouragement needs to be specific, not general.* When I say, "Greg, you did a nice job leading the worship service today," that's helpful. But it's better to say, "I could tell you worked hard to prepare that transition into communion. When you said, 'This is a safe place,' I could hear a pin drop." When your encouragement is specific, it motivates your team member to excellence and encourages future effort.

2. *Encouragement needs to be honest, not flattering.* If you don't mean it, don't say it. Once when I was the guest speaker at a church, I was talking with the worship leader afterward when the young woman who had sung the special before my sermon walked by. The worship leader said to her, "Great song!" After she walked away, he turned to me and said, "She wasn't very good. I don't think we'll ask her to sing again." Naturally, when he said to me, "Really good message tonight," I wasn't encouraged! People are perceptive, and eventually they'll figure out whether you are encouraging them or flattering them.

3. *Encouragement needs to be occasional, not incessant.* I know what it's like to have the same person tell me every week, "Good sermon." After a while it doesn't mean anything. Proverbs 25:16 says, "If you find honey, eat just enough—too much of it, and you will vomit." Many people don't encourage enough, but too much encouragement can make you nauseous.

4. *Encouragement needs to be balanced with occasional correction.* If

people know that you will tell them the truth when they need to be corrected, then your encouragement means a lot more to them. Paul told Timothy, "Preach the Word;... *correct, rebuke* and *encourage*—with great patience and careful instruction" (2 Tim. 4:2, author's emphasis). A good leader does both—rebukes and encourages. The encourager shouldn't be just a Pollyanna cheerleader.

John Foster, chairman of our board of elders, is an excellent encourager. One of the reasons I like his encouragement is that he's not afraid to correct me on occasion. On a recent Saturday night, I used the slang phrase "shacked up" to talk about two people who were living together without the benefit of marriage. John came to me and said, "That phrase doesn't sound like Bob Russell to me." He didn't think it was very dignified for me to say "shacked up." So I changed it. I had no problem receiving that criticism because John also encourages me often. And when I know John will occasionally correct me, his encouragement is more genuine and means more to me.

Prepare them properly. Another way to encourage your workers is to make sure they receive proper training. Any worker can easily become discouraged if no one takes the time to tell her exactly what's expected of her or leaves her unprepared. If you're a supervisor or ministry leader, be sure to communicate with your workers regularly about your expectations. And give them the proper tools to do their jobs effectively.

Almost every evening the activities center is opened to members and their guests. We built a first-class facility, equipped with basketball courts, racquetball courts, and weightroom facilities, so we could create a healthy environment for relationship building and good, clean fun. (I'm convinced that people get to know each other more naturally as a by-product of playing sports together or participating in a common activity than if they meet for the specific purpose of relationship building.)

The activities center is run in the evenings mostly by volunteers. Eugene DePorter has learned that volunteers get frustrated if they feel unprepared, so he prepares them for the kinds of questions they will be asked while running the center. He said people will call or come into the building asking a myriad of questions about different activities, some of which aren't even in the center, but the main building. So Eugene prepares the volunteers by giving them a list of every activity the church has for that day. Then when someone comes into the activities center looking for a support group, the volunteer can give them specific directions. Or when the neighborhood fast-food restaurant calls (this happened recently) to ask why so many people are flooding their restaurant, the volunteer can explain that it's the week of the Christmas program and mention exactly when the program will be ending each night so the restaurant can be prepared.

Eugene also provides for the volunteers a three-ring binder, equipped with tabs on every activity their ministry offers. When someone who has come to play basketball asks when the softball leagues begin, the volunteer can find the answer. Nobody likes to be asked a question he can't answer. But imagine how encouraged those volunteers are when they feel prepared to answer all those questions!

In their training sessions, Eugene will say to the new volunteers, "Here's your information notebook. There will be one available at all times. I am confident that every question you are ever asked will be answered in this book. But if I'm wrong and you get a question you can't answer, let me know, and I'll add it to the book later." The volunteers are encouraged because they've gained confidence that Eugene is not going to leave them unprepared.

Eugene told us that some volunteer positions are given a written job description. Then volunteers know exactly what is expected of them. The job description will list the assigned tasks, tell the volunteers when they are to be on duty, and remind them that they are committing to a one-year service.

My son Rusty and his wife volunteered this year to help serve in the nursery. Shortly after Christmas they received the following letter from the children's department reminding them of their commitment for the second semester in the "ARK" program:

> Dear ARK Volunteers,
>
> Happy New Year to all of you! As we look ahead to 2000, I want you to know I'm looking forward to a great year of working together in the ARK!
>
> Enclosed you will find the schedule for January. Check your schedule carefully! If you have any questions about it, please talk to your coordinator or call me here at the church.
>
> As of this mailing, the lesson books for the upcoming weeks have not arrived. Enclosed you will find "the plan" for January 5, and I will let you know when the books come in. Sorry about the inconvenience!
>
> This past year over 265 children between the ages of 6 and 11 have been baptized. Many of these children have grown up in our children's programs. Some might have had you for a teacher in the past. And someday the little ones you teach right now will have an opportunity to accept Jesus, too. Thanks for planting seeds in their lives now!
>
> In Him,
>
> Diane Mansfield

The letter contained not only the schedule for the semester, but also a detailed schedule of the first week's activities and the lesson plan for the week. That letter was a great example of how to encourage and prepare your volunteers. Things never work perfectly, and Diane had to explain that her plan hadn't worked out the way she hoped with the lesson books. But she went the extra mile to make sure the volunteers were still prepared for the first week, and she took the time to explain in detail why they should feel encouraged.

Reward them generously. You can't give volunteers a raise, but you can do creative things to reward them. Brett DeYoung, the administrator who oversees many of our education and children's ministries, encourages his leaders to reward their volunteers regularly with creative thank-you notes. On any given week a volunteer is likely to get a note with a roll of mints attached that says, "You're a breath of fresh air! Thanks for volunteering!" or a roll of Lifesavers with a note that says, "You're a real lifesaver for volunteering!" or some other creative reminder that they're appreciated.[2]

Several of our ministries throw a volunteer appreciation banquet at the end of every year for all their volunteers. They budget generously for it and make it as elegant as possible. The volunteers and their spouses are invited to a sit-down dinner in the fellowship hall, which will be decorated like a first-class banquet room. The volunteers come with their spouses and sit down to a catered dinner, with glass plates, real silverware, and *cloth napkins!* Sometimes there might be a few minutes of entertainment or creative encouragement at our appreciation banquets. Our guests are impressed that someone took the extra time and money to treat them to a nice dinner in appreciation of their year of service.

The volunteer teachers in the fourth-and-fifth-grade department were treated to a banquet recently. When they arrived, each of them received at their place settings a gift binder containing fifteen or twenty letters of encouragement. Then several fourth- and fifth-graders filed by the microphone, each one speaking directly to their teacher sitting in the audience about how much they appreciated that teacher.

But most often the banquets are just for the purpose of fellowship and encouragement. Our volunteers save us thousands of dollars each year. It's a wise investment to spend a few hundred dollars making sure they know they're appreciated.

People assume that a church that is growing as fast as ours must be "a mile wide and an inch deep." But I've discovered that the larger our church has grown, the more dependent it has become on every member to grow spiritually so that they in turn can do the work of the ministry. It's exciting to see nearly four thousand people involved in ministry. And I'm convinced that the ministry is done more effectively by those volunteers than when it was all done by the paid staff.

Recently Wayne Nally, who had been a member of Southeast for only two months, was admitted to the emergency room of a local hospital. He was seriously ill and nearly died. But he survived three operations and spent four days on a respirator. Later, in tears, he told me how people from the church came in streams to visit him—quietly, not intrusively, just praying for his healing. While he was in intensive care between operations, someone slipped in and placed on his nightstand a note that he read when he regained consciousness. It said, "Good morning. This is God. You take the day off and rest. This is in my hands. I love you." The other side of the note indicated that "Carol B." had stopped by.

Wayne said to me, "I realized that while I was brushing with death's door, my church took the time to plead my case when I wasn't able. My church had the foresight and the kindness to pray." Three weeks after the surgery, Wayne said to his wife, Lou, "I want to go to church and find out who 'Carol B.' is. I want to thank her for that note and her prayer." Wayne told me about some others who visited him. The church ministered as the church should; and as Wayne said, "If our church can continue to do that, what an unstoppable force it's going to be!"

If your church is going to reach its maximum potential and be an "unstoppable force" for Jesus Christ, then all its members must begin to see themselves as ministers and priests, doing their part to see that the work of the ministry is done.

- ❖ Stronger Than Our Diversity

- ❖ The Need for Fellowship

- ❖ Three Circles of Fellowship

- ❖ Create Atmospheres for Relationship Building

- ❖ Minister to the Hurting

8

FELLOWSHIP:
Continually Practice Agape Love
for One Another

In 1997 Chris Brodfuehrer and Andrew Nelson, sons of two of our staff members, were killed in an automobile accident. An estimated two thousand people stopped by the Highlands Funeral Home during the visitation hours. Many stood in line for hours just to express sympathy to the families. David, a young man from Poland who was serving a yearlong internship on our staff, waited for almost two hours in line to give his condolences. But when he got to Andrew's mother, Jacque Baumgardner, David was so overwhelmed with sorrow and sympathy that he couldn't say anything. So he got back in line a second time and waited another two hours to say what he wanted to say.

The outpouring of love on those two families has been overwhelming. More than two thousand people also attended the funeral. The families received more cards and flowers than they could count. Though our church is very large and most of our members didn't know the families well, when such a tragedy causes two families to grieve so deeply, the entire church grieves together.

Chris and Andrew were both active in our youth ministry, and their deaths had a significant impact on the high-school kids at Southeast. Several of them gathered together over the days after the accident, grieving together. They attempted to comfort each other and reached out in love to the parents of the two boys. Chris was a talented musician who loved to play the guitar. A few days after his death, several students with whom he had played music were playing a melody he had written when words to the melody began to come to them. A beautiful song came out of that grief. "Don't cry for me," they sang, as if singing from Chris's perspective.

> Don't cry, don't mourn for me
> I am here in eternity
> Don't cry, don't mourn for me
> I'm with the Father and I'm waiting for you to join me
> I'm home, I am home.[1]

Jim Burgen and the rest of the Southeast youth ministry staff wisely and compassionately ministered to the youth during that time, and more than fifty young people were baptized in the few months that followed.

In a healthy church, the love that flows from the heavenly Father and through his children is deeper, richer, faster, and more authentic than that which is found anywhere else in the world. Anne Ortlund, in her book *Up With Worship*, says that the average church is too much like a bag of marbles—we scratch against each other and make a little noise, but we really don't affect each other much. She says the church should be more like a bag of grapes that mesh together, producing a sweet-tasting wine because of the interaction.[2]

STRONGER THAN OUR DIVERSITY

Despite the diversity among God's people, they enjoy the richest fellowship imaginable because it is based on a common commitment to

Jesus Christ. It's possible to have good fellowship outside the church—through family relationships, athletics, business, or military service—but the most meaningful fellowship is available in the church because of our mutual dedication to Christ. John wrote:

> We proclaim to you what we have seen and heard, so that you also may have fellowship with us. And our fellowship is with the Father and with his Son, Jesus Christ. We write this to make our joy complete.
>
> This is the message we have heard from him and declare to you: God is light; in him there is no darkness at all. If we claim to have fellowship with him yet walk in the darkness, we lie and do not live by the truth. But if we walk in the light, as he is in the light, we have fellowship with one another, and the blood of Jesus, his Son, purifies us from all sin. (1 John 1:3–7)

There is a common goal among believers—to glorify Christ and to spend eternity with him someday. There's a common lifestyle—"if we walk in the light…we have fellowship." There's a common sacrifice—we've given up time, money, and some pleasures of the world for something we agree is greater. There are common values, common world-views, common habits, and traditions that bind us together.

The twelve apostles were a diverse group. Simon the Zealot was a patriot—a kind of redneck who hated the Roman government. Matthew was a tax collector—a collaborator with Rome. That would be like Rush Limbaugh and Ted Kennedy serving on the same committee! They'd about slit each other's throat! But Jesus united them. Thomas and Peter were opposites too. Peter was impulsive, a sanguine personality, quick to believe, and often fickle. Thomas was melancholy, a thinker, slow to respond but deeply committed. All these personalities must have occasionally unnerved each other. But they were united by a cause bigger than their own egos and personalities—the deity of Jesus Christ.

Jesus united that diverse group of disciples by motivating them to sacrifice their egos in service to each other. Once when they were bickering about who was the most important team member, Jesus called them together and said, "You know that the rulers of the Gentiles lord it over them, and their high officials exercise authority over them. Not so with you. Instead, whoever wants to become great among you must be your servant, and whoever wants to be first must be your slave—just as the Son of Man did not come to be served, but to serve, and to give his life as a ransom for many" (Matt. 20:25–28).

The twelve apostles form a kind of microcosm of the church. In the church we enjoy fellowship in spite of our diversity. At Southeast we have old and young, wealthy and poor, healthy and disabled, Democrats and Republicans, black and white, baby Christians and mature believers. Sometimes there is little in common except the high calling of Jesus Christ. But that is enough.

Jesus insisted that the outstanding characteristic of his followers should be their love for one another. "A new command I give you," he said. "Love one another. As I have loved you, so you must love one another" (John 13:34). Jesus didn't want his followers claiming loyalty to him while bickering and competing with each other. He intended his church to be a closely knit family where people genuinely care for each other despite their different backgrounds.

Christian Schwarz, after studying a thousand churches covering six continents, listed "loving relationships" as one of the necessary qualities for a growing church. He wrote:

> Some years ago, when we published materials to help individuals, groups, and entire churches learn how to express Christian love, some specialists said that these were not "church growth materials." Yet our research indicates that there is a highly significant relationship between the ability of a church to demonstrate love and its long-term growth potential. Growing churches possess on average a measurably higher "love quotient" than stagnant or declining ones....
>
> Unfeigned, practical love has a divinely generated mag-

netic power far more effective than evangelistic programs which depend almost entirely on verbal communication. People do not want to hear us talk about love, they want to experience how Christian love really works.[3]

The early church was distinguished by its fellowship:

> They devoted themselves to the apostles' teaching and to the fellowship, to the breaking of bread and to prayer. Everyone was filled with awe, and many wonders and miraculous signs were done by the apostles. All the believers were together and had everything in common. Selling their possessions and goods, they gave to anyone as he had need. Every day they continued to meet together in the temple courts. They broke bread in their homes and ate together with glad and sincere hearts, praising God and enjoying the favor of all the people. And the Lord added to their number daily those who were being saved. (Acts 2:42–47)

The church exploded in growth because the people loved being together. When you get a group of people together who genuinely believe something and who really enjoy each other, it's such a contagious atmosphere that you can't keep people away from it. People assume that smaller churches must have better fellowship and stronger relationships because everybody knows everybody. But churches that genuinely love one another don't stay small very long.

If you want your church to grow—if you want to attract people to Jesus Christ and to your church—then learn how to love one another.

THE NEED FOR FELLOWSHIP

Christian fellowship satisfies our intense need for love. Clara Null, a young single mother from Oklahoma City, described what she called one of the worst days of her life. She said,

> The washing machine broke down, the telephone kept ringing, my head ached, and the mail carrier brought a bill I had no

money to pay. Almost to the breaking point, I lifted my one-year-old into his highchair, leaned my head against the tray and began to cry. Without a word my son took his pacifier out of his mouth and stuck it into mine.[4]

Today we have a record number of single adults in America. Vance Packard calls America "a nation of strangers." As a result we're experiencing an epidemic of loneliness in our society. A Gallup poll showed four in ten Americans admitted to frequent feelings of intense loneliness. Americans are in fact the loneliest people in the world. There are so many people, and so little personal concern. People feel that they're just a number. In Dave Stone's book *I'd Rather See a Sermon*, he wrote:

> As times have changed, so have people. In *Time* magazine, Robert Wright said, "These days, thanks to electric garage-door openers, you can drive straight into your house, never risking contact with a neighbor." He's right. We used to build a front porch with a swing, now we build a back deck with a privacy fence.[5]

Your church is to be a contrast to that coldness. The church should be a place where we genuinely care for each other. Jesus said, "A new command I give you: Love one another. As I have loved you, so you must love one another. By this all men will know that you are my disciples, if you love one another" (John 13:34–35).

I hear people claim they don't need the church. Years ago there was a saying, "Christianity—yes, but 'churchianity'—no." The December 23, 1999, issue of *USA Today* carried the following headline: "In Search of Faith: For many, self-defined 'spirituality' is replacing a church-based faith." The article reported on a Gallup poll survey that found:

> For many people, God has been detached from "religion." Where once a community of believers shared a common vocabulary, many feel free to define God by their own lights. The survey finds a largely Christian nation partaking of the

feasts of faith—its challenge, inspiration and comfort—a la carte. Denominational lines are blurring and church-free "spirituality" is on the rise.[6]

One man said, "I can go on a forty-mile bike ride and get as much from it as I can from going to church." Another admitted that he was turned off to his childhood churches by "the hypocrisy of organized religion. I have deep moral beliefs about what is right and wrong. I try to live my life (with integrity). I don't feel that I need to belong to any organized religion to do that."

A psychologist claiming to be a Zen Buddhist bragged, "People say they want ABC (anything but church)." I'm not sure that's the majority opinion, but there's certainly a significant number of people who believe they can get spirituality without being part of a church.

But the Bible refers to the Church as the Body of Christ. How can you love Christ and yet hate his Body? Yes, it is possible to be saved without having fellowship with others. A prisoner in solitary confinement or a missionary just entering the mission field may have little or no contact with other believers. But that's not the ideal. God knows it's not good for man to be alone, and he has provided companionship for his people.

To say, "I don't need the church," is to completely miss the purpose of the church. You need the fellowship of other believers to grow and to be held accountable, and other Christians need you. Paul said, "The eye cannot say to the hand, 'I don't need you!' And the head cannot say to the feet, 'I don't need you!' " (1 Cor. 12:21). The Lord hasn't given you the option to say, "I believe in Jesus, but I don't want anything to do with the church." When you attach yourself to the head, that makes you a part of the body. The body may have scars, blemishes, inadequacies, and maybe even paralysis. But you can't have life apart from the body.

The New Testament is replete with "fellowship" commands, revealing in detail how we are to love one another. Consider many of the "one-another" commands:

- Be devoted to one another in brotherly love. Honor one another above yourselves (Rom. 12:10).

- Live in harmony with one another (Rom. 12:16).

- Accept one another (Rom. 15:7).

- Instruct one another (Rom. 15:14).

- Greet one another with a holy kiss (Rom. 16:16).

- Agree with one another (1 Cor. 1:10).

- Serve one another in love (Gal. 5:13).

- Be patient, bearing with one another in love (Eph. 4:2).

- Be kind and compassionate to one another, forgiving each other (Eph. 4:32).

- Speak to one another with psalms, hymns and spiritual songs (Eph. 5:19).

- Submit to one another out of reverence for Christ (Eph. 5:21).

- Bear with each other and forgive whatever grievances you may have against one another (Col. 3:13).

- Teach and admonish one another with all wisdom (Col. 3:16).

- Encourage one another and build each other up (1 Thess. 5:11).

- Live in peace with each other (1 Thess. 5:13).

- Try to be kind to each other and to everyone else (1 Thess. 5:15).

- Spur one another on toward love and good deeds (Heb. 10:24).

- Confess your sins to each other and pray for each other (James 5:16).

- Love one another deeply, from the heart (1 Pet. 1:22).

- Live in harmony with one another (1 Pet. 3:8).

- Offer hospitality to one another (1 Pet. 4:9).

- Clothe yourselves with humility toward one another (1 Pet. 5:5).

How are we to obey those commands unless we regularly fellowship with one another and build relationships with each other? The world can be a discouraging place. You can get the impression that everybody's cheating, everybody's doing drugs, everybody's greedy. You can begin to think you're all alone, that there's no one left in the world who believes like you do. No one disciplines their children, no one abstains from immorality, nobody gives their money away. But when you have fellowship with Christians, you realize you're not alone. It's a boost to your spirit if every week you see hundreds of people who share your values and are trying to walk in the light.

Remember when Elijah was so discouraged that he wished that the Lord would just take his life? One of the reasons Elijah was despondent was that he thought he was all alone. He told God, "I have been very zealous for the LORD God Almighty. The Israelites have rejected your covenant, broken down your altars, and put your prophets to death with the sword. I am the only one left, and now they are trying to kill me too" (1 Kings 19:14).

God came to Elijah and gave him hope. Besides ministering to his physical needs and giving him a new task, God reminded him that he really wasn't alone. The Lord told Elijah, "I reserve seven thousand in Israel—all whose knees have not bowed down to Baal and all whose mouths have not kissed him" (v. 18). There were seven thousand people still left who were on Elijah's side! With that news, Elijah felt renewed and returned to his duties.

For ten years I taught a Masters of Ministry class at Kentucky Christian College for preachers who've been on the field. They would come to KCC once a quarter for a week of training to try to enhance their ministry. I always invited my friend Wayne Smith to come one afternoon during the course and talk about preaching. Wayne is the dearly loved preacher who recently retired from Southland Christian Church in Lexington, Kentucky. He has a great sense of humor, a contagious laugh, and a wonderful ability to encourage people.

Usually Wayne would encourage us with his laughter and funny stories. But one year when he came, he was really discouraged because his elders had recently confronted him about his preaching. They had taken him aside and told him that his sermons had grown a little too shallow and repetitive and that he needed to deepen them. It just crushed him. He told the preaching class, "I don't feel like being here today."

He started telling them what had happened, and this man who was a mentor to many of those in the room broke down and cried. The mood was solemn as we tried to encourage the one who had been so encouraging to us. I thought to myself, *Well, this is going to be a real downer for these preachers.* But at the end of the week, almost all the evaluations had Wayne Smith's visit as the highlight of the week, with many writing specifically that "The highlight of the week was when Wayne Smith came and encouraged us."

Encouraged us? Those preachers were encouraged that day because they witnessed a man they respected, who preached in a church with thousands of people, dealing with criticisms and rough times just like they did. They witnessed a man who hungered for fellowship just like they did. And they had the opportunity to minister to him as he had so often ministered to them.

The Bible talks about bearing one another's burdens. There's a love that happens in the fellowship of the church that doesn't happen often in other circles, because we are willing to confess our faults and our problems to one another.

THREE CIRCLES OF FELLOWSHIP

The followers of God need the fellowship of other believers.

Therefore, it becomes the duty of the church to create as much opportunity for fellowship and relationship building as possible.

Most of us have three different levels of relationships: *acquaintances* (people we recognize and greet in public); *friends* (people whose names we know and with whom we have spent quality time); and *companions* (people who are very close to us—family members, spouses, and intimate friends). Most people have scores, maybe even hundreds, of acquaintances; we have fewer friends, and only a handful of companions over the course of a lifetime. But all three levels of relationships are important. And those three levels mirror the three circles of fellowship that should be available in the church.

Congregation

Few things are more exciting and encouraging than gathering with a large number of like-minded people for an agreed-upon cause. That's true in the secular world as well as the church. When I attend a University of Louisville basketball game, I'm hoping the arena is packed with twenty thousand loyal fans. When every seat is filled and everyone is excited about being there, the game is even more fun.

My son Rusty traveled to Washington, D.C., a couple of years ago when Promise Keepers had their rally in the nation's capital. One million Christian men gathered to worship God and pray together. Everyone who was there talks about how inspiring it was to see so many Christians gathered in one place. With a touch of humor, Rusty said, "One of the most inspiring moments for me was when I peeked during one of the prayers and saw nothing but men's backsides—as far as I could see—because hundreds of thousands of men had knelt together with their faces to the ground to pray for the healing of their homes and their nation."

In the congregational setting, people can be encouraged, inspired ("spurred on," as the Hebrew writer commanded), and taught God's Word. When we attend revivals or conventions, we hope there is a packed house, with hundreds of worshipers and eager hearers of the gospel message. You can imagine how encouraging it is every weekend to see fourteen thousand people gather together for worship at our church, or three thousand gather in our midweek service.

But if this is the only type of fellowship people have, they're being robbed of the deep relationships God intended us to have in the church.

Class

This is a group, usually between twenty and two hundred, that gathers for the purpose of study and ministry. It might be a Sunday-school class, a weeknight Bible Study, or a special elective series.

Many churches have dismissed the need for this middle circle, claiming that they only need the congregation and small groups for proper ministry. But that may be a mistake. Thom Rainer, in his book *High Expectations*, revealed the results of his study of retention factors among almost three hundred churches. He determined that the most effective way of closing the back door and assimilating people was the old fashioned Sunday-school method. He said, "Let it be said with clarity and emphasis that no single methodology was as effective in closing the back door.... Sunday school is the most effective assimilation methodology in evangelistic churches today."[7]

Don Cox added, "Many church leaders have helped perpetuate the myth for twenty or so years. The myth is that Sunday School is no longer effective evangelistically or as an assimilation tool. And those who believed the myth are suffering the consequences today."[8]

Dr. Rainer quoted a pastor in California who had concluded the same thing:

> Our church has tried everything to create relationships among the members: small groups, dinner clubs, family ministries, you name it. But we keep coming back to the Sunday School. That's where people get to know one another best. We've

finally gotten smart enough to decide to put our best efforts in relationship building there.[9]

The class level of fellowship provides some important ingredients that can easily be missed if only the large and small circles are present.

A natural first step. This medium-sized group is often a natural first step for people who want to move from the congregation to deeper relationships. Just as it is difficult for you to try to become an intimate companion with someone who only yesterday was merely an acquaintance, so it can sometimes be a challenge to put together a successful small group with people who don't know each other. It can happen, and sometimes it works beautifully, but a certain amount of time must be invested up-front in the relationship building—finding common interests and spending time together outside of the group—if companionship relationships are to be developed. And some people will shy away from such an awkward step. They may, however, be willing to visit a class where twenty to two hundred people are gathered. In the class setting, you can still maintain a certain amount of privacy and anonymity when you first attend, and you can take the time to develop natural friendships.

Objective Bible study. The middle circle provides an important Bible-study environment. The class setting is the only environment where a certain type of objective study of God's Word can be accomplished. In the congregational setting, the depth of Bible study is limited because of the varied backgrounds of the listeners and their inability to interact. (In our culture it is inappropriate and awkward if someone in a congregational setting interrupts the speaker to ask a question. It's especially awkward for the preacher!)

In the cell group (the smallest circle), Bible study is often more subjective and less instructive. The facilitator is likely to be someone who is willing to lead a group discussion, not necessarily someone gifted to teach.

When Jethro encouraged Moses to delegate his responsibility, he told him to find leaders of hundreds, leaders of fifties, and leaders of tens. Some are more gifted to teach than others. The middle circle of the class provides an atmosphere for objective learning under a teacher that is gifted to teach. We need Christians who are grounded in the Word of God and who have been instructed in Christian doctrine.

Opportunities for ministry. Our Adult Bible Fellowship program (our version of adult Sunday school) encompasses almost half of the adult members. We have forty-five ABF classes, ranging in size from fifteen to two hundred. Because of the size of our congregation, we encourage the ABF classes to act as small congregations, small churches within the church. Class members minister to one another—praying for each other, visiting the sick among them, and even caring for financial needs. Many view their ABF teacher as their pastor.

In addition to our ABF classes, we have more than seven hundred women involved in weekday women's Bible studies. Lynn Reece, our director of women's ministries, has done an outstanding job encouraging women to get involved in these weekly Bible studies.

Several years ago Cecil McGee came to me with an idea for a different kind of group at the class level. He said, "I want you to start a Saturday morning men's Bible study. We'll get together for donuts and coffee at 6:30 A.M., and then you teach for an hour starting at seven o'clock."

I thought it was a crazy idea. *Nobody wants to get up at 6:30 on Saturday morning for a Bible study!* I thought. But Cecil was very persistent, so I agreed to try it. I couldn't believe the response! We now have almost five hundred men coming to this weekly Bible study. They come as early as 6:30 for fellowship, and then at seven I teach for an hour. It's an informal setting with a lot of interaction. We laugh a lot together and sometimes cry. One of our guys referred to it as a kind of a Christian stag party. Men invite their friends to come, and some first-timers at the Bible study have never even been to our church.

This class has become another small community, as a class is intended to be. A few months ago we discovered that one of the regular attenders was having some financial troubles. We spontaneously collected an offering for him—over three thousand dollars that day! A class, when it is gathered for in-depth Bible study, often results in genuine Christian fellowship, deeper relationships, and a caring community.

Cell

Although I'm convinced that both of the first two groups are necessary elements of Christian fellowship, if we neglect this third circle, we will miss the most important ingredients of loving one another. The "cell" is a group of twenty people or fewer, where members get to know one another on a deeper, more personal level. The average size of our small groups is fourteen people. In a group this size, it's impossible to maintain much anonymity, and the dynamics demand more interaction and personal involvement of each member. In a small group you get to know each member, and everyone ministers to one another.

I get together every week with eight ministers from our area, and we work on sermons together. A by-product of the group is fellowship. Over the years we have come to know each other well. Many times before we leave, someone will say, "I'm struggling with something in my church right now. Will you pray for me?" We'll listen and then pray together. The next week we'll ask him about his problem and follow the progress. A lot of ministerial associations have attempted to create that kind of fellowship without much success. But we've discovered that the richest, most natural fellowship is often a serendipity of a purposeful activity.

A couple of years ago, I preached a sermon titled "Fellowship Is More Than Coffee." Sometimes we get together for a Sunday-school class, eat a donut, drink some coffee, and say that we've had "fellowship" together. Bill Hybels, in his book *Rediscovering Church*, pictured the typical conversation between two men on the church patio:

"So how's it going at work, Jake?" one of them would ask.

"Fine, Phil. Say, you driving a new pickup?"

"Used," Phil would reply. "What do you have going on this week?"

"Not much."

"Well, great fellowshiping with you, Jake."

"Same here."

Hybels concluded, "But the Bible says true fellowship has the power to revolutionize lives. Masks come off, conversations get deep, hearts get vulnerable, lives are shared, accountability is invited, and tenderness flows. People really do become like brothers and sisters. They shoulder each other's burdens."[10]

We all need that kind of fellowship, but most of us don't want to confess our deepest secrets to two hundred people! That's why the smallest circle is necessary. There should be a sense of authenticity and accountability in all three circles, but the deepest relationships are built in the smallest groups.

Lately our small-groups ministry and our adult-education ministry have been working together to encourage the Adult Bible Fellowship classes to develop small groups within their classes. The most natural way to experience companionship is to first develop a friendship with someone, discover your compatibility and similar interests, and get to know them on a surface level. The most natural place to develop *cell* groups is at the *class* level, where friendships are already beginning to develop.

Southeast has about 250 Home Bible Fellowship groups and about one hundred accountability groups, for a total of more than 350 small groups. We estimate conservatively that about 50 percent of our adults are committed to some kind of group within our church where deeper relationships are being developed. (We want to have an even better percentage than that, so we continue to search for ways to get people plugged into places of community.) The purpose of these groups is to provide a structured way for people to move beyond the "news, weather, and sports" level of relationships. Murphy Belding, our small-groups minister, said to us:

> Think about the one-another passages: love one another, serve one another, honor one another, etc. That's the blueprint for the Christian life. In order to fully live out that blueprint, we've got to know one another. The best place to know one another is inside a small group, in the context of a small group relationship. My purpose as a small-groups minister is to help people form healthy relationships around a Bible study. Relationships that are formed around a Bible study will last forever. When people have spent quality Bible study time together...the Holy Spirit tends to cement those people together. That group becomes not only a Bible study, but also a caring place.

Men in particular benefit from involvement in accountability groups, where they pledge to be transparent with each other and weekly ask one another tough questions about their personal lives. Accountability groups aren't foolproof, and they can be too forced on occasion, but they provide the vehicle to the quickest and deepest kind of fellowship for those who are willing to take the plunge.

CREATE ATMOSPHERES FOR RELATIONSHIP BUILDING

Every church can create new ways to bring members together for relationship building. But I think we can try too hard sometimes. I mentioned earlier some of my concerns that the church not manipulate people. If they feel manipulated or forced into being in a small group or intimate conversation, they will immediately put up walls, and the relationship won't penetrate the surface. For the most part I think it's better to leave relationship building to the two smaller circles.

But there are some ways to create an atmosphere within the church where relationships can begin to be built. You may have ideas that are even better than the ones I've listed here, but here are some things that have worked for us.

Large Atrium

We are now in our third location in twelve years. Each facility has had a nice gymnasium, classrooms, a fellowship hall, and a worship center. The most notable difference in our current building, besides its size, is the large atrium. In order to enter or exit the worship center from the main entrance, you must walk through a huge welcome area that measures over sixteen thousand square feet—comparable to half a football field.

None of our previous buildings had a large enough area in which people could stand and fellowship before or after services. You can hear the buzz of the crowd long before you arrive in the atrium. It's exciting to watch people milling around, running into acquaintances from work or their neighborhood, not knowing they were also members of our church. People can stand and talk without worrying about disturbing a service, being in the way, or hiding from the elements. Had we known what a tremendous advantage the large atrium would be, we would have built our foyers in the first two buildings much larger. If you are in the process of building a new facility, consider building near your main entrance an atrium or foyer much larger than seems necessary, for the purpose of fellowship.

Recreational Opportunities

Some people think that the only excuse for having a recreational ministry is for outreach. If it brings people into the church, then a sports program is beneficial. That is one benefit, but it's not the only benefit. Recreation also provides wonderful opportunities for relationship building within the church.

We've learned through the years that people will join in recreational events like softball leagues and volleyball leagues more quickly than they'll join a Sunday-school class. And when people begin with a common interest, it is easier and more natural for them to develop deeper relationships. I'm more likely to develop a relationship with someone who likes golf, because I love to talk about golf. I'm less likely to find common ground with someone who quilts, because I don't quilt. So our activities ministry has golf outings and quilting classes, where people with each of these interests can find other Christians with that interest.

Our activities ministry does an outstanding job of providing opportunities for people to develop deeper relationships out of those common interests. They have insisted that good sportsmanship be a part of every activity. They've gathered teams for prayer before and after the games and required them to ask if there are any prayer requests. They've carefully selected qualified coaches and team leaders. They've equipped Little League coaches to give a devotional and prayer before every practice. Those little things are creative reminders that we gather for something more important than sports, and they create a better atmosphere for relationship building.

The great thing about recreational events is that they don't force or require intimacy. The main event is playing the sport, and the ministry aspect of relationship building is subtly added. People don't feel manipulated or forced into being more intimate with others than they are ready to be.

Eugene DePorter, our activities minister, loves to share testimonies about people who have come to Christ and developed deeper Christian relationships through the activities ministry. Here are some stories he has shared with us:

> *Deepest Christian friendships.* A family member invited Kenny Parker to come to Southeast. He liked the service, but he was kind of nervous and uncomfortable at the church. In fact, he asked his brother-in-law, "Do you think they would let me come back next Sunday?" But then Kenny got involved in the men's

basketball league, and he started feeling more comfortable at the church. He began developing relationships with Christian men, and he saw the joy and peace people can have when they know Christ; and in 1979, Kenny committed his life to Christ and was baptized. His brother-in-law, Gary Whitenack, claims that Kenny would never have stayed with the church if it hadn't been for the basketball program. Now Kenny has played in the men's basketball league at Southeast for twenty-two years, and he told me it's where he has developed his deepest Christian friendships! Kenny and his wife, Donna, have been very active in the church. They have four kids who have been raised in the church, and each of them has accepted Jesus. You see, this tool called the gymnasium and the relationships developed there have definitely had an eternal impact on this man and his entire family.

Physical exercise leads to spiritual commitment. Several years ago Dorleen Garrett and her husband, Gene, didn't attend church anywhere. But a friend invited Gene to come shoot basketball in our gymnasium for some exercise. He met a few other Southeast members, and they encouraged him to attend a worship service, so he decided to investigate. While Dorleen went to play in her Sunday morning tennis league, Gene would sneak off to church. When Dorleen found out what he was doing, she was shocked. You see, Gene had never been a member of a church in his entire life. Dorleen started attending with Gene. God's Word penetrated her heart, and in 1990, she became a member of the church. (And now she is employed by Southeast in a staff support role!) Two years later Gene made his commitment to Christ and was baptized. This all began with an invitation to shoot basketball in the gym.

From aerobics to missions. Patty Anderson and two other ladies were looking for a good exercise program, and they had heard about the aerobics at Southeast, so they started coming. Several days a week they came to aerobics in our family-life center. They never came in [the sanctuary], nor did they have any intention to. Then Patty got involved in a weight management program we offered called First Place. This required a weekly Bible study, daily prayer, and Scripture memorization. Her life began to change as she started coming into this building for worship services, and on October 1, 1989, she stood in the baptistry, confessed Jesus as her Lord and Savior, and was baptized. Meanwhile her daughter, Shani, had started attending the Senior High Vision program with a friend from school. Patty's husband, Gary, and her three sons loved to play basketball, so she encouraged Gary to play in the men's basketball league, and her boys began participating in the youth league. Eventually Gary started attending our worship services, and God changed his life. In November of 1992, he accepted Christ. One week later their oldest son, Scott, accepted Christ. Shani had accepted Christ after her senior year in high school. [And since then the two other sons have also confessed Christ as Lord.] It all started with Patty attending some aerobics classes. Today the Andersons fulfill leadership positions in the church and have been on short-term mission trips. Shani got so involved in missions that she met and married Daniel Ramirez, a minister from Colombia, South America, and plans to serve as a full-time missionary there with her husband.

A difference in the people here. Steve Parks was invited by his longtime friend Don Rowe to play in our basketball league. After resisting at first, Steve finally consented and began playing. Steve came from a very rough background. In fact, he had never been to any kind of church in his life. He noticed a difference in the people here. Since he was playing in our league, he felt obligated to come to our worship services. He heard the gospel, and it penetrated his heart. A few years ago, as Steve describes it, he walked down the aisle "with weak knees and a nervous stomach" to make a commitment to Christ. If we hadn't had the basketball program, I wonder if Steve would still have never been to church in his life.

As you can see, it can be an easy step from our activities ministry to relationship building and on into deeper involvement. Occasionally we even have cell groups spring from the activities ministry. Guys who meet each other playing basketball decide they need to start an accountability group or Bible study together, and deeper relationships are formed.

Eugene gave us an interesting insight into the benefits of recreation for keeping *men* in the church. He said, "Recreational ministry is especially beneficial to men. A lot of churches have problems recruiting men to be actively involved in their congregations. Recreational ministry has a "glue" effect, keeping men connected to the church. Over a period of time, barriers begin to break down, and they start developing deeper relationships with Christ and other Christians."

Meaningful Activities: Service Projects and Mission Trips

A few years ago we began an annual churchwide program called a "Great Day of Service." In October of 1999, more than a thousand Southeast members spent a Saturday volunteering at forty-four local ministries. We painted rooms, cleaned windows, stuffed envelopes, planted flowers, and served in whatever capacity was needed. Not only do such service projects help to meet the needs of the community and provide great opportunities for witness, they're also great times of fellowship. You feel a kinship with someone who stood beside you painting all day, who planted flowers with you, or who helped you clean windows.

Along a similar line, about five hundred Southeast members went on short-term mission trips in 1999, and we hope that as many as 650 will go in 2000. Short-term mission trips have obvious benefits—they provide encouragement to the missionaries you visit and opportunities to win people to Christ and experience individual spiritual growth. But they also provide great atmospheres for relationship building.

Author and Christian counselor Gary Smalley says that every family should go camping together because deeper relationships are built during times of shared suffering! It's rough while it's happening, but you have shared experiences that build deeper relationships later. The same is true for mission trips. They aren't easy, but the shared experiences often result in deep friendships among those who go on such trips together.

MINISTER TO THE HURTING

The New Testament tells us that Jesus was filled with compassion toward the people, seeing them as "sheep without a shepherd" (Mark 6:34). Paul described God as "the Father of compassion and the God of all comfort" (2 Cor. 1:3), and he commanded the church to express this kind of compassion too:

> Therefore, as God's chosen people, holy and dearly loved, clothe yourselves with compassion, kindness, humility, gentleness and patience. Bear with each other and forgive whatever grievances you may have against one another. Forgive as the Lord forgave you. And over all these virtues put on love, which binds them all together in perfect unity. (Col. 3:12–14)

We live in a world full of hurts, and the church should be a place of healing. Often the pastor tries too hard to be the only one ministering to the hurting when it should be the duty of the entire church. If the church is to be the Body of Christ, then when one member hurts, we all should hurt. Paul said, "The eye cannot say to the hand, 'I don't need you!'" (1 Cor. 12:21). Imagine hitting your thumb with a hammer and your eye saying, "Oh, who cares? I'm not hurting—it's just the hand that hurts. Let's just ignore it!" No way! If you're a healthy person, when you hit your thumb, your whole body will react. Tears will come to your eyes, your stomach will ache, and your knees might even grow weak. When one part of the body hurts, the whole body is affected. The same should be true in the church.

Here are some of the things we have done at Southeast to help people minister to each other's hurts.

Support Groups

When Bill Wilson founded Alcoholics Anonymous, he discovered a need that is deep in the heart of many hurting people. Among other things, he discovered that those who are battling against sinful habits or who are dealing with deep emotional hurts deal best with those hurts if they can surround themselves with others who are fighting and *winning* similar battles. The Bible tells us to "spur one another on toward love and good deeds" (Heb. 10:24). We have more than twenty regularly scheduled support groups that are responding to this exhortation. They include:

- AA (Alcoholics Anonymous)
- Al-Anon (Family members and friends of alcoholics)
- Cancer (Support for those affected by cancer and their families and friends)
- Chronic Pain (Sufferers or friends and family members of sufferers)
- Freedom from Smoking (Accountability and ongoing support for smoking abstinence)
- GA (Gamblers Anonymous)
- Gam-Anon (Family and friends of gamblers)
- Homosexuality (Support for families and friends of homosexuals)
- HOPE (He Offers Peace Everlasting—Support for those battling depression)
- Hopeful Hearts (Support and information for those experiencing infertility)
- Learning Differences (Support for those with children who have learning differences)

- Life After a Death (Grief recovery)

- Love Hunger (Support for those with eating disorders)

- MS Support Group (For multiple sclerosis victims)

- Pilots' Wives (Support and fellowship for wives of pilots)

- Public School Educators (Network and support for teachers)

- Rebuilders (Support for those dealing with divorce)

- Restorative Justice (Support for victims of violent crimes, offenders, and their families)

- Serenity Seekers (12-step group for co-dependency)

- Sugar Babes (Support for those with juvenile diabetes and their families)

- WORTH (Women survivors of rape or abuse)

Ephesians 4:15–16 is a great passage for this ministry. Paul said, "Speaking the truth in love, we will in all things grow up into him who is the Head, that is, Christ. From him the whole body, joined and held together by every supporting ligament, grows and builds itself up in love, as each part does its work."

The goal of support groups is to speak the truth in love. But we also become the body of Christ in those groups—the ligaments, in this case—holding one another together.

Benevolence Ministry

The Bible indicates that we are being hypocritical if we attempt to minister to someone's spiritual needs but are unwilling to minister to their physical needs (Matt. 25:31–46; James 2:16). We receive over a thousand calls a year for some kind of financial help. We are resolved to help every legitimate need we possibly can, but it's not always easy to determine which needs are legitimate. A man who is unwilling to work shouldn't be helped (2 Thess. 3:10), and we don't want to enable some-one to continue making bad choices, so we try to be as discerning as possible about legitimate needs.

Every person who requests help must fill out an application for assistance and then be interviewed by the benevolence committee. Usually about half of those who call will take the time to fill out the application. Last year, 550 people applied for assistance. After review-ing their applications and interviewing them, we decided to help about three hundred of those who applied. The benevolence committee prays with all who interview and gives them a Bible, tracts about how to become a Christian, information about the church, and notices about upcoming financial seminars. The committee never gives out cash, but instead writes checks directly to the creditors. We also have a food pantry on site, gas vouchers available, and gift certificates to a local dis-count store if items are needed like winter coats or shoes.

Only about a third of the people we help are members of Southeast. We asked Tina Bruner, the director of our missions and benevolence ministry, why more people from Southeast don't ask for assistance from the benevolence committee. She said, "Our members often don't want to take money away from what could be going to someone else whom they imagine might be 'more in need' than they are. Also, if they're plugged into the church, then the community they're in—the small group or ABF [Adult Bible Fellowship] class—often ministers to the need of that family or individual."

Pastoral Care

I mentioned in the last chapter that when the church was smaller, I did all the work. I still try to do as much pastoring as I can. I still visit the hospitals, although it's usually only when someone is very ill and facing death. I also try to contact every member who has lost a close relative in death. But as the church has grown, that's become more dif-ficult to do, and I've depended on elders, staff members, and volunteers to help with the pastoring of the flock. I'm convinced they do a better job than I would at many aspects of ministry.

Counseling ministry. We have a counseling ministry in which professional counselors assist people who have deep emotional scars or who are going through a certain crisis in life. Don Delafield, the director of our counseling ministry, reflected on the reasons we started the ministry and why we continue it:

> We started a counseling ministry several years ago for two reasons: First, the ministry staff was overloaded in trying to respond to the pastoral care and counseling needs of the congregation. Much of their time was being spent in pastoral counseling. We wanted to free the time of the ministers so they could focus on their areas of ministry. The second reason was so that we could minister more effectively to the people in need. A number of the concerns the ministers were facing in counseling sessions were in areas they didn't feel properly equipped to deal with. So the counseling ministry was brought on to relieve them and to provide a more specialized type of care.
>
> The goal of the counseling ministry is essentially to help accomplish the third arm of the mission statement—to minister to those in need. We're trying to minister to the deeper needs of people. We try to help people who are going through crisis—maybe family crisis, relationship problems, or some form of grief. We also minister to people who are carrying around baggage from their families of origin, dealing with dysfunction from the past. Basically, we're meeting people who are stuck in their spiritual life, and we're trying to help them get "unstuck" and to be able to grow in their relationship with the Lord.
>
> You don't have to have a very large church to have a wide variety of counseling needs represented. In our leadership conference, when I teach a seminar on counseling, it amazes me how many smaller churches are having to respond to some fairly

major counseling issues—marital breakups, abuse, addiction, and things like that. If you've got a church of just a few families, you've probably got some counseling needs. We believe the church has been called to minister to people, and we believe the counseling role is a way to effectively accomplish a part of that ministry. There's a proverb that says, "The thoughts of a man are like deep waters, but a man of understanding can draw them out."

We have four paid counselors on staff and four volunteer professionals who provide free counseling services to about 250 people a month.

Marriage-mentoring ministry. Don Delafield recently developed a marriage-mentoring ministry in which a Christian couple is matched with a couple going through marital problems. We have thirty mentoring couples right now. Rich Shanks, our pastoral care minister, has also trained almost forty couples to mentor those planning to be married at Southeast.

Paraclete ministry. Because of the number of problems in our culture, the counseling ministry at Southeast has fought for enough time and counselors to meet the needs. We've had times when every counselor was booked and waiting periods were as long as six weeks. Thankfully that has changed, and we are meeting the needs better today. We added some new counselors, and recently Dennis Kaufman, one of our counselors, began what he calls a paraclete ministry. *Paraclete* is a Greek word which means one who "comes alongside." Dennis wanted to find a way for caring, discerning Christian people in our church to help with the counseling load and to be able to use their gifts in the Body of Christ. Dennis told us,

> There's been a re-thinking about the whole "private practice" thing. Christians [in the counseling field] have begun to say, "You know, there's a lot of this counseling that could be done by mature Christians." We need to rediscover that concept.

Allowing mature Christian people who have biblical knowledge and wisdom to do most of the counseling is more consistent with the New Covenant than a lot of what the counseling
world has been chasing after.

The paracletes go through nearly fifty hours of intensive classroom
training, along with reading and writing assignments, over a nine-
month period in order to be a part of the ministry. Then they are
matched up with people seeking counsel, who need a listening ear and
some wise advice, but who don't necessarily have deep emotional scars
that take professional expertise to handle.

Care ministry. Not all who hurt need a counselor. Sometimes they
just need a friend—someone to talk to. I heard about a preacher who
once dialed a wrong number. When he didn't recognize the voice of
the elderly lady who answered, he said, "Oh, I'm sorry—I think I've
dialed the wrong number."

"Wait," she said. "Please, just talk to me for a minute."

There are a lot of hurting and lonely people in your church. In
fact, there's probably a broken heart in every pew. A few years ago we
began a care ministry so that anyone who was hurting could pick up
the phone and talk to someone who would listen to, encourage, and
pray for them. The volunteers in the care ministry have completed
fifty hours of training to prepare them for this ministry. Many of them
have endured hurts of their own and want to minister to others out of
their own experiences. When a hurting person calls who doesn't need
counseling but just needs someone to talk to, they're introduced to a
care-ministry volunteer.

Marlena Woodmansee, who has been a care-ministry trainer for
eight or nine years, summarized the goal of the care ministry:

> When people come into our ministry, it's usually because their
> lives have been through some kind of turmoil or crisis. We
> arrange for a Christian friend to be with them through that

trial. The care-ministry volunteer tries to be "skins" for God, so there's somebody to give them a hug, to walk with them through their trial, and to reveal Christ to them.

Telecare ministry. Because our church is so large, we have to do some creative things to make sure that no one falls through the cracks. We recently began a telecare ministry. Volunteers go line by line through the membership directory, more than five thousand households, and call each one about twice a year. The volunteer says, "I'm representing the telecare ministry from Southeast. We just wanted to know how you're doing and if there is anything we could be praying about for you." They don't talk long, don't ask for anything, and simply give an opportunity for the member to express any concerns. The callers involved with the telecare ministry are convinced that the Holy Spirit has often guided them to the families that needed a phone call. Claudia Tyler, the volunteer director of this ministry, told us about one incident when a lady in the church answered the phone the night that her unmarried daughter announced she was pregnant. The caller happened to be one of the volunteers at our Crisis Pregnancy Center. The mother of the pregnant girl opened up and poured her heart out to the caller because she was willing to listen. The telecare caller was able to minister to her and supply her with a lot of information about the care that her daughter needed and how she could receive some good counseling. Claudia Tyler concluded,

> We don't believe in coincidences. Those are God-incidences. So we say that the Holy Spirit is really involved in this ministry. The timing couldn't be otherwise. So many times we've called when there is a sickness in the family, an accident, a pending divorce, or a death of a family member. We couldn't have known that ahead of time because these calls have been done randomly, so the Holy Spirit has to be involved.

Claudia said that those who are called are often amazed that someone would take the time to call, not for money or to ask them to do a particular job in the church, but to see if there is anything the *church* can do for *them*.

Hospital-visitation ministry. A Southeast member who enters the hospital is visited almost every day, sometimes more than once a day, by a volunteer from the hospital-visitation ministry. Our members tell me that the volunteers do a much better job of ministering to them in the hospital than the paid staff! The volunteers stay and talk, pray with them, and offer to help in various ways. The paid staff often visit out of duty and don't stay long. Our paid ministers are not always great at pastoral care. They've been hired because of gifts they have in other areas. Although we should all minister to the hurting even if we are not gifted to do so, when you are in the hospital, you'd much rather have someone visit you who has the gift of mercy and who wants to be there!

After their son Chris died in 1997, the Brodfuehrers almost immediately began ministering to other parents who lost a child. Out of those visits began an informal support group that meets regularly and ministers to one another. When they learn of the death of a young person, they immediately visit the home of the parents. The members of that group can resonate with them because they've been there.

Randy and Judy Coy had very little church affiliation two years ago when their daughter—a popular cheerleader at Western Kentucky University—was killed in an automobile accident just a couple of months after Chris died. They were devastated. During that tragic time, the people who meant the most to them were the members of the Brodfuehrers's group. The group members were introduced by some mutual friends and visited the Coys right away, even though Randy and Judy weren't active members of our church, and began an ongoing ministry of love to that family. The Coys became a part of the church a few months later and have continued in fellowship with that informal support group.

Two years later, over the Christmas holidays in 1999, the Coys' twenty-year-old son committed suicide. I called on them the next day to try to comfort them. There were six or seven cars in the driveway and on the lawn. There in the living room were those families who had lost children. They spent most of the day just being there and comforting the Coys. They were the people who knew how to minister at a time when the rest of us didn't. The Coy family has now had three children die—their three-day-old baby died several years ago from illness, their daughter died two years ago in an automobile accident, and now their son has committed suicide. I cannot imagine the grief they must be experiencing. Neither can I imagine how anyone could make it through such an experience without the love of Christ as expressed by the members of his Body.

Have you ever seen the giant redwood trees in California? They are hundreds of feet high and so large at the trunk that our family of four, holding hands, couldn't reach all the way around the base of one. You would think that such giant trees must have a massive root system. But compared to other trees, the redwoods don't have many roots, and they don't go very deep. Yet those trees have stood for centuries because the roots of the trees are interwoven with each other. They've stood against the storms because they are literally holding each other up. If your church is to be a place where needs are met, it must have an intricate infrastructure of relationships like those redwoods, where people's lives are interwoven and therefore able to reinforce each other against the storms of life.

- ❖ Spending Too Much on Buildings?

- ❖ Why Preachers Hate to Talk about Money

- ❖ Five Reasons to Preach on Stewardship

- ❖ Some Practical Advice

9

STEWARDSHIP:
Give Generously of God's Resources
as a Church and as Individuals

One morning a local talk show host was using
Southeast Christian Church as his main target
for the day. He was criticizing our huge
expenditure on a new building and asking, "What is
this church doing for the community? Why aren't
they giving that money to the poor?"

The director of a local benevolence ministry who
is not affiliated with our church called the show. "I just
want you to know," he told the host, "that without the
generous support of Southeast Christian Church and
its members, we'd have a hard time doing our job.
They do a lot for this community, and you need to get
off their backs." I wish I could have seen that host's
expression! He moved on to another target.

SPENDING TOO MUCH ON BUILDINGS?

When we decided to spend ninety million dollars
on a new location for the church, a lot of people said
we were spending too much on buildings and that the

229

money should instead be given to the needy. We wrestled over those concerns and prayed to God for guidance. We didn't come lightly to our conclusion to relocate, but we finally reasoned that we were following the leading of the Holy Spirit.

If a church of one thousand people spent nine million dollars on a building, few people would criticize. So why can't a church of ten thousand (which was our membership at the time) spend ninety million dollars? Jewish Hospital in Louisville spends eight to ten million dollars *each year* on capital improvements. Nobody says that money should have been spent on medicine for the sick. The building is necessary for carrying out the mission of the hospital. Our church building is not a monument for people to see; it is a vehicle through which we minister to people and evangelize the lost. Is any cost too high for accomplishing that mission?

People forget that every cause generates its own funds. We didn't have ninety million dollars sitting around and decide to spend it on a building rather than to give it to the needy. People gave sacrificially for the purpose of building a facility that would help reach the lost for Christ. Jesus said, "Man does not live on bread alone, but on every word that comes from the mouth of God" (Matt. 4:4). Our primary purpose is not to give physical food but to provide the bread of life. If we feed hungry people but don't save them from sin, they're still lost for eternity.

But we're also convinced that the sacrificial gift people made toward the new building will do more to help the poor than if Southeast had not continued to grow. In 1999 we gave more than two million dollars to missions. A significant percentage of that money goes to causes that help alleviate suffering in third-world countries where poverty is many times worse than it is anywhere in the United States. In one month we sent five hundred pairs of shoes and 450 bags of clothes to the needy in Ukraine. In another month we had our annual Great Day of Service, when more than a thousand members volunteered to help local ministries.

Additionally, we give thousands of dollars a year to benevolent causes in our local community, and as outlined in the preceding chapter, we help the needy from our food pantry and clothes closet. We also have ABF classes, small groups, youth groups, and families who minister on their own to the poor and needy. Had those people not been transformed by Jesus Christ, it's unlikely they would be so generous with their time and money.

WHY PREACHERS HATE TO TALK ABOUT MONEY

My wife oversees our Living Word tape and radio ministry. Shortly before we moved into our new building, she received a letter from a preacher who was angered because I had preached four straight sermons on money. He wrote, "You better tell Bob he'd better quit preaching on money, or there won't be anyone left to occupy that new building."

The letter exasperated her, so she wrote him back: "Dear Sir: You may be interested in knowing that during the month Bob preached on giving there were 176 responses to the invitation, about double the normal number. Did you know that half of Jesus' parables were about money? Maybe you should preach more on the subject!"

Wise stewardship of God's resources is an important part of a healthy church. We live in a materialistic culture where people are battling daily the god of money. Biblical stewardship and generous giving can transform lives and significantly advance the Kingdom of God. Yet most preachers don't even want to broach the subject of money.

Preachers I know hate to talk about money. A lot of us make sure there's a note in the bulletin that says, "If you are a guest, please feel no obligation to participate in the offering. We want you to enjoy the service." We don't say, "If you're our guest, don't feel like you have to sing and don't feel like the invitation is directed at you." We don't say, "This sermon is on sexual purity. If you're a guest and that makes you feel uncomfortable, there are ear plugs available." Why, then, is money such a sensitive subject?

Reputation of Television Evangelists

Television evangelists have a reputation for exploiting people financially. It is not universally true, but that doesn't matter. The media has so stereotyped televangelists that we want desperately to disassociate ourselves from them.

I heard about a farmer who called the office of a televangelist asking to see "the Head Hog at the trough."

The receptionist said, "Sir, if you're talking about our beloved minister, you may call him Reverend or Pastor, but I don't think it would be proper to refer to him as 'Head Hog at the trough.'"

"Well, all right," the farmer said. "I just sold a few sows and was going to donate ten thousand dollars to the building fund, so I was hoping to catch him."

"Oh, just a minute, sir," the receptionist said. "I think the Big Pig just walked in!"

Since some pastors, especially televangelists, are perceived to be always focusing on money, many preachers go to the opposite extreme of not wanting to talk about money at all.

Fear of Offending People

Sometimes preachers don't want to talk about money because they're afraid of turning off the visitors. They're convinced it's not "seeker sensitive," so they avoid the subject entirely in their sermons and make sure that the offering is downplayed as much as possible.

I've had people say to me, "I worked for months to get my friends to come to church with me, and wouldn't you know the day they came you preached on money! I tried to tell them you don't preach often on money, but they haven't come back." I hate to hear that because I hate to lose anyone. But if they had said, "You preached on the resurrection, and they didn't believe it," or "You preached on disciplining your children, and they disagreed with you," I wouldn't stop speaking the truth.

I got an anonymous letter once following a stewardship sermon. I hate to get anonymous letters. I think they're cowardly and unchristian. (Dwight Moody once got an anonymous letter containing only one word: "Fool." He said many letters have a message and no signature; but that was the first time he had received an anonymous letter with the signature and no message!) The letter I received said, "I came to the church needing comfort. All I heard was more money pressure." He called me a moneygrubber and promised never to return to any church. That hurt, but as I mentioned in an earlier chapter, I've learned to put up with such criticism.

FIVE REASONS TO PREACH ON STEWARDSHIP

I used to brag that I only preached about money once a year. Then when I had my annual stewardship sermon, I'd apologize and bring it up as gently as I could. "I'm sorry," I'd say, "but we need to talk about giving today. If you're a visitor, please don't feel that we are asking you to take responsibility for the giving at this church." But I've changed my mind about how often I should preach on money for these five reasons.

1. God's Word Speaks Often about Stewardship

Paul said, "For I have not hesitated to proclaim to you the whole will of God" (Acts 20:27). I feel led to do the same thing—to preach the whole counsel of God. And the Bible talks a lot about stewardship. *Jesus talked about stewardship more than any other subject.* He talked more about handling your money than he did about heaven, hell, or even loving your neighbor. He knew that "where your treasure is, there your heart will be also" (Matt. 6:21). And as my wife wrote the critic, more than half of Jesus' parables relate to the issue of stewardship.

Brian Sluth, former president of the Christian Stewardship Association, said,

> There are 2,350 passages in the Bible dealing with money and material possessions—more than on any other subject—but it's the least talked-about subject in the church. The church has been silent for so long that people don't understand the responsibilities that undergird a generous lifestyle."[1]

Preaching on money isn't very popular, but it wasn't popular in Jesus' day either. When the rich young ruler came running up to Jesus, the disciples must have been excited. "We could really use this guy. He could bankroll our entire mission! I hope Jesus doesn't say anything about money for a while—it might turn him off!"

But Jesus knew the young man's heart, and he said to him, "Go, sell everything you have and give to the poor, and you will have treasure in heaven. Then come, follow me" (Mark 10:21). The young man left sad, and the disciples must have been disturbed.

It takes courage to speak the truth about money because it is such a god to so many. But we are commissioned to preach the whole counsel of God. Someone said, "It's better to be sobered by the saddest truth than deluded by the merriest lie."

According to Jesus, it is the truth that "no servant can serve two masters. Either he will hate the one and love the other, or he will be devoted to the one and despise the other. You cannot serve both God and Money" (Luke 16:13). If you fail to communicate that truth to people, you are doing them a disservice and failing to preach the "whole will of God."

2. Generosity Transforms People

One of the reasons I'll never quit preaching about money on a regular basis is that I've seen generous giving transform the lives of people.

There's an old illustration about a technique Africans use to capture monkeys. They put a banana in a small-mouthed jar chained to a tree. The monkey will reach in to get the banana, and get his hand stuck in the jar. Because he refuses to let go of the banana, he is captured. He could have easily set himself free if he had just been willing to let go of his prized possession.

When people release their grip on the things of this world, they are so liberated. Shortly after we celebrated our thirty-one-million-dollar commitment, a man approached me with tears in his eyes. He had been only on the fringe of the church for some time, but he got caught up in the campaign and made a six-figure commitment to the church. He embraced me and said, "Did you ever dream that I would be a part of something like this?"

Jesus was right when he said, "Where your treasure is, there will your heart be also." I used to think it was the other way around—if I could just get people to give their heart to Jesus, their treasures would follow. But Jesus knew that for many people, the treasure must come first.

Shortly after our elders approved the launching of a twenty-six-million-dollar capital campaign, Mount Davis said, "The worst thing that could happen to this campaign would be for one person to decide to give the entire twenty-six million." Mount recognized that such a gift would rob a lot of people of the opportunity to participate and experience the joy of giving. All the elders nodded in agreement.

Then Jack Webster, another elder, said, "I move that if one person offers to donate twenty-six million to the building fund...[he paused]...that no one tells Mount Davis!"

Jesus also said that "it is more blessed to give than to receive" (Acts 20:35). He promised, "Give, and it will be given to you. A good measure, pressed down, shaken together and running over, will be poured into your lap. For with the measure you use, it will be measured to you" (Luke 6:38).

Jesus didn't necessarily mean that we would receive back monetary gain if we give to the church. But generosity will result in an overflow of spiritual, emotional, and relational blessings in your life—and God promises to take care of your physical needs too. If we fail to tell Christians about those blessings and motivate them to test God in this (Mal. 3:10), then we rob them of a chance to experience the joys of generous giving.

3. Money Is Often Necessary to Advance the Gospel

In the article in *Kiplinger's Personal Finance Magazine* cited earlier, reporter Sean O'Neill wrote, "Immediately following World War II people gave proportionately more of their income than they do today." O'Neill reported that the average evangelical Christian today gives only 3.5 percent of his income. As a result, the average church has cut back its giving to outreach and missions by more than 50 percent.

Talk show host Dave Ramsey once spoke about how different America would be if all the Christians tithed. He said, "There would be no more welfare in North America. In ninety days there would be no existing church or hospital debts. In the next ninety days, the entire world could be evangelized. There would be prayer in schools, because Christians would buy all the schools!"

Almost every program, almost every plan for communicating the gospel, costs money. How many times have good ideas been turned down and our vision limited because we're worried about how much it costs?

In April of 1999, we had a guest speaker come from out of town for four straight Wednesday nights to talk about Bible prophecy. It was unbelievable. Attendance at our Wednesday night services doubled that month. We had eighteen baptisms, and a spirit of revival swept the congregation. But that month was costly. There were air flights, motel bills, an honorarium, meals, and promotion costs. Without regular, sustained giving, such an event could never have taken place, and we would have missed a golden opportunity to advance the gospel.

I mentioned earlier a program Southeast has for the year 2000 called "2,000 in 2000." Our goal is to involve two thousand church members in missions over the course of the year. That seems simple, but we needed an additional staff member to organize the program and two additional secretaries to handle the enlistments and assignments. They needed computer terminals, office space, salaries and benefits, office supplies, and telephones. If the congregation were not giving regularly and generously, our elders would have never considered such a venture.

I've previously mentioned that our worship department performs an annual Easter pageant. It's a spectacular portrayal of the life of Christ. More than thirty-six thousand people witnessed it in 1999, and we had more than sixty thousand in 2000. It's a great evangelistic outreach, and I would estimate that hundreds, if not thousands, have come to know Christ because of the pageant. But it got to be so costly that a few years ago we had to make a change. We had already been distributing tickets because seating for that many people without reserved tickets is a nightmare. But after much discussion, we decided to charge for tickets. We continued to make them available free to those who cannot afford the fee, but we ask everyone else to purchase their tickets in advance. Some people wondered aloud why we had to charge a fee, but our elders decided it was the most cost-effective way of continuing the pageant.

I once asked our men's Bible study, "What things related to the Easter pageant cost money?"

Somebody called out, "The stage!"

"That's right," I said. "That elaborate stage costs $250,000!"

Someone else said, "The animals!" We have live animals at our pageant—camels, horses, a donkey, sheep, and even a dove that comes and lands on Jesus' shoulder after his baptism.

"That's right," I said. "Those animals don't work for free. They're our only paid actors." Then I added, "There's something else you might not think of. We have five hundred choir members and actors who come every night for more than two weeks of dress rehearsals and performances. They arrive at 5 P.M. and leave at 10:30. What happens between those times?"

"Supper!" someone hollered.

"Yes, if you're going to require them to be there at those times, you need to feed them. How much pizza do you think it takes to feed five hundred people? That gets expensive!"

We listed some other costs like buses, parking security, costumes, makeup, insurance, and special effects. Those men began to see why the church wasn't making money off those ticket sales! Even with the ticket sales, we usually lose money on the Easter pageant, and the church has to cover the loss. But it's worth the expense because of the tremendous outreach it has become. In order to advance the gospel, we have to be willing to discuss money.

4. Generous Giving Is a Positive Testimony

One man who is now an active member of Southeast told us when he first started coming, "I'm not yet sure what I think of your doctrine, but I see what you do for the community and that's what attracted me." Many are afraid that preaching on money is going to turn off the world, and sometimes it does. But sincere efforts to help people overcome their addiction to the stuff of this world will result in attracting people to Jesus Christ, and a congregation of sacrificial givers is a powerful testimony to the community.

After we committed to giving thirty-one million dollars for our new facilities, we still had to borrow an additional twenty-two million. Several bankers in town tried to form a consortium so they could lend us the money, because everyone assumed that no one bank would lend us that kind of money. But then one bank owner, who was not a Christian, contacted me and said, "Bob, I want to be your banker. I want to lend it all." That bank proceeded to lend us the money at the lowest possible interest rate.

The owner joked with me privately, saying, "Bob, how did you raise thirty-one million dollars? I'm Jewish, and I can't raise that kind of money!" That banker was so impressed by the generous giving of our church members (and our financial department's record of integrity) that he was willing to support us even though he doesn't share our faith in Jesus Christ. We were stunned! A financial expert who was on our church finance committee told me, "Bob, this is truly a miracle!"

5. People Need Stewardship Advice

Mike Graham, our stewardship minister, told us,

> One of the reasons people don't give to the church like they should is that they are caught in the grips of debt. They're strapped with a house payment they can't afford, they owe more on two cars than the cars are worth, their credit cards are at the maximum. They feel like a yoke has been strapped to their shoulders and they're constantly carrying this burden. It robs them of the joy of giving and results in guilt and bondage. Biblical teaching on the avoidance of debt and responsible giving will help lift that yoke from their shoulders and give them a new zeal for the Christian life.

That's one of the reasons we offer financial counseling at Southeast. It's also a good reason to preach God's truths about handling money. Solomon's advice in the Proverbs and Jesus' words in the Gospels still apply today—don't trust in riches, don't wear yourself out to get rich, stay out of the slavery of debt, earn your money honestly, spend and save wisely, and give generously. Those are basics that people need to hear again and again because money can be such a trap.

That's why I've changed my mind about preaching on stewardship. People need to hear God's Word clearly spoken. We don't hound people for money (the offering is still a low-key part of our service), and we don't take up many special offerings. But I preach four or five sermons every year on stewardship. Not all of those sermons are on giving. Some are about earning money honestly or spending and saving it wisely. But I make sure that money is a regular topic of my preaching.

We anticipated having some financial strain when we moved into our new building. There are usually costs for which you can't adequately plan—like new furniture and fixtures and higher operation and maintenance costs. But our congregation has given generously, and God has provided. We have experienced a 33 percent increase in giving since the move.

After we had been in the building for three months, we needed to make some major changes in our staff because of the dramatic growth. We went to the elders and said, "We have some good news and some bad news. The bad news is that we need eighty-two more employees. The good news is that we've narrowed that down to twenty-six!" They approved the hiring of an additional twenty-six staff members! We couldn't possibly have done that if people hadn't been giving generously to support the work of the ministry.

Some Practical Advice

Focus on Regular Stewardship, Not Crisis Giving

Most churches make the mistake of only pleading for money when there's a crisis. They think people will respond when they hear about the need. And they might. But if we are manipulating people to respond to a crisis, they often do so reluctantly—the opposite motive for which we should be searching. Paul said, "Each man should give what he has decided in his heart to give, not reluctantly or under compulsion, for God loves a cheerful giver" (2 Cor. 9:7). We want people to give because they have decided in their hearts to give generously, out of love for God and a sense of duty to give back to him some of what he has so generously given to them.

Here are three things we do on a regular basis to keep people focused on stewardship:

1. We preach regularly about giving. As I mentioned, I preach every year, usually in January, a series of sermons on stewardship—how Christians should earn, spend, invest, and give their money.

2. We send out offering envelopes once a month. This is more expensive than asking the members to pick up their offering envelopes at the church building, but it is more likely that the envelopes will be used, and it serves as a gentle monthly reminder to our members of their duty to give.

3. We conduct stewardship seminars and provide financial counseling. We offer budget counseling to people who are struggling with their finances. We offer free seminars on how to write a will, and we encourage people to remember the church in their wills. We've even had an affluent member of our church lead a financial seminar for those who have abundant means to teach them creative ways in which they can help advance the Kingdom of God.

Handle the Money Wisely

Poor money management will have devastating effects on your church's giving. If the people don't trust those who are in charge of the finances, they won't give.

Have proper accountability measures in place. Use checks and balances to ensure that the church's offerings are being counted properly, to avoid the opportunity for someone to embezzle money, and to avoid even the appearance of evil. Make sure that more than one person counts the money, that there's not a hefty petty cash fund that goes unaccounted, and that staff members are kept accountable for the money they spend and are not given preferential treatment.

I have never seen the list of who gives what at Southeast. All the recording of individual gifts is done by two people whose integrity and trustworthiness are without question and who are not in leadership positions. And I don't have special privileges when it comes to the church treasury. I have to endure the same red tape as every other staff member to handle an expenditure.

Prayerfully spend money on the priorities. No church has as much money as it has needs. Every church is forced to make decisions about which expenditures are the most important. Should we repave the parking lot or repaint the sanctuary? Should we give to the local children's home or to the one in Romania? Should we hire a youth minister next or a worship leader? How your leaders make these decisions, and what decisions are ultimately made, sends a powerful message to the congregation.

Financial decisions should always be made with these priorities in mind. And the top priority is the advancement of the gospel. Make the financial decisions based on what is best for the Kingdom of God, not what will receive the least amount of criticism. The congregation will respect such decisions and, in the long run, will give better.

Give a greater percentage of the church offerings to trustworthy missions. Develop a global mind-set. Americans live in the richest nation in the world. Christians in America have an opportunity and responsibility to fund the advancement of the gospel around the world. Get your congregation excited about missions, then promote the fact that the church leaders are committed to giving a higher percentage of the budget to missions. I'm confident you will see your offerings increase.

At a staff retreat in 1993, we were brainstorming about the future. Our church had been stagnant for almost a year, with very little growth, and we were searching for answers. We had always said we would give 10 percent of our budget to missions, but we had fudged on that a little in the last building campaign. We started considering certain items "missions giving" that we hadn't considered missions giving before. I said, "Let's increase our missions giving 1 percent a year until we're giving 15 percent. And let's look for some open doors to relocate."

The staff agreed. We took it back to the elders, and they approved it. We now give 15 percent of our offerings, almost three million dollars annually, to support missions at home and abroad. And it seems the more we give, the more God blesses. We believe that what's true for the individual is true for the church—give and it will be given to you.

Conduct Only Purposeful, Well-Planned Capital Campaigns

We've had several very successful capital campaigns over the years. In 1983, we became one of the first churches in America to raise a million dollars. We raised an additional four hundred thousand dollars just a few years later. Then in 1993, we set a goal to raise over twenty-six million dollars. After we made that decision, we learned it was the largest amount a church had ever set out to raise at that time. But people sacrificed, God answered our prayers, and we raised more than the twenty-six million dollars we needed. Through those experiences I've learned some things about capital campaigns. I'd like to share with you what I believe are seven reasons our campaigns have been successful.

1. Each campaign had a tangible and exciting purpose. I'm convinced that capital campaigns should be rare and only for tangible goals such as building a new education wing, enlarging the sanctuary, or purchasing a facility for a ministry such as a Crisis Pregnancy Center. For which cause would people rather sacrifice—enlarging the sanctuary so more people can be brought to hear the gospel, or paying down the debt? Toward which cause would you rather your money go—buying a Crisis Pregnancy Center or replacing the carpet in the nursery? The debt may need to be paid down, and the carpet may need to be replaced. But a special campaign should be for a cause that generates its own momentum and support.

2. We prayed for God's guidance. Before the elders decided to lead the church into a capital campaign, they bathed the decision in prayer and asked for God's guidance. If we weren't convinced that God was in it, we didn't want to move forward.

3. We hired consultants. We used the services of Resource Services Incorporated when we organized our twenty-six-million-dollar campaign called "Beyond the Open Door." RSI asked me to do three things I didn't want to do. First, they asked me to preach four straight sermons on giving. That was back when I was convinced I should only preach once a year on giving. But after I followed their advice and saw the positive results, I began to change my attitude, and I've been preaching four times a year on stewardship ever since!

4. The leaders set the pace. The second thing RSI asked me to do was to visit twelve major contributors and ask for large gifts. They said we needed five one-million-dollar donations, and I was to do the asking. That made me feel very uncomfortable because I had never done any fund-raising at all. But I did it, and I'm glad I did!

Counting the major donors and the leadership of the church, we raised almost fourteen million dollars in leadership donations! We were able to ask the rest of the congregation to raise the remaining amount. At first we were concerned that they would see the large amount the leadership had pledged and conclude they didn't have to give as much. We reminded them that hundreds of families—about four hundred elders, deacons, staff, major contributors, and their families—had already pledged, so the remainder was squarely on their shoulders. And they responded beautifully!

The third thing RSI asked me to do was to give a personal testimony of what I had decided to give. I protested. I said, "The right hand isn't supposed to know what the left hand is doing." I had prided myself on my humility—I had never known what others were giving and had never bragged about what I was doing with my own finances.

But the guys at RSI responded, "What about the passage in 1 Chronicles [chapter 29] where David announced exactly what he was going to give to the cause in order to inspire the people to give generously?" I wrestled with how I could discreetly announce what I was giving without sounding like I was bragging. Finally I thought of a way to do it. During one of the four messages on stewardship, I said to the congregation, "In the last campaign, I joined with three other leaders in borrowing ten thousand dollars each to give to the church. This campaign is five times larger, so I've decided to give five times as much."

The church needed to know that the leaders, myself included, were 100 percent behind the campaign. When they saw our commitment, exciting things began to happen.

5. We shared testimonies of sacrifice along the way. A single mother stood before the congregation and gave a testimony about her Beyond the Open Door commitment. She said, "I have three teenagers and hardly any money. My husband doesn't support us, and we barely make ends meet. We decided that we couldn't support the campaign but we would pray every day for this campaign to be successful." You could feel the spirit of the congregation move as she shared her powerful testimony.

Then she concluded, "But then one of the kids said, 'Mom, we have cable television.' We all agreed that was something we could sacrifice for the campaign. So for the next three years, we're going to do without cable television so we can give something to the campaign." It was a modern-day version of the widow's two mites. A spirit of revival swept over our church as people began to ask themselves what was really important to them. We began to hear stories of people selling their second homes, delaying retirement, and breaking "alabaster jars."

6. We asked the congregation to pray. We held twenty-four-hour prayer vigils at the church as we asked God to bless our giving efforts. We prayed in people's homes and in our Bible classes, as well as in our worship services, for an outpouring of God's Spirit in the hearts of people through generous giving.

7. We celebrated the victories. In an earlier book, I shared a story that has been told around the country.

Our church has also experienced the joy of giving. We have had four special offerings for new buildings over the past fifteen years, and each time, when the totals are announced, everyone has rejoiced and celebrated. The most dramatic incident occurred about twelve years ago when we came to our congregation just a few months after raising more than a million dollars to build our present building. Because of a rise in construction costs, we were going to need four hundred thousand dollars more than we had originally anticipated to complete the project. We decided to have a special offering, and people again sacrificed. We heard stories of people canceling vacations, taking on extra work, selling boats and sports cars, and postponing retirement so they could give more to the church.

When the total was announced at a Sunday night service, we had raised about three hundred forty thousand dollars, just sixty thousand short of our goal. We rejoiced and celebrated.

But I will never forget what happened next. You must understand that our church is very reserved. People don't speak out from the pews. Ever. The wildest thing that ever happens in our church is spontaneous clapping during an upbeat Southern gospel song. After we applauded the announcement of our total, our song leader was about to start another song when Emory Cockerham, an older gentleman who had never spoken out in our church before, walked up to the song leader. (Remember, *no* one had, and Emory was the least likely one to do so.) "Can I say something?" he asked.

"Well, I guess," our song leader said a bit reluctantly and handed him the microphone.

Emory said, "You know, that was a great offering, but it didn't quite reach the goal. That's not like us. We were so close I think we ought to pass the hat again tonight and see if we can reach the goal."

I headed for the front, preparing to say, "That's a fine idea, but I think we should just rejoice in how God has blessed us, and if you want to give additionally, you can see our building chairman afterward."

But before I could get to the microphone, Jack Coffee, the building chairman, beat me to it. He said, "I think that's a great idea, Emory! We don't have to start making our payments till January 1, so if you want to make pledges tonight, effective January 1, to help us reach that goal, you can do that. Ushers, get the offering plates."

By that time it was too late. I couldn't do anything about it. They passed the plate again and went off to count the second offering. We sang a few more hymns and waited for the announcement.

About fifteen minutes later, the counting crew came back in and announced that we had pledged an additional seventy-five thousand dollars, including sixteen thousand given in cash! I don't know who carries that much money around on Sunday nights, but we've done a lot more Sunday night offerings since then!

When the announcement was made, the congregation exploded from their seats. People were cheering, giving each other high-fives. I saw one of the elders and one of my sons standing on the pew above the crowd with their fists in the air![2]

Emory Cockerham passed away in 1999. He could tell you today better than anyone else that Jesus' words really are true—it's more blessed to give than to receive.

- ❖ The Main Thing

- ❖ Some Qualifiers

- ❖ Practical Suggestions

- ❖ "This Ship Is Going Down!"

Not until we burn
with a passion,
which is almost a
pain, to reach people
with the gospel,
will they be likely
to take the
matter seriously.
—MICHAEL GREEN[1]

10

EVANGELISM:
Commit Enthusiastically to
Evangelism as Your Primary Mission

Liz Curtis was a new radio personality in Louisville in 1981. Before moving to Louisville, she was the "Motor City Mama" in Detroit, billed as "Detroit's number one lady of Rock-n-Roll." Liz confesses that she was anything but a Christian. In fact, her lifestyle involved everything the world had to offer. Liz said, "As a one-sentence summary of how low my values had plummeted, even Howard Stern [the shock jock who hosted a morning show at the same station in Detroit] once shook his head at me and said, 'Liz, you've got to clean up your act!' It wasn't my on-air show that was shocking…it was my lifestyle."

But in Louisville, Liz met Tim and Evelyn Kelly, a sharp young couple who hosted a morning talk show at her new station. The Kellys had recently become Christians and were openly enthusiastic about their relationship with the Lord. They invited Liz to come with them to Southeast. Liz later admitted that as a newcomer to Louisville, she was lonely, and the prospect of going out to eat afterward with Tim and Ev was what really appealed to her!

The first Sunday Liz came, I was preaching through the book of Ephesians. Paul's emphasis on wives submitting to their husbands in chapter 5 happened to be the text for that day. I talked about husbands being the leaders in their homes. Liz admits she struggled with some of the concepts as a single woman. But then I said that husbands are called to be like Christ—to sacrifice for their wives and even lay down their lives for them. Liz leaned over to Ev and jokingly whispered, "If I ever met a man who'd die for me, I'd marry him in a minute!"

Ev whispered back, "Liz, a man has already died for you."

There was something about the excitement of the people and the inspiration of the worship that intrigued her. When the Kellys invited her to attend with them again the next week, she agreed. Soon she met some people who invited her to join the choir. God began to work on her heart, and a couple of months later, Liz stepped out of the choir loft and gave her life to Christ! In her testimony about that event, she writes, "When we closed the service singing, 'I Have Decided to Follow Jesus,' I did just that. Walked right out of the choir loft and down to the baptistry, as the whole alto section gasped: 'We thought she was one of us!' Finally, I was. I was delivered, body and soul, from one location to another—from the gates of Hell to the gates of Heaven."[2]

From that moment, Liz Curtis's life took fascinating turns. She was offered a job on WHAS, the powerful fifty-thousand-watt AM station in Louisville, as their morning personality. She became extremely popular in our community, and she used her status to speak for Jesus Christ as often as possible. Several years later she disclosed to me that she was interested in branching out as a public speaker. We arranged for her to speak at some Christian events: Christian school chapels, mother-daughter banquets, youth groups, and Sunday-school classes. She was hilarious and thought provoking. Soon she was in such demand that she quit her job as a radio personality and joined the National Speakers

Association. Within a few years she became one of the most popular speakers in America and was elected to N.S.A's Speaker Hall of Fame.

Liz married Southeast member Bill Higgs and has two wonderful children. A few years ago she began writing and has authored more than a dozen best-selling books, including *The Pumpkin Patch Parable* and her latest book, *Bad Girls of the Bible and What We Can Learn from Them*.

Liz Curtis Higgs has touched thousands of people for Jesus Christ—all because Tim and Ev Kelly urged her to come and see what they had discovered at Southeast Christian Church.

THE MAIN THING

It's easy for any enterprise to get sidetracked from its main thrust. I ate at a restaurant recently called The Pancake Factory. You know what their luncheon special was that day? Grilled chicken sandwich with spicy Mexican sauce. I was convinced that they had lost their focus.

What's the primary purpose of the church? Jesus said his main mission was "to seek and to save what was lost" (Luke 19:10). He gave his church the same mission just before he left this world when he said, "Therefore go and make disciples of all nations, baptizing them in the name of the Father and of the Son and of the Holy Spirit, and teaching them to obey everything I have commanded you. And surely I am with you always, to the very end of the age" (Matt. 28:19–20).

The church, like that restaurant, can easily get sidetracked and forget its primary mission. Over the years I've been asked to get involved in antidrug, antialcohol, antipornography, antihomosexuality, antiabortion, and antigambling causes. I've occasionally been involved in some of those causes because I believe the church is called to be a conscience in the community, and I'm a citizen in our community. But we are not called *primarily* to stop sin in the world. Our primary call is to preach the gospel and bring people to salvation in Jesus.

The larger our church becomes, the more some people in our community want us to become politically active. We try to tell them that Southeast Christian Church has never been and doesn't intend to become a giant political-action committee attempting to force legislation. We will speak out about moral issues and occasionally encourage our people to become involved in their community as good citizens, but I'm convinced that the best thing that could happen to our community is for revival to break out in our churches.

Satan is more intimidated by a church faithfully preaching Christ crucified than by a thousand demonstrators protesting one facet of the devil's program on the steps of the state capitol. The best way to change the community is to win one soul at a time to Jesus Christ. Besides, better legislation can't save anybody—only Jesus can. The Bible says, "Salvation is found in no one else, for there is no other name under heaven given to men by which we must be saved" (Acts 4:12).

Not only should the church refrain from being a political-action committee, we also are called to be more than just a social agency to care for welfare needs. One of the church's missions should be to minister to people's needs—first to those in your congregation and then to others. But if you feed every hungry mouth in your community without bringing them the bread of life that feeds them for eternity (John 6:35), you haven't fulfilled your mission.

A wise man once gave this practical advice for success in any organization: "The main thing is to keep the main thing the main thing." That's brilliant! Every church needs to remember that the primary mission—the main thing—is evangelism. When we bring people to Jesus Christ, we are bringing them something more important than an improved legal system or a better diet. We're bringing them hope for eternal life.

In Acts 5, when Peter was imprisoned for preaching the gospel, an angel came and released him. The angel didn't say to Peter, "Go now and tell people how corrupt this political system is," or "Go protest in the streets against the Sanhedrin," or "Go feed the poor." The angel said, "Go, stand in the temple courts, and tell the people the full message of this new life" (Acts 5:20). He told Peter to get back to evangelizing the lost. And Peter obeyed. "Day after day, in the temple courts and from house to house, they never stopped teaching and proclaiming the good news that Jesus is the Christ" (Acts 5:42).

Some people hear about how large our church has grown and they say, "Shouldn't you concentrate on building up the people you have there now?" They don't understand that one of the primary ways a person can grow as a Christian is to share the gospel with other people. We want our new people to be evangelists—and they're usually the best evangelists we have!

A young woman who was a new member of our church brought her best friend to our What We Believe class. At the end of the three-week session, she brought her friend to me after class and said, "My friend has some questions for you." Her friend proceeded to ask me some familiar questions in an attempt to challenge the legitimacy of the Christian faith—*Why do good people suffer? What about science and the scientific "proofs" for evolution? What will God do with those who have never heard the gospel?* It was obvious that this woman wasn't quite ready to become a Christian but was raising questions in order to evade her own responsibility. So I suggested a book for her to read that would provide answers to her questions and tried to end the conversation. Then I glanced at the young lady who had brought her, and she had tears in her eyes. She said, "I want her to become a Christian so bad I can just taste it!"

Jesus told a parable about a shepherd with a hundred sheep. That was a large flock in those days. I've read that the average flock was fifteen or twenty. But when the shepherd lost one sheep, he didn't say, "Well, I've got too many sheep anyway. One sheep doesn't matter." Instead, Jesus said of the shepherd,

Does he not leave the ninety-nine in the open country and go after the lost sheep until he finds it? And when he finds it, he joyfully puts it on his shoulders and goes home. Then he calls his friends and neighbors together and says, "Rejoice with me; I have found my lost sheep." I tell you that in the same way there will be more rejoicing in heaven over one sinner who repents than over ninety-nine righteous persons who do not need to repent. (Luke 15:4–7)

People ask us why we keep trying to grow when we have so many members already. "How big do you want to get?" they ask.

We answer, "We don't know how big God wants our church to be, but we'll keep evangelizing until everyone in our area has come to Christ. We're still searching for that one lost sheep—and we'll rejoice when he or she is found."

The highlight of my summer in 1999 came when both of my daughters-in-law announced on the same night that they were expecting a baby—just two weeks apart. We had been praying for Kellie for three years. She and Rusty had been told by the doctors that their son, Charlie, was a miracle child and that hopes for another child were slim. We thought our prayers had gone unanswered. Phil and Lisa were trying to have their first, and for almost a year their prayers, too, had gone unanswered. Then one night we were all eating together, and after the meal Rusty looked at my four-year-old grandson, Charlie, and said, "Charlie, tell Nana and Pop our secret."

Charlie said, "Mommy is going to have a baby!" I knew they had been pursuing adoption and concluded that they must have finalized some plans.

Rusty said, "Tell them where the baby is."

Charlie said, "In Mommy's tummy!" We all squealed, cheered, wept, and rejoiced together.

Then about five minutes later, after everything calmed down, Lisa, who already knew about Kellie's pregnancy but hadn't told any of us about her own, said, "We have a gift we'd like to share with the grand-parents in honor of this occasion." My wife, Judy, reached into the gift bag and pulled out a pair of baby shoes. She looked in the bag and saw a second pair of baby shoes. She said, "Kellie, are you expecting twins?" Then everyone (except me) suddenly realized that Lisa, too, was expecting. There were wild cheers and more embraces and tears and raucous laughter, and I couldn't figure out what was going on! I said, "Is Kellie going to have twins?"

Rusty grabbed me from behind and shook me. "No, Dad, wake up! Lisa is pregnant too!" Then I was overjoyed. I embraced Lisa and laughed and cried. I said, "I'm so thankful—I've been praying for you both every day, and I'm tired of praying!" I didn't realize until later that my son Phil had recorded the whole event on video. There I sat, look-ing like such a doofus while everyone else rejoiced. "Duh, is she going to have twins?"

But you know what I *didn't* say when I realized that both Lisa and Kellie were pregnant? "Hey, I think one is enough. Lisa, it's not appro-priate for you to have a baby at the same time as Kellie. The way Judy spends money on the grandchildren, we'll go broke with three. It's going to be a burden to baby-sit all these kids." No way! I was ecstatic. We rejoiced over the new life. We're happy the family is going to increase—that's part of the reason we exist.

That's why the Christian family, the church, exists too. Jesus said there's more joy in heaven over one new birth than over ninety-nine who are already alive. God, the perfect Father, loves the beginning of new life. The church should too. That's our ongoing mission until Christ returns.

SOME QUALIFIERS

Although evangelism should be your church's priority, let me underscore some qualifiers about evangelism.

Evangelism Should Not Take Precedence over Truth

Noah was an evangelist who saved only eight people. I'm sure he wanted many more to come onto the ark. But he didn't entice them to come by promising a brief cruise or a free ticket to the Ark Zoo. There was a prerequisite to getting on the ark—you had to believe the message and repent of your sin. We can get so desirous of growth that we sacrifice doctrine to make the message more palatable or rely on gimmicks to attract people. We are to go into all the world and make *disciples*, not just add numbers.

Evangelism Is Not the Church's Only Purpose

Evangelism is the church's primary purpose, but it's not the only purpose. Jesus commanded us to make disciples and teach all of his commandments. The church exists to edify Christians and minister to people's needs as well. You shouldn't measure your church's effectiveness totally by the number of new members.

Evangelism Is Not Measured by Comparative Statistics

Jesus said that some seed will fall on hard ground and not grow at all. Other seed will fall on fertile soil—but even the fertile soil will produce different results—some producing thirtyfold, others sixtyfold, and others a hundredfold (see Matt. 13:3–9). Some fields are more receptive than others. Some have more potential than others because of the size of the population or different cultural conditions. I'm convinced that I could take my entire staff and plant a church in certain parts of the country and experience very little growth. I think we'd still grow, and we'd still concentrate on doing the things I mention in this book, but I don't think we'd grow at the same rate.

It's also possible that we could transplant our staff to another location and grow even faster! Some evangelism is local, and some is international. Consider a church in a rural area that has never grown but has sent missionaries all over the world because those who grew up in that church were trained to be evangelists. A church's effectiveness isn't measured in local statistics but in eternal impact.

I'm really proud of my home church in Conneautville, Pennsylvania. My parents helped start the church in that little town of one thousand people. The church began with thirty-five people in 1956. I was in the eighth grade. We met in a house for eight or ten years before we built our first building. That church went through some tough times. One preacher left town with a lot of unpaid bills. My dad, concerned about the church's reputation in the community, borrowed twenty-five hundred dollars from the bank to pay off the preacher's debts and took a second job working in a sawmill to pay off the loan.

Then a few years later, our preacher, Gerald Comp, who was very well-liked and had great credibility in the community, drowned at the annual Sunday-school picnic. The next preacher had two little girls who were killed at a freak accident at the county fair. But the congregation kept going, determined to evangelize in very difficult circumstances.

Slowly the church has grown and has had a tremendous impact in the community. Their present minister, Bill Geiger, has been there for fifteen years. He's an excellent preacher who loves the people in that church. They're now averaging over two hundred people in their two Sunday morning services. They're singing contemporary choruses and having dramatic presentations in their worship services. In March of 1999, I went home to be the dedication speaker for their new gymnasium. It has a full-size basketball court and new kitchen facilities, and it's the talk of the town. On the day I was present, they had 360 in attendance.

You've probably never heard of Bill Geiger or the Conneautville Church of Christ, but in God's economy that church is one of the most effective evangelistic churches around. Not only are they winning an impressive number of souls for that small town, but they've also seen more than forty of their young people attend Bible college to study for ministry and mission work.

My mother is eighty-three years old. Several weeks ago she took a class on personal evangelism offered at her church there in Conneautville. She became convicted that she had not been vocal enough about Christ with some of her neighbors and relatives. (Those closest to us are often the most difficult to approach.) Mom took her Bible and went to the neighbors. They received her well but continued to keep her at a distance when the conversation came to spiritual matters. Refusing to be discouraged, she went again to talk to my Uncle Tom, who has been a spiritual project of my family's for years. Uncle Tom again had a condescending attitude toward any spiritual matters. He even returned unread the Bible in which my mother had underlined several passages for him to read.

But Mom also went to talk with my cousin Deane, a sixty-two-year-old retired schoolteacher, a graduate of Allegheny College, and a very intelligent woman. My mother boldly but gently said to her, "Deane, you need to become a Christian." Deane got tears in her eyes and said, "I know."

When I talked to my mother on the phone several days later, she was elated. "It was a wonderful day in church. There were 240 people in attendance, and Deane Lint was baptized!" My eighty-three-year-old mother has grown up attending church, but she has never lost the passion for evangelism. She's still seeking the lost, still keeping the main thing the main thing.

PRACTICAL SUGGESTIONS

Every culture is different. What works in winning people to Christ in America may or may not work in Zimbabwe or Ireland or India. What works in Louisville, Kentucky, may not work in Indianapolis or New York or Los Angeles or Horse Cave, Kentucky. But we've done some practical things at Southeast that I would be tempted to try almost anywhere. And if a thought mentioned here doesn't help your effort to evangelize in your culture, perhaps it will spark a new idea that *will* work for you.

Preach to the Christians in Your Congregation

Don't just preach evangelistic messages. Some preachers mistakenly believe that if their church is to be evangelistic, then every sermon must be directed toward the few in their congregation who don't yet know Christ. You certainly need to explain the basics of salvation regularly. But the primary thrust of most sermons should be directed toward those who are already Christians.

Growing Christians are more evangelistic than evangelistic sermons. Inspire the members of your congregation—get them on fire for Jesus Christ and excited about growing spiritually in your church—and then they can't help but tell their friends about it. The best evangelism is that which comes as a natural outpouring of believers' excitement about what they've discovered. Like the shepherds who saw the angels and found the baby Jesus, like the healed leper whom Jesus tried to keep quiet, like the two on the road to Emmaus after they discovered who had been their traveling companion, when people have had an encounter with Jesus, they can't help but tell others about it. That kind of evangelism is authentic and contagious. If the preaching is true and applicable to their lives, as I emphasized in chapter 1, and if the worship is inspirational, as I explained in chapter 2, then your people will become great evangelists. If they're inspired, you won't be able to keep them quiet.

Adopt the "Come-and-See" Method of Evangelism

Butch Dabney's son Bob, a longtime Sunday-school teacher in our church, once decided to trace the "spiritual family tree" of one of our members. He asked Major General Dick Chegar, at the time commanding general of the 100th Division and a member of Bob's

Sunday-school class, "Why did you begin coming to Southeast Christian Church?"

General Cheger replied, "My brother-in-law, Jim Hatfield, had been coming and was so enthusiastic that whenever my wife, Carol, and I were in Louisville, we attended."

Bob Dabney then went to Jim Hatfield. "Jim, why did you start coming to Southeast?"

Jim said, "I ran into John Sampson, whom I had known from high school. Johnny was kind of a 'rounder' in high school. His life was so changed that when he invited me to come to Southeast, I decided I had to check it out."

"John Sampson," Bob asked, "Why did you start coming to Southeast?"

"I met a guy named George Fields at the fitness center where I used to work out," John said. "Our kids were the same age, and he started talking about what a good youth program Southeast had, and he invited me to come."

"George Fields, how did you get to Southeast?"

George said, "We were friends with Darrell and Betty Weaver. They were so fired up about the church that when they invited us, we knew we had to come see."

"Darrell and Betty Weaver, what brought you to Southeast?"

"We knew Robert and Mary Helen Vaughn through the real-estate business, and they invited us to come to Southeast," they said.

"Robert and Mary Helen Vaughn, how did you start coming to Southeast?"

Robert explained, "Mary Helen used to teach high school with Sallie Wortham. Sallie's husband, Junior, was singing in a musical group, and she invited us to come hear them sing. We've been coming ever since!"

"Junior Wortham, how did you start coming to Southeast?"

Junior said, "Elizabeth Harvin, one of the teachers at my school, kept bugging me to come visit her church, and I finally did."

"Elizabeth Harvin, what brought you to Southeast?"

Elizabeth Harvin said, "One day I was driving down Hikes Lane. I saw a sign that said 'Southeast Christian Church,' and I just pulled in!"

I guess that's the end of that "family tree"! Everyone in it except Elizabeth came to Southeast because someone was so excited about the church that they naturally invited someone else to come. Imagine how many people wouldn't have come to know Christ, how many children wouldn't have grown up in the church, how many marriages wouldn't have been saved, if Elizabeth Harvin—or anyone else in the chain—hadn't been inspired to invite one friend to "come and see"!

I was once leading a workshop where I talked about why our church was growing. At the end of the class when I asked if there were any questions, one man said, "I see all the great things you're doing, but what about *evangelism?*" After I asked him to explain, I realized he couldn't get beyond his traditional thinking. He was convinced that the only true method of evangelism was door-to-door calling. If we weren't doing that, we weren't really evangelizing.

Maybe you live in an area where Tuesday night visitation still works and your church is winning hundreds of people to Christ. If so, keep it up. But in most of America, door-to-door calling doesn't work. In most areas in our culture, it's no longer acceptable to "stop in" on people—especially if you're a stranger. Americans don't like having unplanned guests, and their time is their most precious commodity; so the last thing they want to do is engage in an hour-long conversation about religion with a total stranger. Also, people in America distrust anyone selling anything door to door. Churches have successfully discovered newer models that work in their culture—from mailing campaigns to neighborhood barbecues. But I'm convinced that the best method today is the word-of-mouth method—what we could call the come-and-see method of evangelism.

As I have mentioned, some of the greatest evangelists in the New Testament were those who simply said, "Come and see." There is no mention of any great sermon by the apostle Andrew. But he is the one who said to Peter, "We've found the Messiah—come and see." When Nathanael asked if any good thing could possibly come out of Nazareth, Philip told Nathanael to "come and see." And the Samaritan woman at the well told everyone in her town to "come and see."

A new Italian subs restaurant recently opened near our church building, and several guys on our staff can't get enough of it. They love to take someone there who's not yet discovered it. When you first find a place like that, you can't help but talk about it. The best restaurants don't have to advertise. If the food is good, the people will come back, and they'll bring their friends. Pretty soon the restaurant will be crowded with people. Yogi Berra once lamented that his favorite restaurant "is always so crowded that nobody goes there anymore"! If you are serving fresh spiritual bread at your church, people will bring their friends.

One of the benefits of the come-and-see method is that hardly ever does one person get the credit for winning someone to Jesus Christ. It's almost always a team effort. Nobody is tempted to brag, "I've won twenty people to Christ this year." Someone might say, "I brought twenty people to my church this year, and ten of them accepted Christ," but he has to acknowledge that the preacher and the worship leader and the Sunday-school teacher and the greeters had something to do with it too.

Paul said, "I planted the seed, Apollos watered it, but God made it grow" (1 Cor. 3:6). When your church adopts the come-and-see method, suddenly every person who has a role in the church has a part in evangelism. The entire church is a body, attempting together to be a place of evangelism. An evangelist is not just a preacher, or even some-one who brings his friend, but any person who has a part in making the church an inspiring place.

Another advantage of the come-and-see method is that it takes no training! Anybody can invite someone to come to church. The evangelists who are most successful in using this method are the new Christians—those who are the most excited about what they've discovered and who have the most contacts with non-Christians! They don't know very much about the Bible yet, they can't explain the steps to salvation, and they can't argue theology. They may not even know what the word *theology* means! But they can invite their friends.

Even those of us who have been Christians for a long time have enough contact with non-Christians to successfully use the come-and-see method. Christian Schwarz, in his book *Natural Church Development*, reported on an extensive study done on the characteristics of healthy churches. He wrote:

> It is particularly interesting to note that Christians in both growing and declining churches have exactly the same number of contacts with non-Christians (an average of 8.5 contacts). Challenging Christians to build *new* friendships with non-Christians is most certainly not a growth principle. The point is rather to use *already existing* relationships as contacts for evangelism. In each of the churches we surveyed—including those that lamented having little or no contact with "the world"—the number of contacts outside the church was already large enough so that there was no need to emphasize developing new relationships with the unchurched.[3]

We do almost no marketing campaigns or advertising in our community. Our primary dynamic is that *90 percent* of our members invited someone to come to church with them in the past year. The most common reason cited among new members as to why they started coming to Southeast was the invitation of a friend. Our most successful form of evangelism, by far, has been the come-and-see method.

Make the Church Experience Inspiring

Make the church experience something for which people will want to return. Do everything you can—short of watering down the gospel—to make it easier for your church members to bring people with them to church. Make a special effort to see that everything is done with excellence (see chapter 5). But do it with a bent toward evangelism. Don't just tell the greeters to be friendly—remind them to be friendly because they are doing it to the glory of God and are a part of the evangelistic process. Don't just ask your facilities people to clean the grounds the best they can—remind them that we're doing everything with excellence so that people want to come back.

One of our staff members, Gary Whitenack, recently attended a Notre Dame football game with his two sons. He talked about what an awesome experience it was. He was impressed with the beauty, the sense of tradition, and the huge crowd, but he was most impressed with the customer service. When he handed his ticket to the ticket taker, she said proudly, "Welcome to Notre Dame." That one statement impressed him. Gary said that it set a mood for everyone entering the gate. You couldn't help but think, *There's something special about this place.*

And it didn't stop there. When Gary went to get something at the concession stand, the attendant said, "Welcome to Notre Dame. May I help you?" When he walked to the top of the aisle, his usher said, "Welcome to Notre Dame, sir. Do you need help finding your seat?" Gary said he did need help. His usher looked at his ticket and told him he was in the wrong section. But instead of giving foggy directions, the young man left his post and *escorted* Gary and his sons to the correct section.

Wow! What a sense of pride and excellence was communicated because those workers took the time to say, "Welcome to Notre Dame," and to go out of their way to serve. You know what we're training our volunteers to say now? You guessed it. Greeters at the door say, "Welcome to Southeast." Attendants behind the counter at the welcome center say, "Welcome to Southeast. May I help you?" Those passing out bulletins are instructed to say, "Welcome to Southeast."

We want everyone who comes to Southeast to have such a positive experience that they want to come back. I was thrilled to hear from Don Waddell, our new-member minister, that in two hundred surveys of new members, almost all of them said that Southeast is "a friendly place." Despite our size, we've successfully created a friendly atmosphere for people when they first arrive. We want the entire experience of the first-timer—from the time he enters the parking lot to the time he leaves—to be surprisingly pleasant, done with excellence, inspiring to his heart, and relevant to his life.

Remind the Members of the Mission

Both the leaders and the congregation need to be constantly reminded of the primary mission of the church. The mission statement of Southeast Christian Church reads like this: *We exist to evangelize the lost, edify the saved, minister to the needs of others, and be a conscience in the community.* In a churchwide survey to which I will allude several times, we discovered that over 90 *percent* of our members understand and agree with the mission statement of the church. That's incredible! Our members know that we exist primarily to evangelize the lost. Everything else comes second. Our people know that mission because we make our mission statement visible and repeat it often. We've even had several sermon series dedicated solely to reinforcing the mission statement of the church.

But I think even more importantly, our people know the mission because our staff and leadership believe in the mission. Before we hire a new staff person, we ask, "Do you agree with the primary mission of this church? We want to continue to grow. Can you reinforce that philosophy?" If they can't agree with that philosophy, they're not hired. It would be really damaging to the morale and mission of the church if a staff member began to communicate that we had grown too big. It's imperative that all staff members agree with the primary mission of the church so that they can communicate that mission effectively to the congregation.

We also encourage every ministry to find ways to implement evangelistic outreach in their department. The activities ministry had a member-guest golf outing this past year. You could only participate if you brought with you someone who was not a member of Southeast. The youth ministry often allows the kids to come to their social events at half price if they'll bring a friend, and it occasionally won't allow them to come at all *unless* they bring a non-member with them.

Not that every event has to be evangelistic. Sometimes it's healthy and necessary to have events that are simply for the purpose of relationship building, deeper study, or discipleship. But we want every ministry to be conscious of ways to reach outsiders, make the guests feel welcome, and evangelize the lost.

Many years ago I read a Herschel Ford book in which he wrote about a tour guide showing a group of people through Westminster Abby. After the guide boasted about the classic architecture, the expensive appointments, and the famous celebrities who had worshiped there, the guide asked, "Are there any questions?"

One plainly dressed, elderly woman said, "Yes, sir. Has anyone been saved here lately?"[4] Our primary mission is not to build beautiful buildings or impress important people but to save the lost.

Remind Them to Invite Their Friends

While Johnny Jordan built a home for a couple moving to Louisville, he said to them, "I want you to come to Southeast with me next Sunday. If you don't like it, I'll buy you a steak dinner." That was a bold invitation! He called me during the week and said, "Listen, Bob, I've got a couple coming this week to visit for the first time. You better be good, or it's going to cost me a steak dinner!" They became an active part of our church!

Remind people to invite their friends and acquaintances to weekly services and special events. When people are growing as Christians and inspired by what is happening in the church, they are naturally going to want to bring others. But we all forget sometimes, or we get lazy and procrastinate. So don't be afraid to remind your congregation about upcoming events or a special sermon series that will provide positive opportunities for the come-and-see method of evangelism.

Unchurched people are more likely to come with you to a special Christmas or Easter program than they are to a regular church service, so we usually make a point to remind our members to invite people to those special programs.

Whenever we start a new series of sermons, we try to remind people of the relevance of the topic to their lives and ask them to bring with them someone who might need to hear the message. For one of our recent sermon series, we printed invitation cards for people to pass along to others. The invitations were postcards with a classy-looking picture and the title of the sermon series on the front side. On the back was a detailed description of the series and some information about service times and directions. We borrowed this idea from some other churches who had discovered that this is a great tool for a person who wants to invite his friend. It's tangible. It can serve as a method for opening up the conversation, and then it's a good reminder for the person who's been invited. We hope the card will go home with the potential visitor and get placed on the refrigerator or sit on the coffee table for a few days as a visible reminder of the special invitation they received.

Be Considerate of the Guests

Be sensitive to the guests, but don't program primarily for them. I'm convinced that the regular church services should be for the purpose of worship. We shouldn't attempt to make them entertaining so that more visitors will come. The believer and the unbeliever both benefit from genuine worship, as we discuss in chapter 3. One of the most powerful methods of evangelism is an authentic worship service, so our programming decisions should be made primarily on the basis of what will help our members worship God, not what will attract more visitors. Yet in 1 Corinthians 14, Paul made it clear that we are to consider the impact that our worship service has on "unbelievers" who might be visiting (see especially vv. 22–33). So make sure your guests feel welcomed and comfortable when they visit your church.

When our church was much smaller, we used to have every first-time visitor fill out a roll-call card and place it in the offering plate. At the end of the service, we would recognize every visitor and have them stand. We stopped doing that, not because we got too large, but because we realized that in our culture most visitors would rather remain anonymous. Now at the end of our service, during the announcement time, we say something like this:

> If you are here for the first time, we want you to know that we're really glad you are here. The ushers have some information about our church and one of our church newspapers that they'd like to give you, if you would just raise your hand as they make their way down the aisle. That's all we're going to ask of you. We want you to know we're glad you're here and that we want you to come back.

We've observed that many visitors won't raise their hands the first time they come. They'll wait and watch what *really* happens to those who raise their hands. Then maybe the second or third time they come, they'll be brave enough to raise their hands.

When someone does raise his hand, he's given a church newspaper, a pamphlet about our church, and a cassette tape. On one side of the tape is a welcome from Dave Stone and me and several choruses that our congregation sings regularly. On the other side is one of my sermons titled "How to Become a Christian."

Our associate preacher, Dave Stone, loves to tell about the time one of our ushers came up to him with a worried look and said, "Hey, Dave, we've got a problem. You know those tapes that we give to first-time visitors? Well, some of the ushers are sneaking in during the week and taking big handfuls of those tapes and *giving them to their friends at work!*"

Dave grinned and said, "Boy, that's a problem! We can't have people giving out that tape on 'How to Become a Christian,' can we?"

The usher picked up on Dave's sarcasm, laughed, and said, "Oh yeah, I guess we'll let them take those tapes!"

We've made several changes to our services over the years in an effort to be sensitive to the many visitors and new believers among us. But instead of watering down the gospel, we've tried to do just the opposite. We take greater pains to make sure the basics of the gospel are clearly explained. We also take more time to explain the purpose of the Lord's Supper, and we're more careful to explain why we baptize. But we haven't stopped serving communion or baptizing in our services because we're convinced that these practices are basic to the purpose of worship. A visitor expects to see you worshiping God and fulfilling your purpose—not catering to his need for entertainment.

For several years even after our church grew quite large, I would stand out in the vestibule after services and greet people, hoping to meet some of the newer members and visitors. But I discovered that often the same two or three people, who had been in the church for years, would stand in line to say hello while the visitors who were reluctant to wait walked by me. So when we moved to our new building, we began offering a guest reception every week. At the end of every service, the person giving announcements tells about the guest reception. (By the way, we limit our announcements to just one or two every week, besides the announcement about first-time visitors and the guest reception. We tell the congregation that the rest of the announcements are in the bulletin and they can get the information they need there.)

When we first started offering the guest reception, our worship leader, Greg Allen, would say, "If you'll go to the fireside room, you can get a chance to meet Bob Russell and Dave Stone." But that sounded too pious and self-serving—"You get to meet these important men." That's not the kind of atmosphere we want to create around the ministers. So we worked on the wording and purposely changed that announcement. Now Greg will say, "For those of you who are visiting, we have a guest reception in the fireside room right after the service...Bob Russell and Dave Stone will be there, along with some of the other ministers, and *they would love to get the chance to meet you*." We don't want our guests to feel manipulated or singled out, but we do want them to know we care about them.

Offer a "What We Believe" Class

People in our culture generally don't want you to come into their home and talk about religion for an hour. But we've discovered that they'll attend a *six-hour class* on our basic beliefs! That's even better! Which person do you think is going to have a better understanding of the gospel? The person who listened to me for an hour in their living room while nervously worrying about what I think of their home or preoccupied with the dessert they're going to offer me later? Or the person who attended a six-hour class complete with a workbook and outlines for future review?

For the last several years, I taught the "What We Believe" class about four times a year. (We've recently changed the format slightly.) We usually had more than three hundred attend. Although the class is not a requirement, we encourage everyone to take it at least once. New members will often come, and even some older members who want to review the basics will attend for the second or third time. But most of those who attend are people who have been coming for a while and are curious about our basic doctrines. They are usually thinking, *All right, I like this church and want to become more involved. But before I go any further, I need to know what they* really *believe.* After this series we always see a leap in responses to the invitation. A great percentage of the class members decide to put their faith in Christ and be baptized.

Have Private Decision Counseling

Every week we still offer an invitation at the end of the message.

Ours is a twofold invitation: for those who want to turn their lives over to Jesus Christ and be baptized or for those who have already done so and want to become members of our church. When someone responds to the invitation at our church, they're taken to a side room where a trained decision counselor asks them about their relationship to Christ and leads them through the plan of salvation.

We have people coming forward in our church who know almost nothing about the Bible, who have never been in church before. About 25 percent of those responding to our invitation have never made any kind of profession of faith in Christ. Most of the rest were not actively involved in another congregation before coming to Southeast. They may have some limited Bible knowledge or some knowledge that has been skewed by their longtime membership in a liberal congregation that doesn't accept the Bible as God's Word.

In that private setting, our decision counselor can lead a person through a basic understanding of the gospel. They usually use an adapted version of the "bridge" illustration.[5] The counselor will ask, "Where are you on this illustration?" From there the decision counselor talks about repentance and baptism. Through that process we can be sure that every person coming to Christ or becoming a member of Southeast has a good grasp of the gospel and really understands what he or she is doing.

Sometimes we discover that a couple coming forward have different last names but the same address. We explain gently but honestly that repentance means a change in lifestyle and that if they are to come to Christ or be members of our church, they need to separate until they get married. Believe it or not, many of those couples will say, "Oh really? All right. We'll do that." End of discussion. They come from a background where they're so ignorant of the gospel that they don't even realize what they're doing is outside the will of God! We preach about marriage and against "live-in" relationships several times a year, but sometimes those people coming forward are so new they either missed those sermons or ignored them at the time. If we were to immediately take their confession of faith in front of the whole congregation like we did in the past, handling those kinds of situations would be extremely awkward.

Our decision counselors report that about 10 percent of those who respond to the invitation decide that they are not ready to make the kind of commitment to Jesus Christ the Bible describes. They just wanted to "join the church." We encourage them to keep attending, and we contact them later to see if they're progressing toward becoming a follower of Jesus, after which they can become members of Southeast.

Many other problems and questions can be handled in a thorough and dignified way through the decision-counseling process. If your church is smaller, the preacher may still be able to act as everyone's decision counselor, and that is great. But as your church grows, you will need to involve more people. Although anyone can invite a friend to "come and see," there will be a select few in your congregation who have the gift of evangelism and who have a passion for leading people to Christ. They would love to be decision counselors. They need to receive thorough training and be accountable to the church leadership, but you may see tremendous benefits in your evangelism outreach as a result.

Have a Decision Day

We've had considerable success with decision days or decision weekends. Every few years, about six weeks in advance, we will begin announcing that the first weekend in January will be a decision weekend. We'll say to the congregation, "We know that some of you have considered making decisions for Christ but have procrastinated for one reason or another. The beginning of a new year would be a wonderful time to make a positive, life-changing decision."

In early December we write letters to those who have been attending for a while or those whose names have been submitted by friends.

In the letter we inform them that the first weekend of the month will be a decision weekend, that many others will be responding to the invitation, and that it might be a good time for them to respond if they have been contemplating a decision. People who have been procrastinating are often willing to set that weekend as a target date and are more likely to respond along with the scores of others who come forward. Some of our most dedicated leaders today say that they first came forward on a decision day.

Be Prepared for the Spirit of God to Move

My son Rusty spent a couple of years right out of Bible college ministering to a small congregation in South Carolina. When he first arrived, he had to have the baptistry cleaned out and filled up because it hadn't been used for so long. He had to insist that plans be made for what they would do should someone respond to the invitation. That little congregation had become so accustomed to having no responses that they didn't even prepare. When people began responding to the invitation and being baptized in that beautiful, clean baptistry, some of the longtime members of the church admitted they had never witnessed an adult being baptized!

When you expect evangelism *not* to happen, it probably won't. And you won't be ready for it even if it happens by accident. You may be in a challenging area where converts are rare or perhaps in an area where almost everyone is already a believer. Praise God! Still, the primary purpose of the church is to evangelize, and as long as there is one lost soul, your church should be prepared for the Spirit of God to move on that lone heart.

"THIS SHIP IS GOING DOWN!"

Let's imagine that you could take a quantum leap in time and that you landed in Southhampton, England, in mid-April, 1912. You see a newspaper headline that reads, "Titanic to set sail on maiden voyage today." What would you do? You would race to the harbor and try to persuade as many people as possible not to get on board. You'd probably have very little success. "What do you mean you know the future? An iceberg? Fifteen hundred people die? Come on! Quit trying to spoil my vacation! Didn't you hear? Even God can't sink this ship!" You'd watch hundreds sail away on the ill-fated vessel, headed toward certain death.

Then what would you do? If you cared about those people, you'd go rent a boat and chase after them. What size boat would you get? Would you go after them with a motor boat that would hold six people or a houseboat that would hold thirty? You'd rent the biggest yacht you could possibly afford. You'd risk everything, knowing that hundreds of lives were in the balance.

If it is true that man's sin has separated him from God for eternity, and if it is true that Jesus is the Son of God who came to this earth to die for sin, and if it is true that only through Christ can we have forgiveness of sin and the hope of eternal life, then the task of bringing people to Jesus Christ is the highest mission of the church. The Bible says that this world with all its pleasures is going to perish. It's going to be destroyed by fire. People whose hopes are in this world are doomed. Our only hope is through Jesus Christ. If we really believe that is true, we're going to do everything we can to persuade as many people as possible to come to Jesus Christ while there is time.

When someone asks me why we built a huge, nine-thousand-seat worship center, I tell them it's because we couldn't afford to build it any bigger! We're trying to get as many people off the sinking ship of this world and into God's yacht as we possibly can.

> For Christ's love compels us, because we are convinced that one died for all, and therefore all died. And he died for all, that those who live should no longer live for themselves but for him who died for them and was raised again. (2 Cor. 5:14–15)

Conclusion

YOUR CHURCH AND THE TEN PRINCIPLES
Where Do We Begin?

Kurt Parker began ministering at the New Hope Christian Church in Memphis, Tennessee, in 1989. At the time, the church had about 150 people. He brought the elders and deacons from his church to our leadership conference at Southeast in 1989, when he first began ministering at New Hope, and has brought a large group from his church to our conference every year since. In the last ten years, the church has grown to more than seven hundred people. They are about to complete a new facility with a sanctuary that will seat twelve hundred and a gymnasium, and they are enthusiastic about what God is doing in their church. Kurt said,

> Initially our leaders were overwhelmed at what they saw at Southeast. But after they came awhile, they concluded, "Hey, those people aren't any smarter or stronger than we are. They just have more faith!" That was the best thing the leadership conference did for

us. We began to believe that God could be God and do any-thing. When our people saw and heard about the modern-day miracles that were happening at Southeast, they asked, "Why couldn't God do that for us?" We took a few baby steps of faith and saw significant results.

Kurt cites several dramatic ways God has blessed their faith. As the church grew to over seven hundred people, they bought more than twenty acres of land, launched out in faith, and went through a capital campaign to raise the million dollars needed for the property. The people responded, pledged more than the million needed, and paid for the land ten months ahead of schedule.

Their new eight-million-dollar complex was a step of faith, but God has provided many generous gifts. One such gift came from a ninety-one-year-old Jewish attorney who became interested in the church. He pledged three hundred thousand dollars to the project! Two days before suffering a stroke, the man gave his life to Christ. In less than ten days, he died. Then his foundation gave an additional million dollars to the church! Kurt said, "Our people have come to believe in miracles. God honors those who walk by faith!"

Maybe you've been challenged by this book but are tempted to think it doesn't apply to your situation. You've been saying to me under your breath, "But, Bob, I'm in a small church. I don't think we could ever do the dramatic things you have done. We're never going to be a Southeast." God doesn't want you to be a Southeast. (Maybe he wants you to be even larger!) But He does want you to walk by faith and begin to believe that he can do great things through a few faithful people.

Maybe you're thinking, *There's so much to do. Where do I begin? How do I put these principles into practice in my church?* If you are convinced that God wants to do a mighty work through your congregation, then consider the suggestions below. They are specific things almost any church can begin to do immediately to implement positive change.

Pray for a Vision of What Your Church Can Be

Gather your leaders together and pray for a vision of what your church can be. Go to your knees together as a leadership body and ask the Holy Spirit to guide you to become the Body of Christ, the church that God intends you to be.

Max Lucado wrote:

> Our problem is not so much that God doesn't give us what we hope for as it is that we don't know the right thing for which to hope.... Hope is not what you expect; it is what you would never dream. It is a wild, improbable tale with a pinch-me-I'm-dreaming ending. It's Abraham adjusting his bifocals so he can see not his grandson, but his son. It's Moses standing in the promised land not with Aaron or Miriam at his side, but with Elijah and the transfigured Christ. It's Zechariah left speechless at the sight of his wife, Elizabeth, gray-headed and pregnant. And it is the two Emmaus-bound pilgrims reaching out to take a piece of bread only to see that the hands from which it is offered are pierced. Hope is not a granted wish or a favor performed; no, it is far greater than that. It is a zany, unpredictable dependence on a God who loves to surprise us out of our socks and be there in the flesh to see our reaction.[1]

Put your hope in a big God who can fulfill big dreams. Determine you will try something so big that if God isn't in it, you will fail. Ask God to give you a vision for what you should set out to do.

Discuss the Ten Principles with Your Leaders

Since the ten principles in this book are rooted in Scripture and the very nature of what the church is called to be, almost every church leader will agree that each principle needs to be a part of your church. Begin to discuss them one by one, and pray that God will reveal to you any principle your congregation has failed to implement. When your leaders are together, ask yourselves the following questions:

- Does the preaching at our church consistently teach people biblical truths and how they apply to our daily lives?

- Do our weekly worship services help people connect with God?

- Are our leaders people of character who have the spiritual gift of leadership?

- Are we doing everything with excellence?

- Are we willing to step out in faith, trying something so big that if God isn't in it, we will fail?

- Is there a spirit of harmony and cooperation among the leaders and the congregation?

- Are the members of our congregation actively involved in every facet of ministry, viewing themselves as ministers and participants rather than the recipients of ministry?

- Do our people love one another, and are they seeking to meet one another's physical, spiritual, and emotional needs?

- Are the members of our congregation giving sacrificially to the work of God's Kingdom, and are our leaders setting the example?

- Is evangelizing the lost our primary mission?

As you discuss these questions, I'm confident that the Holy Spirit will guide you to areas where you can improve. It's important that the leaders be able to share in an atmosphere of security and love. This means that some will have to have tough skin and others will have to work at being tactful. Ask God to give you a harmonious spirit as you discuss these issues.

Realistically Evaluate Your Situation

It's healthy for every church to set goals and think optimistically, but you also must be objective. Jesus said that some seed wouldn't grow because it falls on hard ground. But even the seed planted in fertile soil grows at different rates: thirtyfold, sixtyfold, or a hundredfold. Some churches have the potential to grow a hundredfold. But other congregations are limited in what they can do because of location barriers, leadership challenges, lack of facilities, or financial difficulties.

If you have limitations, admit them honestly. Are they barriers you can overcome with God's help, or are they characteristics you must accept and work around? If your church is in an area that is sparsely populated, it's doubtful that you're going to grow to become the largest church in America. But God still calls you to walk by faith and to implement the ten principles in this book. Evaluate your situation honestly, work on the ten principles, and trust God for the increase.

Develop a Mission Statement

Several Christian products are available that will help your church develop its own mission statement. The process itself will have positive results among the leaders. Once the mission statement is complete, make sure it is communicated to the congregation and posted in prominent places where people can be reminded often. Every couple of years we preach a sermon series based on our mission statement, just to remind our people to "keep the main thing the main thing."

Develop a Five-Year Plan for Change

It's been said that we overestimate what can be done in one year and underestimate what can be done in five years. Many pastors and church leaders have made the mistake of trying to change too much too quickly. If your church has been heading down the wrong path for a while, it will take a significant amount of time and energy to turn it around. Don't try to revolutionize things too quickly.

Turning a church around is a lot like turning around a large ship. It takes a long time just to stop the momentum and begin to turn in the right direction. Then the wake from your previous momentum will beat against you until you can pick up speed. Yet I've talked to many preachers of small, established congregations who successfully implemented change and saw positive results.

It usually takes a minimum of five years to turn a dead church into one that is alive and growing. The reason most churches stay dead is that very few leaders are willing to wait that long to see results. They move to a place where the ship has already been turned in the right direction, or they give up and decide to head further down the wrong path. When you create a vision for the future of your church, keep at least a five-year picture in mind. Don't think you can turn the ship around in one year.

Work on the One Hour of Weekly Worship

Your Sunday service is the most important hour of the week. More visitors and members are present, and the tone of the entire ministry of the church is usually set in that hour. Make sure everything that surrounds that one hour is done with excellence and bathed in prayer. The building should be clean, the greeters friendly, and the nursery clean and well-staffed. (The nursery communicates something intangible to the young families in your church. If it is too small, dirty, or not a secure environment for infants, the wrong message is communicated to those young families who are the future of your church.)

In the service, make sure the sermon is biblical and applicable, the worship songs are meaningful, the special music well-rehearsed, and the prayers carefully thought out. Cut out dead time, encourage all the leaders to do their best, pray with the leaders beforehand, and expect God to be present. Create an atmosphere that is both reverent and friendly. You want people to say things like, "I really worshiped God today," "This is a friendly church," "I appreciate you all doing everything with excellence," "I enjoyed being here today," "You can feel the Spirit of God in this place."

When that one hour is done with excellence every week, there is a trickle-down effect. Members begin to come more regularly because they don't want to miss. They begin to feel more confident about bringing visitors with them. New people like what they see and want to come back. Offerings can improve relatively quickly. And leaders in other areas of the church will catch the spirit and begin performing their tasks with excellence as well.

Find a Worship Leader

Put as much effort into choosing the leader of your worship services as you do into choosing the person who will be preaching the sermons. Because the impact of that one hour of worship is so important to the atmosphere of the entire church, and because spiritual blessings begin to occur when people are inspired to worship God in an authentic way, you should ask God to guide you in finding just the right worship leader.

A small church usually hands the job of "song leading" to a person in the congregation who can sing. That person may be the most talented musician in your church but not the best at leading people to worship God. Some churches remedy this by having the minister lead the worship, regardless of his musical abilities. That's an option, but the way some preachers sing, their leading worship could have a negative impact on the church!

If the same person has been leading the singing for years in your church, change will be difficult. Move slowly and with much prayer. Sometimes, when it is possible, the most pragmatic solution is to hire a full- or part-time worship leader to replace the volunteer. It's easier for a volunteer to accept being replaced by a "qualified paid staff member" than by another volunteer.

Small churches often talk about hiring a youth minister as soon as they can afford one. In some cases that might be the right decision, but I'm convinced that most churches will get healthy faster if they focus first on choosing a good worship leader. Don't go out and hire a "music minister" who can lead choirs and sing solos. Find a worship leader. Recruit someone—either a volunteer or paid staff member—who wants to lead people to worship God and who has the heart and talent to do it.

Get the Men Involved in Leadership

I don't intend for this to be a theological debate over the role of women in the church, only a reflection of reality. When men are in leadership in a church, they bring their families along with them. When women are in leadership, the men often stay home. Men attract other men, and those other men bring their wives and children with them.

Not every leadership position in your church has to be filled by a male, but there should be an effort to get the men of your congregation involved. That's one of the reasons why we've maintained the tradition of having only men ushering and serving at our weekend services. When people come for the first time—men and women—they often notice that the men of Southeast are involved in serving and leading. They immediately conclude that if we can convince men to be involved, our church must be different from others they've visited.

Start a "What We Believe" Class

Your people—old-timers and newcomers—need to know the basic beliefs of your church. Begin to offer a three- to six-week course on your basic beliefs. As I mentioned in chapter 10, people in our culture are more likely to attend a two-hour class than to welcome you into their home for a two-hour doctrinal discussion.

Love One Another

The world is attracted to any group of people that sincerely loves others. That's the biggest reason cults can grow so dangerously large— they do one thing right: They care about people. Find tangible ways to love the members of your congregation. If the leaders of your church begin showing love toward one another and the congregation, the people will catch on.

Give Up Control

As I mentioned earlier in the book, one of the greatest challenges in any church is to overcome the temptation to battle over who's in charge. If the pastor has to be an autocratic leader or the elders have to micromanage every ministry of the church, then you will only grow as large as your ability to control things. Your church's influence will be severely limited until each of your leaders is willing to give up control. Follow the biblical guidelines for authority, state them clearly, and then get out of the way. It's time to trust that God is in charge and let go of your power.

Visit Other Churches That Are Alive and Growing

I mentioned this earlier, too, but it's worth repeating. Not only should the preacher be encouraged to occasionally visit other congregations, the entire church board should go. Visit churches in other areas that are offering leadership conferences. Not only will your sights be lifted; the camaraderie your leaders develop from traveling together will benefit your church.

Also, find the local church that is doing the best job of ministering in your community and talk to the leaders there. They've discovered something that's working in your town. If they have the right attitude, they'll recognize we're all on the same team and be happy to share their secrets with you.

Celebrate Victories, Giving God the Glory

From the pulpit, in your newsletter, and in your board meetings, begin to champion the things that God is doing in your church.

Near the end of his Gospel, John said that if all the things about the incredible life of Jesus were written down, the world couldn't hold the books that would be written. I now know in a microcosmic way what John must have felt, because there's no way that in one book I could share all the things I have witnessed Jesus Christ accomplish just at Southeast. I'm convinced that if you implement the principles in this book, you, too, will soon have so many things to champion, so many stories to tell, so many victories won, that you won't have time to tell about them all!

Jesus said, "Do you not say, 'Four months more and then the harvest'? I tell you, open your eyes and look at the fields! They are ripe for harvest" (John 4:35). I pray that your church will see the possibilities, witness the moving of God's Spirit, and reap a bountiful harvest.

APPENDIX

GUIDING PRINCIPLES

These are the core values that represent what we believe about ourselves and our organization. They represent how we will interact with each other to accomplish the Mission Statement and Visionary Goals.

1. We believe the Bible to be our final authority for faith and practice.
2. We believe service to Christ merits excellence in everything we do.
3. We believe both corporate and individual encounters with God are vital.
4. We believe all people have worth and value to God and therefore to us.
5. We believe in the development of our God-given gifts and talents for service to Jesus Christ.
6. We believe the family is God's primary unit for ministry, and therefore, the family should be nurtured.
7. We believe in manifesting the love and grace of Christ in practical ways in the community and throughout the world.
8. We believe that it is God's will that every believer grow to maturity in Christ.
9. We believe in the submission to and active support of godly leadership.
10. We believe in practicing wise stewardship of God's resources.
11. We believe that God has called us to be a people of prayer.
12. We believe in encouraging a prayer-guided faith that is willing to take bold risks.
13. We believe that leaders are accountable first to God and then to the people they serve.
14. We believe God honors a spirit of humility, integrity, and Christlike character in all areas of service.

MISSION STATEMENT

We exist to evangelize the lost, edify the saved, minister to the needs of others, and be a conscience in the community.

VISIONARY GOALS

How we will go about accomplishing the Mission statement over the next three to five years.

In the Area of Evangelism

1. To relentlessly pursue evangelism for Jesus Christ in every aspect of ministry.

2. To create a community that is welcoming and friendly to all people.

3. To provide excellent facilities, infrastructures, parking, and traffic flow for everyone.

4. To continually improve the quality of every aspect of worship, teaching, and preaching for adults, youth, and children.

In the Area of Education

1. To create an environment where the congregation and leadership are focused on daily prayer and Bible study.

2. To create an environment where everyone belongs to a group that provides a caring place.

3. To provide for the spiritual development of our children and youth in a safe, caring, and nurturing environment.

4. To create an environment in which all individuals use their God-given gifts in service to Christ.

In the Area of Leadership

1. To build and nurture highly competent, responsive, and accessible leadership.

2. To become a more intentional church through a process of strategic planning.

3. To enlist leaders to a high level of spiritual discipline.

4. To create an informed and unified congregation relative to our mission and ministry.

5. To create a relationship of clear and open communication between elders and staff regarding roles and expectations.

6. To develop a succession plan for key leadership.

In the Area of Ministering to Those in Need and to the Community

1. To understand and respond to community need in every area of ministry.

Southeast Christian Church Organizational Chart

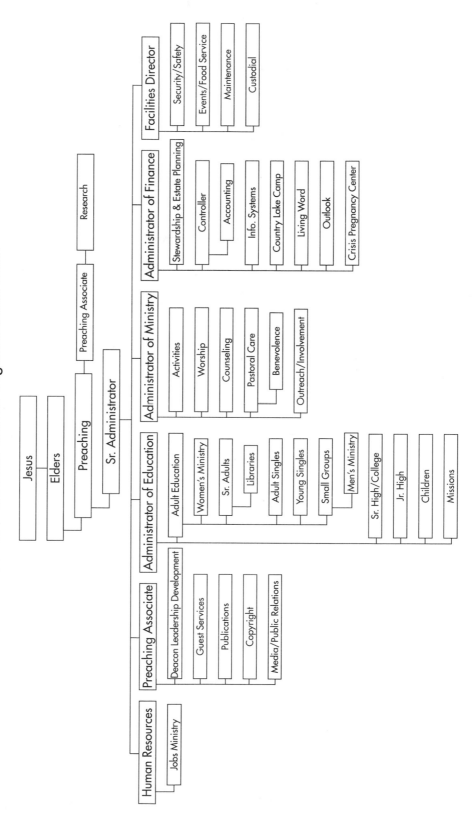

NOTES

Introduction

1. Rick Warren, *The Purpose Driven Church: Growth without Compromising Your Message and Mission* (Grand Rapids: Zondervan, 1995), 68.

Chapter 1

1. Reported by Edward E. Plowman, "Faith at Gunpoint" in *World Magazine*, May 8, 1999 (Vol. 14, No. 18). (http://www.worldmag.com/world/issue/05-08-99/cover_1.asp)

2. R. Albert Mohler, "Fellow Nonbelievers: Liberal Theologian Now a Critic of Liberalism," *World Magazine*, Aug. 8, 1998 (Volume 13, Number 30). (http://www.worldmag.com/world/issue/08-08-98/national_2.asp)

3. All the quotes come from an article in *St. Paul Pioneer Press*, St. Paul, Minnesota, titled "A Popular Crash Course in Christianity; Alpha Leaders Claim 1 Million Students" on August 11, 1999, Main Section, 1A. You can find the article at www.newslibrary.com

4. John R. W. Stott, *Between Two Worlds: The Art of Preaching in the Twentieth Century* (Grand Rapids: Eerdmans Publishing Company, 1982).

Chapter 2

1. William D. Hendricks, *Exit Interviews: Revealing Stories of Why People Are Leaving the Church* (Chicago: Moody Press, 1993), 260.

2. Paul Eshleman, *The Touch of Jesus* (Orlando: New Life Publications, 1996). Excerpts are taken from the audio book.

3. Ibid.

4. Sally Morgenthaler, *Worship Evangelism: Inviting Unbelievers into the Presence of God* (Grand Rapids: Zondervan, 1995), 84. © 1995 by Sally Morgenthaler. Used by permission of Zondervan Publishing House.

5. Tommy Walker, worship leader, quoted by Sally Morgenthaler, Ibid., 241.

6. Mark Pickerill, pastor, quoted by Sally Morgenthaler, Ibid.

7. Raphael Green, pastor, quoted by Sally Morgenthaler, Ibid.

8. Ibid., 214.

9. "Lord, I Lift Your Name on High." Words and music by Rick Founds, copyright © 1989 Maranatha Praise, Inc. (adm. by The Copyright Company, Nashville, Tenn. All rights reserved. International copyright secured. Used by permission.).

10. Patricia Klein, Evelyn Bence, Jane Campbell, Laura Pearson, and David Wimbish, *Growing Up Born Again: A Whimsical Look at the Blessings and Tribulations of Growing Up Born Again* (Old Tappan, N.J.: Fleming H. Revell Company, 1987), 42.

Chapter 3

1. Christian A. Schwarz, *Natural Church Development: A Guide to Eight Essential Qualities of Healthy Churches* (Carol Stream, Ill.: ChurchSmart Resources, 1996), 29.

2. Charles R. Swindoll, *Living above the Level of Mediocrity: A Commitment to Excellence* (Waco, Tex.: Word, 1987), 133.

Chapter 4

1. *Louisville Magazine*, July 1998, 78.

Chapter 5

1. Thomas J. Peters and Robert W. Waterman Jr., *In Search of Excellence* (New York: Harper and Row Publishers, 1982), 119–155.

2. Leith Anderson, *A Church for the 21st Century* (Minneapolis: Bethany House Publishers, 1992), 181.

3. James C. Collins and Jerry I. Porras, *Built to Last: Successful Habits of Visionary Companies* (New York: HarperCollins Publishers, 1997), 93.

Chapter 6

1. Schwarz, *Natural Church Development*, 37.

2. Bob Russell, "The Day I Forgot the Wedding!" in *Leadership Journal*, Fall 1999 (Volume XX, Number 4), 107.

Chapter 7

1. Thom S. Rainer, *High Expectations: The Remarkable Secret for Keeping People in Your Church* (Nashville: Broadman and Holman Publishers, 1999), 23. Used by permission.

2. The two specific ideas given are from Susan Cutshall, *Treat 'Em Right! Tasty Ideas for Encouraging Volunteers* (Cincinnati: Standard Publishing, 1999).

Chapter 8

1. "12/11/97," words and music by Ben Kolarcik and Chris Brodfuehrer (Louisville: Prospect Records, 1998). Available on CD titled *Esther's Request*.

2. Anne Ortlund, *Up With Worship* (This excellent book is now out of print, and we couldn't find further documentation.), 228–229.

3. Schwarz, *Natural Church Development*, 36.

4. Clara Null, quoted in *The Christian Reader* (Carol Stream, Ill.: September/October, 1995 Vol. 33, No. 5), 85.

5. Dave Stone, *I'd Rather See a Sermon: Showing Your Friends the Way to Heaven* (Joplin, Mo.: College Press, 1996), 11.

6. Kathy Lynn Grossman, "In Search of Faith: For many, self-defined 'spirituality' is replacing a church-based faith," in *USA Today*, December 23, 1999. (http://usatoday.elibrary)

7. Rainer, *High Expectations*, 23, 47.

8. Ibid., 29.

9. Ibid., 40–41.

10. Bill and Lynne Hybels, *Rediscovering Church: The Story and Vision of Willow Creek Community Church* (Grand Rapids: Zondervan, 1995), 59.

Chapter 9

1. Cited in Sean O'Neill, "On a Shoestring and a Prayer," in *Kiplinger's Personal Finance Magazine*, May 1999, 99.

2. Bob Russell, *Money: A User's Manual* (Sisters, Ore: Multnomah Books, 1997), 180–181.

Chapter 10

1. Michael Green, *Evangelism in the Early Church* (Guilford, Surrey: Eagel Publishers, 1995), xiv.

2. Liz Curtis Higgs, *Mirror, Mirror on the Wall, Have I Got News for You!* (Nashville: Thomas Nelson Books, 1997). This quote was taken from excerpts sent to us by the author.

3. Schwarz, *Natural Church Development*, 35.

4. This story is from one of Herschel Ford's many "Simple Sermons" books, undocumented. Bob Russell tells this from memory.

5. The Navigators originally developed this illustration, to the best of our knowledge. Southeast Christian Church has adapted this tool for use in witnessing and decision counseling. In Southeast's version, similar to other versions, a man is pictured on one side of a chasm and God on the other. Sins are in the chasm, and the man has fallen into the chasm because of sin. Steps leading out of the chasm end without getting to God because our good works can't save us. Somehow we must make it across the chasm. The counselor explains that only the cross of Christ bridges the gap.

Conclusion

1. Max Lucado, *God Came Near: Chronicles of the Christ* (Portland, Ore.: Multnomah, 1987), 89.